THE REFUSAL OF WORK

T0353310

ABOUT THE AUTHOR

DAVID FRAYNE is a lecturer and social researcher based at Cardiff University. His main research interests are consumer culture, the sociology of happiness, alternative education and radical perspectives on work. Twitter: @theworkdogma

THE REFUSAL OF WORK

The Theory and Practice of Resistance to Work

DAVID FRAYNE

BLOOMSBURY ACADEMIC
LONDON · NEW YORK · OXFORD · NEW DELHI · SYDNEY

BLOOMSBURY ACADEMIC
Bloomsbury Publishing Plc
50 Bedford Square, London, WC1B 3DP, UK
1385 Broadway, New York, NY 10018, USA
29 Earlsfort Terrace, Dublin 2, Ireland

BLOOMSBURY, BLOOMSBURY ACADEMIC and the Diana logo are
trademarks of Bloomsbury Publishing Plc

First published in Great Britain by Zed Books Ltd., 2015
Reprinted, 2021
This edition published by Bloomsbury Academic, 2022
Reprinted 2023, 2024

Typeset in Bulmer by Apex CoVantage, LLC
Index: ed.emery@thefreeuniversity.net
Cover designed by Michael Oswell

A catalogue record for this book is available from the British Library.

A catalogue record for this book is available from the Library of Congress.

ISBN: PB: 978-1-3503-5429-6
ePDF: 978-1-7836-0119-6
ePub: 978-1-7836-0120-2

To find out more about our authors and books visit www.bloomsbury.com
and sign up for our newsletters.

For Jen, who loves life.

Contents

Acknowledgements

I would like to thank everyone at Zed Books, particularly Kika Sroka-Miller and Ken Barlow, for seeing potential in this project and helping to bring it to fruition. I would also like to thank my mentors Finn Bowring and Ralph Fevre for their years of generosity and guidance, along with a number of others who have kindly commented on my work, including Hannah O'Mahoney, Grace Krause, Stuart Tannock, Françoise Gollain, Gareth Williams and Kate Soper. It should also be recognised that this book would have been impossible without the candour of those interviewees who shared their views and experiences so that they could be included here. Thanks to you all.

Closer to home, my warm appreciation goes to my parents, who have long supported my studies, and whose encouragement was especially helpful in the final few months of writing. I would also like to thank my good friends – whether for talking about ideas, listening to me complain, or humbling me with their video game skill. You know who you are, and your ongoing support and wild sense of humour are greatly appreciated.

This world is a place of business. What an infinite bustle! I am awakened almost every night by the panting of the locomotive. It interrupts my dreams. There is no sabbath. It would be glorious to see mankind at leisure for once. It is nothing but work, work, work.

Henry Thoreau – 'Life Without Principle' (1962: 356)

I can't believe what a continual slog it is, just to make a living.

Anonymous (November 2014)

INTRODUCTION

The work dogma

It's eight o'clock in the morning.
When you come out it will be dark.
The sun will not shine for you today.

The above quotation is taken from Elio Petri's 1971 film *La classe operaia va in paradiso (The Working Class Goes to Heaven)*. The film gives a fictionalised account of the struggles of the Italian Autonomist movement: a loose coalition of students, workers, feminists and unemployed people who protested in Italy in the 1960s and 1970s. The quote is a slogan, shouted through a megaphone at eight o'clock in the morning and intended for the ears of the hundreds of workers who at that time were filing through the factory gates for another day of repetitive and hazardous labour. I quote it here as a perfect illustration of what the Autonomists were fighting for. Their cause went beyond the traditional union demands for fairer pay and better working conditions. They acknowledged the need for greater freedom and equality within work, but also fought for the right of workers to lead richer lives *outside* of work. The Autonomists protested at the wasted time, lack of variety, and excessive administration of life in capitalist society. They fought for the right of workers to feel the sun on their skin, to play with their children, to develop interests and skills outside the factory, and to rest peacefully at night. We might say that the appeal of the Autonomists was not just to the injustices of exploitation, but also to the worker's diminished sensory experience of the world.

Mirroring these concerns, a range of social critics (from the authors of the Frankfurt School to related critics such as André Gorz) have set out to question work from an emancipatory standpoint, supporting a vision of social progress based on a reduction of work and an expansion of free-time. These critics did not deny the importance of work, nor did they dismiss the many pleasures to be found in productive activity, but they did propose that a reduction of work might leave people with more time and energy for their own self-development. These critiques of work have provoked their readers by highlighting the casualties of a work-centred society: the time for politics, contemplation, conviviality and spontaneous enjoyment, which have been displaced by capitalism's narrow focus on commercial production and consumption. For today's students, who find themselves pushed through an education system focused largely on socialising the young for a future job role, to read these critiques is to receive an education in desire, and a reminder that time could be spent differently. The radical nature of these theories, however, has earned them a marginal position in academic and public debates. Whilst important issues like pay inequalities and poor working conditions are still discussed, it is rarer for social commentators to question the ethical status of work itself.

Whilst this is certainly true, the alternative vision of social development implied in calls for a less work-centred future has seen a modest resurgence in recent times. Go to any high-street bookshop and alongside those books promising to instruct readers on how to influence others, accumulate fortunes and achieve career success, one can also find a shelf of books telling readers to slow down, find a better 'work–life balance', and seek happiness by consuming less.

In the context of contemporary capitalist societies, narrowly fixated as they are on the activities of working and spending, the ultimate message of these books is a valuable one, tapping into a rippling disquiet about the ways in which work has crept into and colonised our lives. If these popular critiques have ultimately had a limited influence on society's priorities, however, it is perhaps because they have tended to stray too far into the genre of self-help. Their mistake has been to approach the domination of work as primarily a problem of individual habits, and it is fair to say that these books have been rather more conservative when it comes to discussing those systemic economic and political changes which might offer people a more genuine range of lifestyle choices.

More promising than the stagnant discussion of 'work–life balance' is the emergence of a braver critique of the paradigm of economic growth. Conventionally, governments have treated economic growth and life satisfaction as one and the same thing, measuring both of these via the metric of gross domestic product (or GDP) per capita. GDP is an indicator which quantifies a country's overall economic activity. It accounts for the total amount of earning and spending that took place in a given year, and it is tacitly accepted that a rising level of GDP indicates an overall improvement in national prosperity. Whilst economic growth is undoubtedly crucial for less developed countries, in which subsistence needs remain unmet, a range of commentators in more affluent societies have questioned the value of GDP growth as a social goal and an index of progress. A report commissioned in 2008 by the former French president Nicolas Sarkozy argues that 'the time is ripe for our measurement system to shift emphasis from measuring economic production to measuring people's well-being' (Stiglitz et al., 2010). The report stresses, among other things, the important role for human flourishing of health, education, relationships and the environment, and represents just one entry in a growing base of evidence to suggest that happiness, security and human progress will no longer flow in an unproblematic fashion from a growth in GDP (see Jackson, 2009).

This developing uneasiness about the equation of economic growth with life satisfaction has seen sociologists and even some economists returning to the fundamental philosophical question of what it means to live a good life. Critical commentators and the new sociologists of happiness are once again talking about the *ars vitae* or 'art of living', and this has inevitably led them to question whether our well-being is best served by capitalism's single-minded commitment to economic growth. Some have relied (not always convincingly, it must be said) on statistical measures of people's subjective well-being, whereas others have drawn inspiration from more philosophical sources. Aristotle's vision of the good life is a common reference point. Aristotle suggested that humans flourish when they live wisely, justly, and in harmony with the world. According to his notion of *eudaemonia,* a sense of well-being is achieved not simply through sensory pleasure, but also through things like good health, security, companionship, autonomy, a sense of being respected and socially recognised, and a feeling of connection with the community and environment. All these things are important because humans are ethical, social and creative beings, as well as sensing bodies. If the ongoing drive to boost economic growth has become troubling for many, this is partly because of its decidedly anti-Aristotelian fixation on material gain as the route to prosperity.

In an age of material abundance, it seems that there is a troubling disparity between our desire for the good life and capitalism's narrower focus on the constant expansion of production and consumption. What most people crave is more free-time and a greater investment in the social aspects of life, but a growing awareness of this fact has done very little to upset the mainstream political agenda. In the UK (the context in which I am writing), apart from the Labour Party's cursory interest in work–life balance in the mid 2000s, the question of working hours has generally disappeared from the agenda, replaced by a focus on employability and the cultivation of a workforce that will ensure the country's competitiveness in a global economy. The stripping back of the welfare state, which in recent times has seen a phased introduction of increasingly stringent penalties for the non-worker, has also significantly reduced the latitude for resistance to work. The ethical superiority of work seems almost untouchable. Paid jobs continue to be promoted as a vital source of good health and character, the media continues obsessively to demonise the non-working 'scrounger', and an old-fashioned work ethic maintains its anchorage in policies designed to force people off welfare and into employment.

Within this political context, my central goal in this book is to argue that the time has come to challenge the work-centred nature of modern society. As it stands, work represents a highly naturalised and taken-for-granted feature of everyday life. The dogmatic nature of work is revealed when we consider the uncanny resilience of its ethical status, even in the face of some very troubling realities. Consider the woeful failure of today's labour market to keep pace with the desire for jobs that allow for self-expression and creativity. Gratifying work is a fantasy that we have all been trained to invest in, ever since our teachers and parents asked us what we wanted to 'be' when we grew up, yet most of us are confronted with scant opportunities to consolidate our ambitions in the world of paid employment – a world whose signature features are often drudgery, subordination and exhaustion. What is also baffling is the fact that the ethical status of work has still not been significantly destabilised by our disintegrating labour market. Mass unemployment, job insecurity, and low-wage work are making employment an increasingly unreliable source of income, rights and belonging. The orthodox political solution to this situation is 'job creation': the invention of work by increasing output and expanding the economy into new sectors. However, as a range of concerned scientists and economists are now pointing out, constant growth is not only unlikely to solve the problem, but also brings with it a disturbing set of environmental and social implications. Finally, the dogmatic status of work is also graspable when we consider the extent to which we have unconsciously accommodated work's escalating dominance in our everyday lives. Work has increasingly spilled its demands into our homes, drawing upon our emotions and personalities to an extent never before seen or tolerated. As the ethic of hard work tightens its grip once again, employability becomes the motivating force of our ambitions, interactions and education system. A side effect of this is that we, as a society, may be losing our grip on the criteria that judge an activity to be worthwhile and meaningful, even if it does not contribute to employability or the needs of the economy. Those activities and relationships that cannot be defended in terms of an economic contribution are being devalued and neglected.

It is puzzling that none of these troubling realities has led to a significant public discussion of why we work, and of how work should be socially distributed. What has ultimately prompted me to write this book is a sense of concern that these pressing issues – from dubious job quality to social insecurity, to the escalating dominance of work in our everyday lives – have failed to destabilise the central place of work in mainstream political visions of the future. The storm may be rising, but the work dogma still huddles safely in its bunker.

Within this troubling context, there is an urgent need to contemplate some of the taken-for-granted realities of today's work-centred society, to consider alternative ways of meeting the needs conventionally sought in work, and to think about whether there might be more equitable and liberating ways of distributing work and free-time. In the first four chapters of this book, I undertake this task on a mainly theoretical level. In the later part of the book, however, my focus shifts to investigate the lives of real people who have tried to resist work.

Between 2009 and 2014, I spent time with a range of people who were taking significant steps to reduce the presence of work in their lives. Whilst some had reduced their working hours, others had given up work altogether. I wanted to understand what had prompted them to resist work, to find out what they did with their time, and to gain a deeper understanding of the pleasures and difficulties that might be encountered in the process of refusal. Something worth noting from the outset is the relative 'ordinariness' of the people I met. I use the word 'ordinary' with caution here. What I mean to stress is that these people were not ideologically committed activists or members of a coherent social movement. They had no overriding mission or agenda, and whilst a few self-identified as 'downshifters' or 'idlers', most had not heard of terms like these. Some even found them off-putting. What the people I met shared was simply a common desire to work a little less and live a little more.

Overall, were these people successful in their attempts to resist work and live according to their ideals? Here, in the Introduction, is not the place for me to say, but over the course of the book we will see that resisting work does carry significant financial and psychological risks. This is definitely not another one of those sugary books that tells its readers they can lead richer and freer lives by doing more of x and less of y. What I aim to do, rather, is draw upon the views and experiences of the people I met as possible sources of nourishment for a critique and putative refusal of work – a refusal which I ultimately argue must be fought on collective and political terms, and not on an individual basis. I would be pleased if the discussions ahead prompted readers to reflect on their own working arrangements, but there is no implication that the people I met had discovered a key to happiness. More modestly, what the discussions ahead represent are an attempt to remain open to alternatives, and to generate ideas that might contribute positively to a critique of our work-centred society.

As to the real-world possibilities for the development of a politics against work, there are reasons to be hopeful and there are reasons to be pessimistic. I take inspiration from Herbert Marcuse, whose provocative works argued that advanced industrial societies are capable of containing all social change, whilst still maintaining that forces and tendencies exist that can break this containment (Marcuse, 2002: xlv). Freedom, for Marcuse, is always both impossible and possible. Focusing on both sides, I will highlight the alternative sensibilities and practices from which we might derive inspiration for a politics against work, whilst also acknowledging the extent to which certain cultural and structural features of capitalism militate against the development of social alternatives. Ultimately, the discussions and arguments in this book are best understood as a kind of provocation. The book is intended as an invitation for people to join the critical discussion around work, and I hope that the ideas presented here will be debated, built upon and criticised, and that they will ultimately nourish the desire for change at a time when some critical distance from the existing state of affairs is urgently needed.

The structure of this book

Setting aside the empirical investigation until a little later in the book, Chapter 1, 'A Provocation', begins by scrutinising the concept of work. I clarify what I mean by the term *work*, explore some of the ways in which society can be thought of as work-centred, and provide a brief introduction to those key critical thinkers who envisaged a less work-centred future.[1] In Chapters 2 and 3, I move on to engage with a number of key social issues, with a view to underlining the relevance of a critique of work. Chapter 2, 'Working pains', examines the phenomenon of alienation. Reflecting on the everyday degradations of working life – be it the repetitive physical tasks of industrial labour, or the more emotionally demanding transactions of modern forms of work – I will consider why the realm of employment might represent an increasingly unsuitable space in which to live out the desire for meaningful and creative activity. Chapter 3, 'The colonising power of work', shifts the focus away from work itself to look at the broader impact of work on our everyday lives. It explores how the colonisation of our lives by economic demands – to work, to recover from work, to spend income, to cultivate employability – leaves a dwindling segment of life free for activities whose value transcends the economic. I argue that the sheer pace and pragmatism of modern life represent another reason to scrutinise the place of work in society.

Chapter 4, 'The stronghold of work', marks the point at which I move on from critical diagnosis to begin considering the scope for resisting this prevailing state of affairs. I begin with the downside, exploring the ways in which the work ethic continues to militate against the possibility of re-evaluating work. Both the relentless stigmatisation of the non-worker in the media and the conservative attachment to work as an irreplaceable factor of social inclusion and good health represent considerable obstacles to the development of a truly open debate. With regard to the prospects for social change, Chapter 4 is certainly the gloomiest chapter in this book, but it also paves the way for the more forward-looking discussions in Chapters 5, 6 and 7. It is here that I detail my independent enquiry into the lives of real people who have tried to reduce their hours or give up working. Chapter 5, 'The breaking point', looks at some of the values and experiences that might cause a person to break from work, introducing the research participants and their motivations. Chapter 6, 'Alternative pleasures', broaches the practical and financial obstacles to resisting work, but also remains open to the idea that there may be new pleasures to be discovered in the shift to a less work-focused, less commodity-intensive lifestyle. Chapter 7, 'Half a person', brings the investigation to a close by examining the experiences of shame and isolation that can arise with attempts to resist work. What, if anything, can we hope to learn from the values and experiences of people who are trying to resist work? What are the hidden benefits and follies of their attempts to go against the grain? In the final chapter, 'From escapism to autonomy', I suggest that a transition to a less work-centred existence could represent a more robust and authentic form of freedom than the superficial escapes and liberties granted to us by the present social system. The question that hangs in the balance, however, is whether people's growing disenchantment with work can be harnessed and developed into a genuine political alternative.

ONE: A provocation

Modern methods of production have given us the possibility of ease and security for all; we have chosen, instead, to have overwork for some and starvation for others. Hitherto we have continued to be as energetic as we were before there were machines; in this we have been foolish, but there is no reason to go on being foolish for ever.

Bertrand Russell – 'In Praise of Idleness' (2004c: 15)

In his 1972 book *Working,* Studs Terkel collected transcripts from over a hundred interviews with working Americans, providing an intricate snapshot of American life from an astonishing range of perspectives (Terkel, 2004). In this enormous book, we hear from welders, waiters, cab drivers, housewives, actors and telephone operators, as each discuss their hopes, fears and everyday experiences at work. Much of Terkel's book is about the little coping strategies that people use to get through the working day, from pranks and teasing to fantasising and other strategies of mental detachment. A gas-meter reader passes the time by ogling a housewife who sunbathes in her bikini. A waitress makes the day go quicker by gliding between tables, pretending to be a ballerina. A production line worker says 'fuck it', and takes a rest without permission. Standing back to reflect on the interviews in *Working,* Terkel wrote:

> This book, being about work, is, by its very nature, a book about violence – to the spirit as well as the body. It is about ulcers as well as

accidents, about shouting matches as well as fistfights, about nervous breakdowns as well as kicking the dog around. It is, above all (or beneath all), about daily humiliations. (Terkel, 2004: xi)

Many of the accounts featured in Terkel's book give substance to his conclusion that work is violence, yet some of the book's accounts also offer glimpses of work's pleasures. In one memorable case, a piano tuner portrayed his work as an artistic exercise, describing how he would enter an almost hypnotic state of concentration and aesthetic delight as he brought harmony to the pianos. His account brings to mind the notion of the 'flow state': a psychological condition of complete and blissful absorption in the task at hand, entered when a work task synchronises with a person's skill level and interests (Csikszentmihalyi, 1990). In the flow, one loses track of time and space, focusing only on the craft. It is the opposite experience to that of the bored worker who watches the ticking clock, unable to shake his physical surroundings from his mind.

The delight of Terkel's piano tuner is a form of pleasure unfamiliar to many people. In modern capitalist societies, access to satisfying and engaging work is profoundly unequal. For those who work in jobs with dubious social utility, subjected to the latest innovations in workplace organisation and control, work often represents a struggle against boredom, meaninglessness and exhaustion. A range of personal tactics help us to survive the working day: we remind ourselves that we are more interesting than the jobs we do, we stage imaginary rebellions against bosses and clients, or we hide away in shells of cynicism. Sometimes we construct elaborate escapes and compensations out of hours in an effort to forget (or 'rebalance', as the life coaches call it). In later chapters I will introduce people who describe work as an external, coercive pressure in their lives. They talk about how they felt 'compressed', 'controlled' and 'forced' in their work.

They said that work made them feel 'watched from behind', 'penned in like battery hens', or 'dominated by a big beast'. The perceived meaninglessness of the work they performed (or that they might, in the future, be forced to perform) represented a significant source of distress. Matthew – only in his mid twenties – said that the thought of working in retail or an office job made him panic about death. His anxieties reminded me of something Terkel once said in a television interview: 'the jobs are not big enough for people's spirits'.

Work is not without resistance, of course. Activists and labour scholars continue to address the pressing need for fairer pay, better-quality jobs, and more democratic relationships in the workplace. These important issues delineate the traditional terrain of trade unions and the politics of the Left. They are all extremely pressing issues and the fight is far from won, but it is crucial that we also think beyond workers' rights to confront a broader and more fundamental set of questions. What is so great about work that sees society constantly trying to create more of it? Why, at the pinnacle of society's productive development, is there still thought to be a need for everybody to work for most of the time? What is work for, and what else could we be doing in the future, were we no longer cornered into spending most of our time working? As we will see, such questions are part of a well-established history of critical thinking on the meaning, purpose and future of work. If such questions are rarely posed outside of this academic clique, however, it is perhaps because they ask us to scrutinise realities that are usually accepted as natural and inevitable. It may feel like there is little incentive to reflect critically on work from a position where most of us, irrespective of our attitudes towards work, are pretty much obliged to perform it anyway. To take a critical stance on work may even seem distasteful or elitist in the context of a society where jobs are so highly sought after. In regions wracked by poverty and high rates of unemployment, what people are feeling is a need for *more* work, not less, but it should be noted that the thinkers introduced here are in no way ignorant or in denial of this fact. It would be senseless to dispute the fact that most of us experience a powerful need to work. What we can dispute, however, is the celebrated prominence of work in the cultural, ethical and political life of advanced industrial societies. What is baffling, from the perspective of work's critics, is the notion that the activity of work should continue to be valued more than other pastimes, practices and forms of social contribution.

The work-centred society

We live in a work-centred society, and this is true in a number of senses. First of all, work represents society's main mechanism for the distribution of income. Work is therefore the central avenue through which people access material necessities such as food, clothing and shelter, as well as the commercial entertainments and escapes offered by modern consumerism. The centrality of work is also grasped when we consider the sheer amount of time spent working – in which I also include the time spent preparing for, training for, searching for, worrying about, and travelling to and from work – as well as the fact that for most people, work represents the main centre of social life outside the family. In affluent societies, work is one of the most conventional and readily available means through which we become part of the pattern of other people's lives. Engagement in paid work also marks the passage to adulthood, showing that the child has matured, gained independence, and accepted what it means to live in 'the real world' (in which we are presumably supposed to forget about our youthful ambitions and knuckle down). The connection between identity and occupation is forged from a young age, with children being prompted by parents and educators to refine their career aspirations and begin cultivating their employability. In the work-centred society, the most readily accepted purpose of education is the socialisation of young people for the successful adoption of a pre-defined work role.

If every society has its own way of measuring achievement, in affluent societies this is usually through work. Conversations with strangers often start with the question 'What do you do?' (a dreadful question to ask a person who does not work, or who dislikes the work that she does), and it is common knowledge that this question represents an abbreviation for 'What job do you perform?'. The tendency to treat occupations as the yardsticks of social status is revealed in the prevalence of clumsy modern euphemisms, often designed to puff up society's less auspicious forms of work. The bin man works in 'waste and sanitation management', the fry cook is 'part of the culinary team', and the unemployed person is 'between jobs'. Reflecting on these quirks of modern usage, Terkel suggested that the people who embrace such terms are not necessarily ashamed of the work they do; instead, they are justifiably defending themselves from a society which is obsessed with measuring status through work, and therefore looks upon them as a 'lesser species' (Terkel, 2004: xvii). It is clear that work represents much more than an economic necessity and a social duty. In affluent societies, work is powerfully promoted as the pivot around which identities are properly formed. It is valorised as a medium of personal growth and fulfilment, and constructed as a means of acquiring social recognition and respect. All of this we recognise, even if work's ultimate function is in most cases to generate private profit.

If work can be described as central on a cultural level, then it is certainly also central at the level of politics. In the UK (the context in which I am writing), apart from New Labour's cursory interest in 'work–life balance' in the mid 2000s, the question of working hours, and the entitlement of people to lead active and varied lives outside work, has long been absent from the mainstream political agenda. Mainstream politics focuses its efforts on job creation and employability, with political rhetoric continuing to promote traditional beliefs about the sanctity and dignity of work. This is particularly evident in the moral tones of discussions about unemployment. In 1985, Claus Offe wrote that the persistence of mass unemployment, particularly if it were concentrated in particular regions, might put an end to the stigmatisation of unemployed people, since the rate of joblessness could 'no longer be accounted for plausibly in terms of individual failure or guilt' (Offe, 1985: 143). Yet we can now see that Offe's confidence was misplaced, failing to anticipate the moral fortification of work in neoliberalism, which has seen a revamped ideological focus on the virtues of 'hardworking people' versus society's so-called scroungers and skivers (Baumberg et al., 2012; Coote and Lyall, 2013; Tyler, 2013: Chapter 6). The ethical lines have been drawn: are you a worker or a shirker? This moralisation of work has been enshrined in the latest social policies, as enforcing work – no matter how dubious its social utility – is adopted as a key function of the state. In recent times, the stripping-back of the welfare system has seen a phased introduction of increasingly stringent audits and penalties for the non-worker. Even groups that have been traditionally exempted from the duty to work, such as single parents and people with disabilities, have found themselves under scrutiny in the drive to move people off welfare and into employment. All of this has significantly reduced the latitude for developing lifestyles based around activities other than paid work. The sociologist Catherine Casey justifiably summarises:

Whether one is in or out of employment, preparing for it, or seeking it, and certainly whether or not one likes one's job, work as it is conventionally organised significantly shapes everyday life experience for most people in industrial societies. (Casey, 1995: 25)

In this chapter, I begin formulating a response to this situation by taking on the task of *denaturalising* work – this most central and taken-for-granted feature of our lives – and opening it up as an object for critical discussion. If work is indeed a central source of sociality, rights, status and belonging, then it is important to recognise that this situation is a social and historical construction, and not a fixed feature of some natural order. First I need to clarify what I mean by the term *work* and, in the process, make some preliminary remarks about what it might mean to engage in a critique of work. Following this, I briefly touch upon a number of studies that chart the historical emergence of work, with a view to developing some critical distance from its central role in modern capitalist societies. In the final part of the chapter, I provide an introduction to those critical authors who have challenged the centrality of work by promoting a radical reduction of working time. In the compelling and unorthodox visions of these authors, work, instead of being central, would be subordinated to the need for human autonomy and the leading of richer, more varied lives.

What work is

The concept of work invokes an extremely varied set of ideas and images, and any attempt to define it quickly leads us into a web of caveats, contradictions and grey areas. For some people, the word 'work' may call to mind the joys of craft and creativity. Marx suggested that, in its ideal form, work is the defining activity of humanity.

In this view, humans are distinguished from other animals by their ability to conceive of and subsequently craft a world of artificial objects, opening up possibilities for new trajectories of development. In artistic circles, the term *work* has a similarly auspicious ring to it, and is often used in its noun form, 'my work', meaning the material embodiment of my talents and sensibilities: my intangible inner world made tangible. Work, in the sense of aesthetic creation, might even be seen as a quest for immortality, expressing the producer's desire to create durable evidence of his or her finite existence in the world. From great structures like churches and bridges to cultural artefacts like novels and video games – all of these things are the product of work.

The trouble with defining work in these terms, however – as a form of creative activity – is that it becomes difficult to know what we should call work that is not creative but menial and routine. Workers who complain about their jobs in call centres, on supermarket checkouts, or at computers, inputting data day after day, are more likely to view their work as a means of self-preservation rather than self-expression. For all of us whose survival depends on submission to the daily grind, 'work' conjures a less romantic set of images. It calls to mind the sense of dread associated with words like 'chore', 'travail' or 'burden'. In these cases, work does not represent a source of joy or a form of self-expression, but that blank part of the day which must be endured until five p.m.: the coveted hour when work releases its grip and we can finally be ourselves again. Adding to the complications surrounding work's definition, we can also observe the morally loaded nature of the term *work*, which is often used to smuggle in ethical views about the respectability of certain activities over others. In a social context where engagement in work is tied with what it means to be respectable, socially included, and worthy of recognition, the question of which activities society chooses to allow into the category of 'proper work' becomes an important one. Domestic work, along with certain forms of artistic, intellectual or care work, continues to sit uncomfortably on the fringes of what society is prepared to categorise as actual 'work', especially in cases where the value of these activities cannot be explained in terms of any measurable social or economic contribution.

If the meaning of 'work' in everyday usage remains ambiguous and contested, this is certainly also the case in the academic realm, where we find a disconcertingly complex history of attempts to define work (see Granter, 2009: 9–11). In this book I will follow André Gorz's observation that the prevailing cultural understanding of 'work' in modern capitalist societies is that it is an activity carried out for a wage. Colloquially, it seems that the label 'work' is most often used to distinguish paid from unpaid activities, and refers to the operations performed in 'jobs' – things that we 'go to' and 'come home from'. Illustrating this definition, Gorz suggested that a market gardener can be said to work, whilst a miner growing leeks in his back garden is carrying out a freely chosen activity (Gorz, 1982: 1). Elsewhere, Gorz has referred to this predominant understanding of work as 'work in the economic sense'. It represents the contractual exchange of a certain amount of productive time for a wage, and is distinguished from the separate category of 'work-for-ourselves' (Gorz, 1989). If one of the key characteristics of a paid job is that it serves society in a general sense, work-for-ourselves is distinctive because the worker performs it for the direct benefit of either himself or others with whom he shares a relationship outside the commercial sphere. Work-for-ourselves is conducted according to principles of reciprocity and mutuality rather than commercial exchange; it has the quality of a gift, performed out of respect for, or a sense of obligation to, others. In today's employment-centred society, work-for-ourselves tends to be limited to domestic chores such as grocery shopping, cooking and cleaning, squeezed unhappily into evenings and weekends (and performed disproportionately by women). However, in a society with more free-time, Gorz believed that this category could in theory encompass a whole host of activities – anything from repairs to community gardening, healthcare and informal education.

Both work in the economic sense and work-for-ourselves are contrasted with a third category, which Gorz called 'autonomous activities'. Autonomous activities encompass those actions which are performed as ends in themselves. They are self-initiated and stem from a conscious choice which nothing forces the person to make. From an individual's perspective, the primary goal of autonomous activities is not to earn money, nor is it necessarily to meet any purpose that can be easily put into words. Instead, autonomous activities pursue the Good, the True and the Beautiful, as defined by the subject performing them. The value of such activities cannot be measured in terms of economic worth or social utility; autonomous activities are undertaken for their own sake, out of pleasure or interest.[1] Gorz suggested that a telltale sign of autonomous activities is that the actions which achieve the goal may confer as much personal satisfaction as actually scoring it (Gorz, 1989: 165).

I have no wish to belabour the differences between work's various guises any further, so it can be summarised that both the theorists and interviewees introduced in this book are turning a critical eye on the first of the categories described above, i.e., work in the economic sense. (For the sake of ease, I will hereafter use the words 'work', 'labour' and 'employment' interchangeably, in order to refer to the phenomenon of paid work). It is important to make these distinctions here, in order to recognise from the outset that the critique of work does not amount to a refusal of productive activity in any general sense – at least not for the critique's more respectable proponents. In 1883, from his cell in St Pélagie prison, the French author (and son-in-law of Marx) Paul Lafargue famously wrote a pamphlet entitled *The Right To Be Lazy*. In the pamphlet, Lafargue attacked the widespread belief in the duty and sanctity of work. He wrote:

> A strange delusion possesses the working classes of the nations where capitalist civilisation holds its sway. This delusion drags in its train the individual and social woes which for two centuries have tortured sad humanity. This delusion is the love of work, the furious passion for work, pushed even to the exhaustion of the vital force of the individual and his progeny. (Lafargue, 1975: 35)

It should perhaps be noted that Lafargue was writing satirically – as a provocateur more than a scholar – yet his contribution is worth dwelling on because it contains a number of elements that are unrepresentative of the critique of work presented in this book. The first point of contention is Lafargue's reference to the 'delusions' of workers and their apparently crazy desire for work. I would suggest that to work diligently is not necessarily to labour under a delusion. As workers, our choices and behaviours are shaped and limited by a specific set of moral, material and political pressures, which is to say that the social system of advanced industrial societies is constructed so that working is often the only way that most people can meet their needs. This includes material needs – for food, clothing, shelter – and also more complex psychological needs, such as the need for social recognition and esteem. As we will see later in the book, attempts to live without work, however enlightened their rationale may be, often carry significant financial and psychological risks. Let us not also forget that work is experienced by many people as a tremendous source of enjoyment and achievement. There is a great deal of satisfaction to be found in clubbing together to get something done, breaking a sweat, using the hands and mind in unison, and so on. The ethical discourse around the pleasure and dignity of productive work is not entirely an accessory of exploitation. Even in cases where the content of a job is relatively meaningless, the job in question might still be enjoyed, or at least valued as an opportunity to break away from the constriction of life in the private domain. It is partly on this basis that feminism has fought for the right of women to work.

> [Work] provides an escape from the narrowness and stifling conformity of the domestic unit or village community, a way of meeting people from other places with whom relationships can be freer, less familiar, than with those who first and foremost see you as daughter or daughter-in-law, sister or cousin, and tie you to a carefully regulated world where everyone must keep to their allotted place. (Gorz, 1985: 54)

To speak of the 'delusions' of workers, as Lafargue did, is to pull the critique in the wrong direction. What is put forward in this book is a critique of work, and specifically not a critique of workers, i.e., what is offered is a critique of the moral, material and political pressures that bear down on the worker, and not a set of judgements about the attitudes of workers themselves.

The second contentious element of Lafargue's contribution is his title's reference to a right to be *lazy*. Once again, we must acknowledge Lafargue's playfulness here, but it is also important to recognise from the outset that the critique of work is not a defence of laziness. It instead expresses a desire to widen the space for autonomous activities and to reclaim the time to work for ourselves. Even if a palatable chunk of time to be lazy has a rightful place in the vision to liberate workers, what is ultimately demanded is less a right to laziness than a right to realise human capacities more fully. Kathi Weeks puts it well when she writes that to critique work is not necessarily to deny that work has any value:

> It is, rather, to insist that there are other ways to organise and distribute that activity and to remind us that it is also possible to be creative outside the boundaries of work. It is to suggest that there might be a variety of ways to experience the pleasure that we may now find in work, as well as other pleasures that we may wish to discover, cultivate, and enjoy.

The critique of work also reminds us that 'the willingness to live for and through work renders subjects supremely fit for capitalist purposes' (Weeks, 2011: 12). If the authors and research participants introduced in this book are critical of work, it is not because they defend the right to be lazy, but because the obligation to paid employment so often precludes the possibility of engaging in activities that are genuinely creative, collaborative and useful.

The beginning of work

We can begin opening up work as an object of critical enquiry by briefly considering its historical contingency. The scholars who have under-taken this task have found that work – even in the broader sense of 'productive activity' – has not always been valued as a personal boon. In the book of Genesis, a life of work was administered by God as a punishment to Adam and Eve. Work was also regarded as a curse in ancient Greece, where it represented a base and menial form of activity. Work was disdained because it symbolised necessity – the enslavement of humans by their bodily need for survival – and it was not something that free people should be forced to perform. It was instead designated to slaves – persons who were cut off from society because their labours excluded them from those pursuits considered to be more worthy of a citizen, such as politics, art, and quiet contemplation. The freedom of Greek citizens to participate in intellectual and political life was to be earned by subjecting others to necessity by force. Hannah Arendt wrote that, condemned to a life of toil, the 'slave's degradation was a blow of fate and a fate worse than death, because it carried with it the metamorphosis of man into something akin to a tame animal' (Arendt, 1998: 84).

One of the most prominent studies on the history of attitudes towards work is Max Weber's classic *The Protestant Ethic and the Spirit of Capitalism*. Originally published in 1904, Weber's analysis focused on the cultural forces that helped to shape capitalism, highlighting the historically emergent nature of the modern attachment to work. Weber compared modernity with what he termed the 'traditional society', in which people moderated the amount of work they performed in accordance with a well-defined set of needs. In the traditional or pre-capitalist society, work was only tolerated in so far as it was necessary: 'a man does not "by nature" wish to earn more and more money, but simply to live as he is accustomed to live and earn as much as necessary for that purpose' (Weber, 2002: 60). The harvester, when offered a higher rate of pay, did not therefore dream of the extra money he could earn, but calculated how much less work he could perform in order to earn the same comfortable amount as before. His main priority was to preserve his free-time, rather than to increase his financial reward. We might say that the harvester worked to live, rather than living to work.

Weber argued that this traditional orientation to work was transformed by the rise of a Puritan morality or a 'Protestant ethic', which began to endorse work as a virtuous end in itself. He traced this

ethical commitment to work back to the Reformation, which saw
Puritan values spilling out of the monasteries and into wider society, teaching people to seek salvation through a dedication to work.
According to this religious morality, work should be undertaken
zealously, as a vocation or spiritual calling, but its financial rewards
were not to be enjoyed or used to finance periods of idleness. Weber
also discussed the influential teachings of the pastor John Calvin,
who famously preached the notion of predestination, the religious
belief that only a limited, pre-determined elect were destined for
salvation in the kingdom of heaven. Calvin taught that success
in work was a sign of God's grace, and he prescribed commitment
to work as a method of calming personal fears about the threat of
eternal damnation. Through this convergence of moral ideals and
religious teachings, work had been elevated to the status of an
ethical imperative.

Whilst there is undoubtedly still a puritanical streak to the modern commitment to work, this is not to suggest that puritanical values
remain a conscious source of motivation for today's workers. Presenting a story familiar to students of social theory, Weber argued
that the ascetic compulsion to work kick-started a legacy of rational
organisation. In their dedication to work, business owners became
more efficient and productive in their labours, installing bureaucra-
cies and standardising working procedures. As capitalism developed,
entrepreneurs who failed to run an effective and competitive business went bust, and the 'idyllic state', where work was performed as a
spiritual vocation, eventually gave way to a 'bitter, competitive struggle' (Weber, 2002: 68). This process of rationalisation produced what
Weber, in the title of his essay, called the 'spirit of capitalism'. Having
established itself as a universe in which people felt destined to participate, capitalism no longer required the Puritan's values to support

it: 'Capitalism at the time of its development needed labourers who were available for economic exploitation for conscience sake. To-day it is in the saddle, and hence able to force people to labour without transcendental sanctions' (Weber, 2002: 282).

Weber's key point was that the morality of work had become embedded in the fabric of capitalist societies: the work ethic prowls about our lives 'like the ghost of dead religious beliefs' (Weber, 2002). Marx made a similar point in his famous reference to 'the dull compulsion of economic relations', which also draws attention to the ritualistic quality of work. We work partly because it feels like the natural thing to do. In more recent times, there has also been some debate over whether workers in affluent societies continue to be motivated by a moral attachment to work, or whether the work ethic has been eroded by a more hedonistic desire to work for material rewards. Analysing the rise of American consumer culture, Daniel Bell suggested that, throughout the twentieth century, the bourgeois values of hard work, frugality and self-control were becoming increasingly irrelevant, and that by the 1950s people were concerned no longer about 'how to work and achieve, but [instead about] how to spend and enjoy' (Bell, 1976: 70). We can note, however, that regardless of the extent to which the traditional work ethic has been surpassed by consumer hedonism, the outcome in terms of people's behaviour remains largely the same. What is retained in either case is a disciplined attachment to working for a wage. Herbert Marcuse recognised this in his book *One-Dimensional Man,* where he argued that the development of capitalism had seen a mounting harmonisation between the desire for sensual gratification and the production of cultural conformity (Marcuse, 2002). Modern consumer culture is perfectly consistent with work discipline, partly because the need to pay for commercial pleasures compels people to commit more of their time and effort to earning money. Indulgence and escapism, far from being cultural taboos, are relentlessly encouraged in modern capitalist societies, but always with the drawback that their enjoyment requires us to heighten our commitment to work. In this account, mass consumption has not killed the work ethic but simply augmented it, taking the place of religion as society's chief distraction from work's more troubling realities.

The value of historical perspectives is that they allow us to achieve some critical distance from the current work-centred state of affairs. Weeks suggests that Weber's *The Protestant Ethic and the Spirit of Capitalism* is particularly valuable in this regard, with its references to periods before and after the heyday of the Protestant work ethic inviting readers to grasp the peculiarity of modern society's attachment to work. Readers are invited to reflect forwards, and consider the lofty status of work from the standpoint of the values inherent in the old, traditional society. What seems startling from this perspective is the limitlessness of the modern desire for material wealth, as well as the fact that work would one day operate as a main axis of identity. Weber also invites readers to look backwards, and consider the emergence of the work ethic from the perspective of the modern, secularised society. What startles in this case is the fact that the most rational and instrumental of all modern activities – the performance of disciplined, productive work – is the product of a religious ethic which is wildly irrational in its origins (Weeks, 2011: 42–7). From the point of view of modern workers and their more secular or self-interested system of values, the Puritan's willingness to sacrifice himself to work, irrespective of its content or material rewards, seems completely bizarre.

Weber's main focus was on the moral fortification of work, but we can note that workers in the 1900s were also bound to labour via new and aggressive techniques of work discipline, developed during the rise of the factory system. Workers' inclinations to self-limit the duration and intensity of their labour were attacked not only by the work ethic, but also by more tangible transformations in the working day itself. The payment of workers became tied to working hours, and labour was regimented and synchronised via the adoption of clock time. By the twentieth century, industrialisation had provided unparalleled opportunities for managers to co-ordinate the pace and procedures of the labour process. Work was divided down into predictable, routine tasks, and the pace of work was dictated by the moving assembly line. Alertness and punctuality were policed via penalties and surveillance technologies, and workers were reminded, as per Benjamin Franklin's well-known dictum, that 'time is money'. Through these combined processes, punctuality, efficiency and productivity became the mottos of the working day (Thompson, 1967). The British economist William Beveridge also played a significant role in the struggle to integrate workers. His system of labour exchanges represented a deliberate attempt to exclude workers who wanted to self-limit their labour. In Beveridge's own words: 'for the man who wants to get a casual job now and again, the exchange will make that wish impossible'. If a worker refused to work full-time, then the exchanges were instructed to deny him work. Beveridge's attack on casual labour was also implemented via his changes to the 1911 National Insurance Act, which was modified to extract higher tax contributions from employers who used casual labourers (Whiteside, 1991: 62–3). These techniques represented a more blatant, coercive kind of discipline than the moral education of the worker described by Weber.

Other authors have dealt with the historical development of attitudes towards work in much greater detail than I have space for here (e.g., Anthony, 1977; Beder, 2000), but what emerges in all of their analyses is the fact that people's subjective reconciliation with work lagged far behind the objective, quantitative expansion of work, witnessed in the industrialising society. It appears that early capitalism faced considerable difficulty in persuading people to adopt regular, disciplined employment, and that resistance to full-time work persisted well into the twentieth century, particularly in industrial sectors that had traditionally relied on casual labourers. The history of capitalism is a history involving the gradual reconciliation of individuals with the sacrifices of the working day. This was not a smooth process, but a struggle requiring a severe restructuring of workers' habits: 'In all these ways – by the division of labour; the supervision of labour; fines; bells and clocks; money incentives; preachings and schoolings; the suppression of fairs and sports – new labour habits were formed' (Thompson, 1967: 90). If the work-centred nature of society has become so naturalised as to seem inevitable, an appreciation of the historical and contingent nature of attitudes to work helps us to achieve a degree of critical distance from this highly normalised state of affairs. Work has not always been at the centre of society's moral, cultural and political life, and I now turn to a range of social critics who have questioned whether it both can, and should, hold on to this position in the future.

The end of work

This book is ultimately concerned with one question: might it be possible, in the future, for everybody to work less and have more time for their own, autonomous self-development? This is not a novel question, but a question that is woven into an intellectual tradition spanning centuries. The thinkers in this tradition hail from a range of different backgrounds, but what unites them all is a broad concern with the emancipatory transformation of society. Regardless of their angle of approach, their ultimate focus has been on the agonising rift between present realities and future possibilities. As Erik Olin Wright writes:

> Let us begin with a simple, indisputable observation: the world in which we live involves a juxtaposition of extraordinary productivity, affluence and enhanced opportunities for human creativity and fulfilment along with continuing human misery and thwarted human potential. (Wright, 2010: 39)

The commentaries introduced here, which have all questioned work's future, are components of (or at least consistent with) the broader project of critical social theory, which has always begun with Wright's indisputable observation. The overall goal of critical social theory has been to submit processes of social development to scrutiny, reflecting upon the obstacles they might pose for the flourishing of human capacities, whether these capacities are physical, artistic, intellectual, social, moral or spiritual.

The critique of work is usually thought of as a Marxist tradition, but in truth a number of its key themes emerged before Marx, in the work of early utopian writers such as Charles Fourier, William Morris and Thomas More. Fourier, for example, believed that work had the potential to become a main source of gratification and the fullest expression of human powers, but was troubled by the rift between his ideal and experiences of the real work provided by industrial capitalism. He referred to the mills and factories of the early nineteenth century as 'veritable graveyards', where the workers were motivated by nothing more than a joyless concern for their own survival. Work was performed with a sense of dreary necessity, producing a weariness in the workers that would also poison their leisure time (Beecher, 1986: 276). Fourier contrasted this miserable reality with his theory of attractive labour, developed in his detailed blueprints for Harmony, a utopian society beyond the historical phase he called 'civilisation'. In Harmony, work would be organised in such a way as to fill the worker with passion and eagerness, rather than dread. Workers would be able to choose their work freely, carrying out a broad variety of productive activities in pleasant surroundings, with both a spirit of co-operation and a healthy sense of competition. Pleasurable work would be the centrepiece of Fourier's utopia, becoming an almost playlike activity, and virtually eliminating the worker's need for rest and escape (Beecher 1986: 274–96).

Fourier's desire to dissolve the boundary between work and play was later echoed by William Morris, who also blamed the joyless realities of labour on its imposed nature, as an activity 'forced upon us by the present system of producing for the profit of privileged classes' (Morris, 1983: 44). Like Fourier, Morris was interested in the prospect of transforming work into a source of pleasure and aesthetic delight: it should become a feature of what he called 'the ornamental part of life' (Morris, 1983: 46). He was more tentative than Fourier on the matter of how this might be achieved, though Morris did deviate from Fourier in one important way. What is significant for the purposes of our discussion is that Morris was one of the earlier commentators to seriously propose the idea of working *less*. Whereas Fourier believed that even the most menial work could be made pleasurable, in a manner that would allow a welcome extension of the working day, Morris argued for the elimination of unpleasant toil through a wholesale reduction of work. This particular theme can actually be traced as far back as Saint Thomas More's *Utopia*, initially published in 1516, well before the advent of industrial society. In More's utopian vision, the need for toil would be reduced by producing sturdier goods, by limiting the production of goods judged to be superfluous, and by sharing the necessary work more equally among the population (More, 1962). It is in relation to the prospects for reducing toil that writers like Morris, witnessing the rapid growth of industry, also began to debate the possible applications of technology. Would the increasing efficiency of production technologies eventually allow citizens a greater degree of freedom from unpleasant toil? Morris thought that it would, such that unattractive labour would 'be but a very light burden on each individual' (Morris, 1983: 51).

Whilst we can find older examples in the work of these early utopian writers, the critique of work is usually discussed in connection with Marx. It is Marx's ideas that inspired the rich vein of theories and research around the spiritual and psychological tolls of working, although there has also been some debate over Marx's exact relationship with the argument for a reduction and decentralisation of work.[2] In one of the more well-known passages from Volume 3 of *Capital*, Marx does indeed appear to foreshadow the argument for shorter working hours. In this passage, Marx relegates work to the mundane 'realm of necessity': he sees it as the obligatory toil that must be surmounted before humans can really begin living in the 'realm of freedom', where they become available for the world and its culture. Marx was explicit in his suggestion that the realm of freedom can be expanded by shortening the working day (Marx, 1981: 959). We also find a similar argument in relation to Marx's mixed views on technology. For Marx, although machine technologies represented an instrument for controlling and degrading work, their tremendous productive capacities could also theoretically be directed towards the reduction of necessary labour, leaving a greater space for freedom outside work: '[Capital] is instrumental in creating the means of social disposable time, and so in reducing working time for the whole society to a minimum, and thus making everyone's time free for their own development' (Marx, 1972: 144).

Marx's mixed views on technology foreshadowed a central premise in what some writers would later call the 'end of work' argument, which is based on the assumption that advances in production technologies are gradually eliminating the need for human labour (Rifkin, 2000). Within the existing structures of capitalist society, the displacement of workers by mechanisation and productivity growth is obviously a grave cause for concern. It leads to forced unemployment (often called 'technological unemployment'), spelling poverty and social exclusion for thousands of people. However, the elimination of human labour by developments in production technology has also been *celebrated* by the 'end of work' authors, because it opens up the theoretical possibility of a huge expansion of free-time.

There have been many versions of this core idea. We find one such version in a famous essay by John Maynard Keynes, for whom the promise of greater freedom from work seemed like a realistic and relatively imminent possibility. In his essay on the 'Economic Possibilities for Our Grandchildren', first published in the 1930s, Keynes predicted that advances in production technology might reduce work time and allow the population as a whole to work less – as little as fifteen hours per week by the year 2030 (Keynes, 1932). Keynes discussed this in terms of the 'economic problem' (of scarcity, there not being enough goods to go around) having finally been 'solved' by society. It would be at this juncture that man would have the privilege of confronting a deeper problem: 'how to use his freedom from pressing economic cares, how to occupy the leisure, which science and compound interest will have won for him, to live wisely and agreeably and well' (Keynes, 1932: 366). Whether the possibility of orienting production towards the end of greater human autonomy can ever be realised, of course, depends not only on the ability of technologies to alleviate the need for toil, but also on society's moral and political commitments. To what and whose ends will new technologies be applied? How will savings in work time be socially distributed? To what extent should society tolerate the unchecked growth of the economy? To what extent does it remain rational to uphold the work ethic as a cultural ideal? If society is ever going to realise the true benefits of technological development, we need to engage in a political discussion. In Marcuse's words, we need to talk about how society's technological and intellectual resources can best be used 'for the optimal development and satisfaction of individual needs and faculties with a minimum of toil and misery' (Marcuse, 2002: xli).

It is these emphatically moral and political questions that defined the terrain of critical social theories after Marx, with writers trying to figure out why, in a time of unprecedented technological possibility, people's lives were still characterised by toil and repression. Just like Keynes, many critical writers found it profoundly irrational that society would continue enforcing a need to work, even in the midst of abundance. Marcuse pointed to the absurdity of this situation in *Eros and Civilisation* (Marcuse, 1998), where he argued that the repression experienced by people in the modern age is an artificial or 'surplus' repression. The word 'artificial' is used here to suggest that the necessity (need to survive) that pushes us to submit large portions of our lives to toil is no longer a harsh, inevitable fact of our existence in nature, but the imposition of an irrational and unjust social system, which not only distributes the available resources unevenly across the social hierarchy, but also manufactures new needs in order to warrant the extension of work.[3] One of the major contributions of Marcuse (and the Frankfurt School of critical theory, to which he was affiliated) was to account for the sheer resilience of capitalism. The extent to which certain structural and cultural forces are mobilised against the possibility of a reduction of work was not always fully accounted for by Keynes and other 'end of work' optimists, and I will return to this point myself in due course, as I consider some of the forces and ideologies which act against a re-evaluation of work in contemporary society. In the meantime, we can get a firmer grasp of critical approaches to work with a look at one of its relatively recent and most consistently engaging proponents, André Gorz.

The politics of time

André Gorz made little attempt to pledge himself to any particular canon, having written under the guise of journalist, economist, sociologist and existential philosopher. He was all of these things, and none of them. What really defines Gorz's thinking is its unswerving commitment to human freedom.[4] For the purposes of our discussion, one of the most striking features of Gorz's thought is a refusal to accept that work's problems can be boiled down to the issues of wages and working conditions. For Gorz, an understanding of work's negative effects has to involve an appreciation of the broader ways in which work dominates our everyday lives. The forgotten struggle of the Left, which Gorz represents, is for the right of workers to lead rich and interesting lives outside of work. As a writer and social critic, his main commitment was to the right of each person to his or her own autonomous self-development.

Gorz pursued these themes across several decades and in a range of publications, each with their own style, influences and points of emphasis, but the underlying coherence of Gorz's project (certainly his later works, at least) lies in his promotion of a *politics of time,* i.e., a critical, open-minded, and democratic discussion around the goals of production and the social distribution of working hours. Like other 'end of work' thinkers, Gorz celebrated the great leaps in productivity afforded by capitalist development. However, in Gorz's view, one of the most pressing questions faced by capitalist societies now, at the pinnacle of their productive capacities, is the question of what should be *done* with the time being saved by these gains in productivity. What meaning and content will we, as a society, choose to give this new-found free-time? Will we use it to enhance our lives outside work, nourish our relationships and pursue our own self-development, or will economic rationality dictate that we spend just as much time and energy on work as we did before?

Gorz's call for a politics of time reflected a belief that these questions should be placed in the hands of the people. Unless humans can acquire the scope to direct them towards humane, societal ends, the savings in free-time provided by capitalism's productive development are essentially meaningless. A politics of time is necessary because 'the development of the productive forces may, of itself, reduce the amount of labour that is necessary [but] it cannot, of itself, create the conditions which will make this liberation of time a liberation for all' (Gorz, 1989: 185). Gorz himself is perhaps best known for advocating a proposal for a politically co-ordinated reduction of working hours, to take place on a society-wide scale. For Gorz, the purpose of a policy of shorter hours should be to channel the free-time saved by productivity gains to humane ends, allowing a greater scope for the free self-development of individuals. Shorter working hours would open up more space for political engagement, for cultural creation and appreciation, and for the development of a range of voluntary and self-defined activities outside work.

The benefits of Gorz's call for shorter hours are manifold. As well as allowing more time for self-development and co-operation outside work, Gorz speculated, a shorter working week might also improve conditions *within* work. A renewed appetite for autonomy, developed outside work, might help to rejuvenate traditional labour struggles by encouraging people to be 'more exacting about the nature, content, goals and organisation of their work' (Gorz, 1989: 93). For professional workers, working less might even represent an opportunity to work with greater efficacy and sensitivity. Tireless application to one's work is not necessarily the best way to ensure success and creativity, and a policy of shorter working hours might give workers time to update their knowledge, try out new ideas, and diversify their interests (Gorz, 1989: 193–4).[5] Gorz's vision was certainly radical, and he was acutely aware of the gulf between his call for shorter working hours and the realities of advanced industrial societies. In reality, what to do with savings in work time is not subject to a serious political debate, as Gorz hoped it would be, but instead is dictated in advance by the economic imperatives of profit and growth.

What happens to the time saved by productivity gains in societies that have failed to develop a politics of time? Gorz offers several answers to this question, presenting an incisive analysis of capitalism: a system in which the pursuit of private profit, rather than a politics of time, dictates who works, how long for, and to what ends. In a capitalist system, one of the most obvious outcomes of savings in work time is the creation of unemployment. The leaps in productive efficiency witnessed in advanced industrial societies mean that fewer and fewer people are required to produce society's necessary goods from one year to the next. If the economy slows for any reason, or fails to grow fast enough to offset this increase in productivity, it becomes increasingly difficult for people to obtain a sufficient, regular income from paid work. Many end up unemployed. The negative personal consequences of this have been well-documented in a range of studies (some of which I will return to later) but it suffices to say that whilst unemployed people are technically outside work, they are not necessarily free from work in any meaningful sense. In the context of a work-centred society, unemployment represents a kind of no-man's-land: a dead time, degraded by financial worries, social isolation and stigma. By maintaining – even in the face of mass unemployment – that work should represent a source of income, rights and belonging, society ensures that 'unavoidable leisure shall cause misery all round instead of being a universal source of happiness. Can anything more insane be imagined?' (Russell, 2004c: 7).

What we are confronted with in contemporary capitalism is a perverse situation in which the highest-ranking workers are plagued by long hours, whilst growing numbers of the people suffer because their labour power is no longer useful for the generation of private profit. These latter people are either without work entirely, or functioning as a reserve army of low-paid, insecure workers for industries that wish to be able to adjust their workforces according to fluctuations in demand. One of the goals of a policy of shorter working hours would be to remedy the maldistribution of work by sharing the available work more equitably among the population. Everyone should work less so that everyone may work, and so that all may benefit from an increase in free-time:

> One of the functions of a politics of time is precisely to share out
> savings in working time following the principles not of economic

rationality but of justice. These savings are the work of society as a whole. The political task is to redistribute them on the scale of society as a whole so that each man and woman can benefit from them. (Gorz, 1989: 191)

Without such a policy, it appears that we are stuck in a society of people who are financially and psychologically dependent on a scarce activity. This is an irrational and profoundly inhumane situation, to say the least. As Hannah Arendt put it: we are trapped in a society of 'labourers without labour' in which, perversely, the most pressing problem for most people is no longer exploitation, but the absence of opportunities to be sufficiently and dependably exploited.

What could be worse than a society of labourers without labour? According to Gorz, what might be worse is a society which, under the banner of progress, responds to unemployment with a relentless programme of economic growth. Throughout the history of capitalism, societies have tended to compensate for the labour-displacing effects of productivity gains either by increasing the output of particular industries, or by expanding the economy into new industries and sectors. Anders Hayden refers to this as the warped logic of the treadmill: 'the need for never-ending economic expansion simply to maintain employment levels' (Hayden, 1999: 33). Hayden's reference to a treadmill reveals the second destination of savings in work time, i.e., their reabsorption into the economy via the creation of *more* work. Free-time in which citizens are neither producing nor consuming commercial wealth is useless to capitalism. For want of being able to make free-time produce private profit, capitalism has historically reacted by snatching back the time saved by productivity gains to create

additional forms of work that are often unproductive, environmentally destructive, and push the realm of commercial activities
more deeply into intimate life (see Bowring, 1999). One of the
things that is troubling from Gorz's perspective is the sheer point-
lessness of many modern forms of employment. Huge proportions
of the labour market are devoted to the production, marketing
and distribution of consumer goods with superficial differences,
limited functions, and short life spans. In his polemic against the
rise of 'bullshit jobs', David Graeber also points to the unprecedented expansion of sectors such as corporate law, academic and
health administration, human resources, and public relations. On
top of this, we can consider the huge numbers of people whose
role is to provide administrative, technical or security support
for these industries, as well those thousands of jobs in the service
industries – from dog-washers to home cleaners and 24-hour pizza
deliverymen – which only exist because the workers who pay for
them are so hellishly busy working (Graeber, 2013). In recent times,
the everyday experiences of the swelling service class have made
for some disturbing case studies (Ehrenreich, 2002; Toynbee,
2003), and Gorz was deeply critical of the injustice inherent in a
society where one section of the population buys their free-time
by offloading their chores on to the other. From his perspective,
it is only a blind attachment to an ideology of work that prevents
people from seeing that, if everyone worked less, everyone could
do their own domestic tasks *and* earn their living by working
(Gorz, 1989: 157).

To summarise, perhaps Gorz's ultimate strength as a social commentator was to keep alive the belief that another way of organising work might be possible. If capitalism has facilitated such huge

leaps in productivity, then why are we all still working so hard? Over a number of publications, Gorz confronted this question by opening up a critical discussion on the politics of time. He hoped to contribute to a political intervention that would finally subordinate the economic sphere to the felt needs of the people, allowing everybody to spend less of their time toiling, and more of their time on activities of their own choosing. Without such an intervention, Gorz believed that we face the prospect of a far more destructive scenario. In this scenario, free-time continues to be a scarce, privileged resource. Work-centred visions of social progress continue to be promoted, even though there are not enough paid jobs to go around, and people's lives become dominated by a struggle to find and keep work. Capitalism continues to seek profits by plundering the environment and spreading the economy into hitherto uncommodified areas of life, and these trends are celebrated as vehicles for job creation. What Gorz and other critics of work prompt us to ask is nothing less than the following question: what kind of society do we want to live in?

...

I have here provided a brief sketch of critical approaches to work that go beyond the Left's traditional concerns with wages and working conditions, to question the future of work itself. Along with those authors who have interrogated the history of attitudes towards work, those writers who have questioned work's future provide a valuable opportunity for some critical distance from the present, work-centred state of affairs. What they provide, above all, is a provocation: an occasion to question whether work can continue to function as the main lynchpin of income, rights and social belonging. This is a particularly apposite question to ask today, at a time where the pressing social issue of 'workers without work' seems here to stay. Statistics released by the International Labour Organisation suggested that 6.1% of the UK workforce were unemployed in 2014, compared with 6.2% in the USA. However, an analysis from the UK's Trade Union Congress argues that the ILO's unemployment figures should be treated as a modest estimate. In 2013, the TUC's own data suggested that the number of unemployed people in the UK was around 4.78 million – nearly double the ILO's estimate of 2.51 million. The variation between the figures from source to source (and also from year to year) is partly caused by the differences in the way that unemployment is measured.[6] However, regardless of exactly how catastrophic the rate of unemployment might be, we can certainly agree that it is significant, enduring, and absolutely catastrophic for the individual.

On top of this, the failure of the labour market to deliver an adequate supply of decent jobs to those who want them is producing all manner of new travesties. The high demand for jobs seriously weakens the power and inclinations of workers to stand up for issues like pay, rights, and job quality. In recent times, we have witnessed the relatively unmitigated rise of the working poor,[7] and the zero-hours contract.[8] For those attempting to insulate themselves from the shifting currents of the labour market by investing in education, the old guarantee that educational credentials ensure a future of secure, well-paid and interesting work is also being eroded. An extensive analysis by Philip Brown and colleagues suggests that a combination of factors – the rapid expansion of higher education, the globalisation of job competition, and the deskilling of work – are leading huge numbers of graduates into an 'opportunity trap', as they fail to find a home for their specialised skills in the labour market (Brown et al., 2011).[9]

Even if economic growth could manage to keep pace with the demand for jobs, what would be the environmental costs of continuing expansion? In recent years, there has been a growing awareness of the ecological implications of never-ending economic growth. Marshalling the swelling body of scientific evidence, the ecologist Tim Jackson suggests that capitalist societies cannot possibly hope to sustain their current rate of production without major ecological consequences. Jackson points to well-established bodies of research on the depletion of vital natural resources, the loss of biodiversity, soil pollution, deforestation, as well as that mother of all limits, climate change, in order to illustrate his conviction that endlessly expanding the economy in order to provide work has become an increasingly unpalatable strategy (Jackson, 2009).

The social construction of work as a key source of income, rights and belonging is unswerving. Yet what is also clear is that, for vast numbers of people, work is becoming an increasingly *unreliable* source of these things. This is a profound crisis, requiring an equally profound re-evaluation of work and its place in modern society. This task – which Gorz has called the politics of time – aims to offer a practical response to today's disintegrating labour market. But more than this, it also invites us to talk about the conditions for freedom, and to engage in a dialogue about the kind of society we want to live in. Like the theorists presented here, I would like to see a fresh, progressive debate unfold on the meaning and future of work. I would like us to remember that the nine-to-five, Monday-to-Friday working week is a relatively modern invention, and to talk about other potential ways of distributing work. I would like us to think about alternative modes of experiencing the pleasure and solidarity which, up to now, have been conventionally sought through work. I would like us to assert a right for varied and meaningful lives outside employment, and to search for modes of fulfilment that render us less complicit in the capitalist's search for private profit. All these things require us to accept an alternative vision of human progress and felicity, based on non-material goods such as well-being, free-time, and the right to realise our human capacities. All these things require a radical departure from the outdated thinking which accepts that the prosperity of a developed country can still be measured in terms of economic growth.

TWO: Working pains

We hated the place and despised everything it had come to stand for, and yet we were terrified of being 'set free' into an economic vacuum where we would struggle to find work and have to present ourselves to other potential employers as similarly enthusiastic, compliant and flexible. I often arrived at the warehouse in the mornings with a mixture of relief that I still had a job and disappointment that the place had not been somehow swept away during the night.

Ivor Southwood – Non-Stop Inertia (2011)

Social critics have long been analysing the spiritual costs of work, and this endeavour has, along the way, been enriched by the first-hand accounts of workers themselves. Studs Terkel's 1972 book *Working* is worth another mention here as a veritable treasure trove of insights into people's everyday realities. I quote here just a couple of examples from the book. Phil Stallings, a spot welder for Ford, describes his daily round:

> The welding gun's got a square handle, with a button on the top for high-voltage and a button on the bottom for low. The first is to clamp the metal together. The second is to fuse it … I stand in one spot, about two- or three-feet area, all night. The only time a person stops is when the line stops. We do about thirty-two jobs per car, per unit. Forty-eight units an hour, eight hours a day. Thirty-two times

forty-eight times eight. Figure it out. That's how many times I push that button. (Terkel, 2004: 159)

Steve Dubi, a steelworker, reflects on his status as an employee:

You're not regarded. You're just a number out there. Just like a prisoner. When you report off you tell 'em your badge number. A lotta people don't know your name. They know you by your badge number. My number is 44-065. At the main office they don't know who 44-065 is … They just know he's 44-065. (Terkel, 2004: 554)

In Chapter 1 of this book I presented a provocation: what if instead of accepting the work-centred society as natural and inevitable, we could open up a serious debate about the future of work? In modern society, work is the main way we acquire an income, form an identity, make a social contribution, and become part of the pattern of other people's lives, but for vast numbers of people work has also become an extremely unreliable source of these things. In this chapter, I continue to build a case in favour of a radical re-evaluation of work, focusing this time on the experience of work itself. In spite of the sanctity and centrality of work in modern society, the harsh reality is that many people continue to experience their jobs in much the same way as Phil and Steve above: as tiring and meaningless forms of activity, undertaken largely out of necessity. This is something that Marx famously recognised with his concept of 'alienation'. With reference to the experiences of work in capitalist society, this chapter suggests that so long as economic rationality continues to dictate the goals and methods of production, existing attempts to humanise working conditions are highly limited in what they can hope to achieve. This is another reason why the prospect of less work, and a greater scope to develop associations and activities outside the confines of work, remains so compelling.

Disengagement and indifference

The concept of alienation is usually associated with Marx. Central to his critique of work was a conception of labour as the 'life of the species' (Marx, 1959: 75). Marx distinguished humans from other animals by their ability to transcend the limits imposed on life by nature and, in a conscious process of self-expression, to craft a world of artificial objects. Through their work, humans are said to purposefully refashion the natural world, extending the possibilities of human life: 'man is forever remolding nature, and with each alteration enabling his powers to achieve new kinds and degrees of fulfilment' (Ollman, 1971: 101). It is on the basis of this moral ideal of self-realisation through work that Marx undertook his critique of work in the capitalist system. In *Capital*, Marx wrote that the possibility of human fulfilment through the exercise of productive capacities was being smothered by industrial forms of work, which 'mutilate the labourer into a fragment of a man, degrade him to the level of an appendage of a machine, destroy every remnant of charm in his work and turn it into hated toil' (Marx, 1906: 708). Marx believed that work had ceased to be an activity that expressed the human need to shape the surrounding world, and was now instead performed joylessly, out of the necessity to make a living. It had, in other words, become an alienated activity. In an often-quoted passage from his *Economic and Philosophical Manuscripts,* Marx suggests that the experience of alienated labour has a quality of detachment:

> In his work ... [the worker] does not affirm himself but denies himself, does not feel content but unhappy, does not develop freely his physical and mental energy but mortifies his body and ruins his mind. The worker therefore only feels himself outside his work, and in his work feels outside himself. (Marx, 1959: 72)

It is not necessary to subscribe entirely to Marx's philosophy of human nature to use the term *alienation*. It is enough to recognise that the act of work represents a potential opportunity for creativity and collaboration, and to experience a satisfaction and rootedness in the world, but that work is often organised in ways which strip it of these qualities. Following Marx, the concept of alienation has been used in a flexible fashion to describe workers' sense of indifference to the work that they do. Authors such as Robert Blauner (1964) and Harry Braverman (1974), for example, helped bring the concept of alienation to bear on the realities of day-to-day life in the factory. A recurring theme in these texts, as well as in Marx's own critique, focused on the alienating effects of the division of labour. Carried to new extremes in capitalist society, the division and subdivision of the production process was said to imprison each worker in a narrow role, shrinking his area of responsibility, draining his work of creativity, and depriving him of any meaningful relationship with his product. The heightened use of mechanical technologies was also criticised for taking the skill out of work, reducing the worker to a mere supervisor or appendage of machines.

As many critics have pointed out, these techniques found their ultimate expression in Taylorism: the set of organisational practices famously developed by the American engineer Frederick Taylor in the late nineteenth century. Capitalism's unscrupulous pursuit of efficiency and profit meant that no decision about the pace or techniques of the labour process would be left to the worker's discretion. The developments associated with Taylorism were perfected in Henry Ford's moving assembly line, which churned out identical Model T cars at a highly predictable rate of production, but not without significant spiritual costs for the worker. As the more uniquely human qualities such as initiative, creativity and cooperation were expelled from the labour process, critics argued that work condemned us to act not as human beings but as impersonal, interchangeable units of labour power. This was brilliantly satirised by Charlie Chaplin in his 1936 film *Modern Times,* which saw Chaplin – an assembly line worker – transformed by his work into a manic, twitching automaton. In order to keep up with the speed and mechanical precision of the machine, Chaplin was himself forced to become one.

Given the transformations in work since the industrial period, the Chaplin example is of course a rather archaic one. We cannot talk about alienation without acknowledging the widely documented shift in the West from an industrial to a post-industrial economy, composed increasingly of jobs requiring the worker to perform services or manipulate information rather than manufacture material goods. If Marxist critics believed that industrial work had stifled the worker's capacities, things changed in the second half of the twentieth century when many commentators greeted the developing era of post-industrial work with a degree of fanfare. Futurologists forecasted the advent of a new 'knowledge economy', which would see a shift away from the standardised manual work of old, towards a higher concentration of smart jobs in the service and computer-based industries (Bell, 1973). Now a political orthodoxy, the notion of a new 'knowledge economy' was first celebrated by economists and sociologists in the 1960s, when it was generally believed that the future prosperity of nations would depend on their ability to produce intelligent, knowledgeable workers for a new era of work. Post-industrial forms of employment would help reintroduce the 'human factor' into work, and jobs would no longer simply be about efficiency and obeying orders; they would draw on the more distinctively human qualities such as social competence,

cognitive ability, practical experience, or consciousness of responsibility, offering workers new opportunities to feel morally invested in
their work (Offe, 1985: 137–8).

With the benefit of hindsight, some commentators have seen
fit to question these claims about the transition to a burgeoning
knowledge economy (Thompson et al., 2001). Whilst the statistical
proportion of jobs in service or information-based industries has
undoubtedly increased, we need to be cautious about accepting this
trend as evidence of a shift towards a more humane, highly skilled
world of work (see Fleming et al., 2004). Occupational categories
do not tell us all there is to know about the ways that particular
forms of work are experienced, and the statistics fail to communicate the more mundane and miserable aspects of many modern jobs.
Workers who today sit at their computers, performing the same
tasks day in day out, may in fact relate to their labour in much the
same way as the alienated industrial worker did. It seems that those
who serenaded the coming era of post-industrial labour radically
underestimated the extent to which computer technologies would
be harnessed to standardise work in the digital age. In many modern workplaces, computer technologies are not used to enhance the
worker's capacities, but to enforce new extremes of work intensification and control. Studies of today's classic example of bad work –
the call centre – document a number of practices that are now
commonplace. Auto-diallers connect both inbound and outbound
calls straight to employees' headsets, with no breaks permitted
between calls. Monitoring software collects data on each worker's
productivity, automatically reporting tardy or under-performing
workers to their managers, so they can be singled out for coaching, disciplinary action or embarrassment. One study describes the
modern call centre as an 'electronic panopticon' (Fernie and Metcalf,

2000), whereas another refers to the 'assembly line in the head' of
the call centre worker, who always knows that the completion of one
task will immediately be followed by the uptake of another (Taylor
and Bain, 1999). In 2013, a public controversy emerged around the
working conditions of warehouse staff (or 'pickers') for the online
megastore Amazon, where handheld computers are used to hold
low-wage workers to unreasonably strict time limits as they trawl
the vast warehouses, scanning and gathering orders. An undercover
reporter writes: 'We are machines, we are robots, we plug our scan-
ner in, we're holding it, but we might as well be plugging it into
ourselves' (BBC News, 2013).

Richard Sennett provided a colourful example of the effects of
computerisation in his case study of a modern bakery (Sennett,
1998). In the bakery that Sennett studied, bread making was accomplished not by mixing and kneading, but solely through the manipulation of icons on a computer screen. The workers were not required
to possess any real knowledge of the baking process, and nor did
they have any occasion actually to touch the dough. Sennett wrote
that the work process, encoded in automated machines, had become
opaque and 'illegible' to the workers, who thus found it impossible
to develop a culture or sense of pride around the job. The workers, he wrote, are 'vividly aware of the fact that they are performing
simple, mindless tasks, and doing less than they know how to' (Sennett, 1998: 70). In his description of the bakers, Sennett resisted
using the word *alienation* in the traditional Marxist sense, where
it represents the spark that ignites the worker's struggle, instead
suggesting that the bakers had merely become indifferent to their
work. What is significant here is that the process of computerisation
and deskilling that Sennett describes can be observed even in
society's most coveted jobs. Even in high-tier jobs, knowledge can

be encapsulated in electronic process manuals, which map out the procedures of the job to the last detail, or by semi-automated computer programs, which perform work tasks with a minimum of human intervention (Brown et al., 2011). If the computerisation of the labour process allows many jobs to be performed without the skills and initiative they may have once demanded, this can have a ruinous effect on workplace cultures, leaving many workers feeling uninterested in and detached from the work they perform. Modern forms of work may be cleaner and quieter than industrial labour, but it is clear that many of the traditional sources of dissatisfaction still remain.

The new intimacy of work

The term *alienation* has traditionally been used to describe workers' detachment from or indifference to the work that they do – a trend that is as prevalent in today's era of computerised labour as it was in the heyday of Ford's assembly line. However, in the twenty-first century we are also now seeing the normalisation of a new form of alienation. This new form is characterised not by the exclusion of human qualities from the labour process, but by the enrolment and exploitation of these qualities. The problem here is not that the labour process presents no opportunities for expression and identification, but that the employer expects workers to become fully involved and invested in the job. The insights developed around this new form of alienation are indebted to C. Wright Mills' classic study *White Collar* (Mills, 1956), though discussions in this area were subsequently popularised by Arlie Hochschild and her theory of 'emotional labour' (Hochschild, 1983). Both authors essentially posed the same question: what are the consequences when instead of being asked to leave their human qualities at home in the morning, workers are expressly asked to bring their emotions, their personalities and their individuality to work?

In her book *The Managed Heart* (1983), Hochschild suggested that in order to function as integrated members of society, people are regularly required to manage their emotions. We might, for example, be required to conjure up a display of gratitude after unwrapping a poorly judged gift, or we might try to squash down a desire to laugh when a friend suffers misfortune. In the social world, we are constantly required to *work* upon our feelings in order to express the socially appropriate emotion or, as Hochschild put it, to satisfy the culturally negotiated 'feeling rules' of a given situation. Hochschild's theory is relevant to modern-day work experiences in so far as the ability to perform emotion work has increasingly come to represent a source of commercial value. The most obvious examples of emotional labour are found in the service industry, where the management of emotions is a core element of the job. Service workers are constantly required to 'induce or suppress feeling in order to sustain the outward countenance that produces the proper state of mind in others' (Hochschild, 1983: 7).

Hochschild developed these ideas by studying the work of flight attendants in the early 1980s. She found that the attendants were being intensively coached to adopt the emotional comportment most appropriate to the provision of a good service: trainees were instructed to present a warm personality, a spirit of enthusiasm, and a 'high moral character' (Hochschild, 1983: 97). Airline advertising promised customers a friendly flight, and the hostesses were also taught to follow precise anger management techniques to help them remain polite to problem passengers. Hochschild argued that managers' attempts to dictate employees' affective behaviour constitutes a kind of emotional standardisation or Taylorism: 'social exchange is forced into narrow channels; there may be hiding places along the shore, but there is much less room for individual navigation of the emotional waters' (Hochschild, 1983: 119). A private emotional system has come to be governed by a commercial logic, and the worker's right to command her own emotional and interactional conduct has been relinquished. We can consider the comparable situation of many of today's high-street retail workers, many of whom will receive training in the simulation of friendliness, or be provided with step-by-step scripts and on-screen prompts that guide them through customer interactions.[1] Adherence to the feeling rules is often enforced via an elaborate disciplinary apparatus, with surveillance cameras, 'mystery customers', customer complaints procedures and employee appraisals all functioning to maintain the predictability of employee behaviour.

Hochschild's main concerns surrounded the potentially stressful or psychologically numbing effects of emotional labour. The daily demand to separate external social performances from internal feelings was seen as a source of mental strain. Attempts to micromanage workers' interactional conduct might also be experienced as a kind of personal violation, because emotion work 'draws on a source of self that we honour as deep and integral to our individuality' (Hochschild, 1983: 7). The forced smile at an awkward customer, the repressed rage towards a vindictive boss, the displays of enthusiasm required to reach the top – these little personal sacrifices eventually stack up, causing mental fatigue, or perhaps even compromising the worker's sense of self. If the rise of service work seemed to signal a welcome reintroduction of human capacities into the labour process, Franco Berardi suggests that emotional (or what he here calls 'cognitive') labour is more like a laborious drama:

Cognitive labour is essentially a labour of communication, that is to say communication put to work. From a certain point of view, this could be seen as an enrichment of experience. But it is also (and this is generally the rule) an impoverishment, since the communication loses its character of gratuitous, pleasurable and erotic contact, becoming an economic necessity, a joyless fiction. (Berardi, 2009: 87).

To my knowledge, one of the most provocative examples of Berardi's joyless fiction can be found in Cederström and Fleming's book *Dead Man Working* (Cederström and Fleming, 2012). The authors discuss a BBC documentary by Louis Theroux, which followed the lives of young women who live and work in a legal brothel in Nevada, USA. In the documentary, the client that the women seem to dread the most is Hank, an apparently gentle and amiable man whose most notable characteristic is that he never actually wants to have sex with the workers. Cederström and Fleming suggest that the women dreaded Hank more than other clients because Hank demanded more than a surface performance for his money. What Hank pays for when he visits the brothel is a form of what Hochschild might call 'deep acting': he is relatively uninterested in bodies and surface appearances; what he wants is a long evening with an authentic girlfriend, complete with kissing, cuddling, and conversations about the future. This was emotional labour at its most intense.

Emotional prostitution is an extreme example, no doubt, but it does not require a great stretch of the imagination to compare the exhaustion experienced by Hank's 'girlfriends' to the negative experiences of a range of workers whose job is to produce a desired emotional state in others. After all, the vocabulary of resistance to work has so often been linked to the idea of prostitution: 'selling yourself', 'selling your soul', surrendering to 'the Man', and so on. When forced to adopt the values of the company or customer, many workers fear the creeping feeling of inauthenticity or indignity that often follows. The scope of this newer form of alienation becomes apparent when we understand that it is not only service workers who are today enduring the risks of emotionally demanding work. Whilst workers of the industrial age were subject to a bodily discipline, their thoughts and emotions were of little concern to the employer, so long as these thoughts and emotions did not impinge on job performance. However, in today's immaterial forms of work, where it is not always easy to quantify a worker's output, it becomes increasingly difficult for managers to assess each worker's productivity. As a result, workers are increasingly measured by their 'character' (Gorz, 1999: 39–44; Weeks, 2011: 69–75). The good worker is one who demonstrates mastery over the social norms of professionalism, displaying commitment, enthusiasm, and an alignment with the goals of the organisation. Since it is difficult to say, objectively speaking, which worker is the most productive, the best employee is the one who is aspirational, affable, dynamic, and a team player.

Catherine Casey explored the high-commitment culture of capitalist organisations in her case study of the Fortune 500 corporation Hephaestus (a pseudonym) (Casey, 1995). Hephaestus's managers were striving to foster a workplace with the solidarity and cohesion of industrial culture but, like in all modern corporations, the managers also wanted their discipline to be smooth and inconspicuous, in order to reduce the possibility of conflict. Casey argues that companies often pursue this ideal with a significant financial investment into efforts to encourage employees to align their values and identities with the company. Workers are, in other words, transformed into 'company people'. In Hephaestus, identification with work was promoted via an organisational rhetoric around ideas like 'team' and 'family', designed to encourage workers to feel a sense of devotion and personal obligation. Ideas like 'team' and 'family' function to reframe the workplace as a field of ethical rather than economic obligation, binding workers more tightly to the goals of the organisation. Casey writes that the archetypal Hephaestus employee is one who is 'unquestionably hard-working, who is dedicated, loyal and committed to the company and its products, and is willing to go the extra mile for the company and for his or her team' (Casey, 1995: 127). Employees responded to these obligations with emotional labour, which saw them engaged in careful, sustained efforts to manage their comportment and use of language. The strong performative requirements of the job were brilliantly captured by the participant Jerry, who carried around a briefcase with nothing in it, simply because it made him look professional. Hephaestus employees also communicated their loyalty by conspicuously working extra hours. Workers who came in on weekends wanted other staff to *see* their cars in the car park, and workers whose family commitments prevented them from arriving early or staying late were compelled to stage theatrical displays of regret and apology in the corridors. Once these high-commitment conventions had been embedded into the workplace culture, it was hard for employees to resist them. Casey observed that the 'family' and the 'team' quickly turned on workers who failed to deliver the goods.

Workers respond to high-commitment organisational cultures in different ways, of course. In the case of Hephaestus, some workers colluded in the workplace culture, others defended themselves against it, and others surrendered to it knowingly, with the understanding that this would probably make their lives easier. Regardless of workers' orientations to the high-commitment workplace culture, however, Casey ultimately argued, Hephaestus was a company rife with psychic anxiety, obsessive-compulsion, and self-admonishment. None of this is terribly surprising: it simply gives substance to a widespread cultural fear that our jobs will consume us. What is especially concerning, however, is the extent to which the high-commitment cultures that Casey and others have described no longer appear to be confined to the upper echelons of the job market. Now the ability to make a convincing display of professionalism is expected of employees in less auspicious, lower-paid jobs too. A person in my own study (Matthew, whom we will meet later) brought to my attention a job advert for shelf fillers at the big-box bargain store B&M. The advert stated: 'If you're ambitious, have great personal skills and a passion for success (just like us), you're sure to like working at B&M!' It seems unlikely that professional qualities such as ambition and passion would be significantly utilised in the stacking of shelves, but the employer nevertheless asks for them. Research by Colin Cremin suggests that this reflects a general trend. His analysis of job advertisements in the *Yorkshire Post* between 1870 and 2001 found that this 'language of personality' had become increasingly commonplace: 'almost every job requires "communication skills" and is placed within a "team" setting' (Cremin, 2003).

If earlier efforts to standardise and monitor work produced feelings of detachment and indifference in the worker, more recent attempts to encourage emotional investment in work carry their own set of risks. There is a clear limit to how far workers can be goaded into investing themselves in alien goals when the personal costs of intensive work – stress, burnout, the inability to relax out of hours – are so well known. In a remarkable display of resilience, however, many of today's managers are pre-empting this reluctance with yet another strategy. In the interests of profit and productivity, this newest strategy promises to permit workers a greater sense of individuality and freedom. The author of a popular management guide writes that 'when people are happy and free to be themselves, they are more productive and give more of themselves' (Bains, 2007). This new ethos sees aspects of workers' personalities that were previously barred or ignored by their employers being dragged into the workplace. 'Being yourself' and 'having fun' are emphasised, and organisations' earlier attempts to create uniform work cultures and a high level of identification with company values are written off as crude and passé. This new ethos is sometimes referred to as the 'Californian ideology', owing to its prevalence in America's Silicon Valley. In the UK, it is perhaps epitomised by the (albeit extreme) example of London's coveted Google offices, which comprise a sort of playground featuring beanbags, allotments, chill-out zones and an old-fashioned sitting room, designed to allow employees to 'work from home' whilst remaining in the office.

Peter Fleming and Andrew Sturdy explored this new fun-at-work ethos in their study of the Sunray (a pseudonym) call centre (Fleming and Sturdy, 2011). Sunray's work culture was governed by the cringeworthy principle of the '3Fs': 'Focus, Fun, Fulfilment' – a slogan repeated in team meetings, recruitment literature, and staff appraisal sessions. Attempts to inject fun into the office gave rise to a range of activities, from quizzes, themed fancy dress events and away-days to Friday afternoon drinking games and decorating the office to look like a jungle. Job advertisements for Sunray were headlined with the phrase 'do you know how to party?', and staff were encouraged by managers to 'be themselves' and express their individuality. It is probably safe to assume that this right to 'be yourself' did not extend to a right to be negative or unhappy. The right attitude consists in a performance which communicates 'a positive personality, a childish playfulness, a bubbly frame of mind and an extroverted and careless disposition' (Fleming and Spicer, 2004: 82). Introverts, thinkers, and people with more wayward or rebellious definitions of fun need not apply. Fleming and Sturdy also found that the call centre's electronic panopticon, with its more traditional controls (automatic call distribution, performance monitoring, and a hierarchical management structure), was still very much in operation. Whilst some of the workers interviewed said they enjoyed the 3Fs ethos, others felt they were being brainwashed.

Fleming and Sturdy were deeply critical of what they observed at Sunray, arguing that the rhetoric of fun and individuality at work ultimately serves two main purposes. The first is to 'capture the sociality' of the worker. By encouraging workers to bring their personalities to work, the managers hope that staff will then offer customers a more personable service. The second and more prominent function is to divert attention away from an otherwise alienating work process: 'The management rationale for the "3Fs" was to compensate for the hard and mundane work required of agents and secured by technical, bureaucratic and cultural controls' (Fleming and Sturdy, 2011: 192). What is telling is the extent to which workers were less permitted than *commanded* to 'be themselves'. The paradoxical injunction to *'be yourself… or else'* confused even the managers. A human resource manager awkwardly bumbles:

> Every 3Fs activity we undertake is implemented in a controlled way and adherence is mandatory – although individualism and creativity are encouraged … we have one Sunray attitude … um … but people can still be themselves. (Fleming and Sturdy, 2011: 191)

It ultimately seems that the much-touted freedom of the Californian ideology is a superficial, carefully administered kind of freedom, which takes place within strict boundaries. To borrow some of

Fleming and Sturdy's examples: it is a freedom to have a unique hair colour, wear a short skirt, or display a surfboard in your cubicle, but not to have a real influence over the labour process. As well as representing a superficial form of liberty, measures to inject an element of fun and freedom into the work environment could also have the detrimental impact of making ethically dubious work pleasurable. As Gorz suggested, it is possible to have a congenial and enjoyable work environment regardless of what is produced, whether it is 'chemical weapons or medicines, Action Men or educational games, pornography or art books' (Gorz, 1985: 52). In the 'humanised' offices of a company known to exploit sweatshop labourers, get children hooked on sugary cereal, or open up new markets for pharmaceuticals, the middle manager might forget any moral qualms by wearing a T-shirt to work, decorating his office, and enjoying the perks of a corporate lunch date. The humanisation of the working day may bring its own superficial pleasures, but it certainly does not guarantee that the job will serve humane, socially valuable ends.

The limits to autonomy in work

We have seen that whilst a range of authors following Marx commented on the alienating qualities of industrial labour, others, anticipating the shift to a new, knowledge-based economy, believed that the future would be brighter. It was thought that emerging forms of employment would present opportunities for a humanisation of work. What is apparent, however, is that there are still strong continuities with alienating forms of mechanical labour in terms of the way the labour process itself is organised and experienced. Taylorism lives on in the age of computerisation, as workers continue to be timed, micro-managed, and forced by a profit-motivated system of production to work on small, repetitive tasks. On top of these more traditional controls we have also seen the emergence of a new form of alienation, consisting in the corporation's attempt to enrol and exploit the worker's selfhood. The rise of service work has also seen a rise in attempts to micro-manage the employee's emotional conduct. Alongside this, strategies of workplace culture management have attempted to elicit full identification with the job role and, where these initiatives have proved limited, a new ethos of play at work has attempted to dress alienating labour in a language of fun and freedom. In each case, work appears to offer the promise of becoming more liberating and humane – to offer people the opportunity to use their communicative abilities; to feel a sense of belonging in the organisation; to be themselves and have fun in their jobs – but in each case, work also appears to have become more invasive, its demands on our selves deepening, and its methods of control becoming more psychologically sophisticated and encompassing.

I should qualify this point by saying that the trends I have identified here are only general trends, of course, and cannot speak for the work experiences of everybody. In the 1960s, Robert Blauner argued that the question of whether work has become alienating is too often posed in a general fashion. Through his comparative research into industrial workplaces he was able to show that workers' experiences varied greatly, both within and between industries, and he thus concluded that it is more appropriate to speak of 'alienating tendencies' in work than to claim that all work has become alienating (Blauner, 1964). Not even the more radical critics of work suggest that modern forms of employment preclude all possibility of expression, initiative and collaboration. Gorz argued that even when the worker is not in control of the goals and methods of production, work can still be congenial and enjoyable: 'heteronomy does not mean that the workplace has to be a hell or a purgatory' (Gorz, 1985: 51).

Whilst we can certainly recognise that it is possible for work to be pleasant and interesting, however, I would still maintain that alienation remains a major source of modern misery, and another social issue which calls for a concerted re-evaluation of the work-centred society. If work can often be gratifying, it is clear that access to rewarding, meaningful employment remains profoundly unequal, and that the moral sanctity of work is painfully out of step with the way that a vast proportion of people actually experience their jobs. The problem here is that the supply of rewarding jobs by capitalist firms is not determined by the human need for settings in which to perform interesting work, but by whether or not these jobs are profitable for the firm. Beyond the incentive to make work at least bearable, so that workers continue to turn up and perform, there is nothing in the logic of capitalism that compels it to cater to the human desire for meaningful, fulfilling work (Wright, 2010: 48). For proof of this, we need only look at how quickly any visage of equity and co-operation between workers and bosses collapses as soon as the company is forced to cut costs and get rid of workers. Such incidents act as crude reminders that the workers are, when it comes down to it, not part of a company family, but disposable instruments for the generation of private profit (Gorz, 1989: 64).

We can define true, meaningful work as work in which people are allowed to carry out tasks in accordance with their own technical, aesthetic and social criteria, i.e., to work in accordance with their own ideas of efficiency, beauty and usefulness. There are clear limitations regarding the extent to which this kind of true, meaningful work can be experienced in the jobs provided by a capitalist economy. Whilst many employers today do call upon workers to consult and reflect, to plan and discuss, and to 'express their real selves', any autonomy that the worker is permitted is always limited by the broader goals of the enterprise, which are always shaped by the company and the economic forces in which it operates. Fleming and Sturdy argued that attempts to inject the human element back into work ultimately amount to the installation of 'freedom *around* control' (Fleming and Sturdy, 2011) – perhaps a deliberate echo of Gorz's earlier reference to 'autonomy within heteronomy' (Gorz, 1999). If modern forms of work invite us to be active, expressive and collaborative, we are only invited to be these things within the confines of the goals that the company has set for us.

> Capitalism calls on [workers] to consult and reflect, to plan and discuss what they do, to be the autonomous subjects of production, but it enjoins them also to confine their autonomy within pre-set limits and direct it towards preordained aims. (Gorz, 1999: 39)

One of the crucial premises of critical social theory and the argument for a reduction of work is the conviction that work will always be alienating to some degree, so long as certain broader freedoms are left unaddressed. Even if workers are permitted a degree of control over the organisation of the labour process, Gorz points out that workers generally still have no place to question the use-value of the products and services provided, or to engage in a debate about the impact of these products and services on society as a whole (Gorz, 1985: 51). A *genuine* autonomy in our productive activities – of the rigorous kind that Gorz argued for – hinges on establishing a freedom to engage with bigger questions. Genuine autonomy consists in a freedom to have a say in what is being produced, and for whose benefit. It consists in a freedom to question the authenticity and the importance of the needs that work is designed to meet (Gorz, 1999: 41).

Finally, we can note that even in cases where workers can be given a greater degree of autonomy in their job roles, the occupation of a full-time job still usually means that our skills and capacities are narrowly focused on one activity to the exclusion of others. Even if work is pleasant, it will still usually confine us to a prescribed and delimited role within the economic system, silencing those parts of ourselves that do not serve our allotted position in the capitalist process of production. The term *role* itself, 'borrowed from the domain of the theatre, suggests that the existence foisted upon people by society is identical neither with people as they are in themselves nor with all that they could be' (Adorno, 2001: 187). A person may find temporary solace in calling himself a teacher, a bar manager, or a policeman, but none of these identities says everything about who he actually is. No matter how hard a person tries to achieve self-actualisation through the adoption of a work role, he will always fail, because – in the words of Renata Salecl – 'there will always be something within him that cannot be defined by an external identity' (Salecl, 2011: 49). As a culture, we have now more or less accepted the idea that many people's working lives will often have little or no relationship to the values and activities that characterise their private lives, i.e., that each of us has a 'work me' and a 'home me'. In this context, paid work is rarely experienced as meaningful in and of itself, but only holds on to its subjective relevance in so far as it is regulated from the outside, by incentives such as income, security and prestige – what are ultimately compensations for the personal sacrifices inherent in the workday itself (Gorz, 1989: 35–6).

In sum, the strict limits within which it is possible to exercise autonomy in the work that capitalism provides represent another reason to remain critical of work. What is clear is that the centrality and sanctity of work – its valorisation as a source of identity, status and social contribution – remain sadly out of step with the way that vast numbers of people actually experience their jobs on a day-to-day basis. For many people, paid employment represents less an expression of their productive and creative capacities than an obstacle to the development of these capacities. If creative, meaningful work is no longer generally synonymous with what people do in their paid jobs, then from a humanist or liberatory standpoint it makes sense to begin exploring the possibilities for a reduction of work and an expansion of leisure time. A reduction of work might allow greater scope for people's talents and capacities to flourish elsewhere, in informal networks of production outside the narrow confines of the job roles provided by a capitalist economy.

THREE: The colonising power of work

Economic rationality has no room for authentically free time which neither produces nor consumes commercial wealth.

André Gorz – Critique of Economic Reason (1989: 115)

In her study *The Outsourced Self* (Hochschild, 2012), Arlie Hochschild interviewed a range of people who were catering to their needs not by spending time or co-operating with friends and family, but by spending money on commercial services. Rich in money but short on time, the people she met were relying on dating services, wedding planners, eldercare managers and birthday party organisers to meet their personal and familial needs. With her signature empathy and eye for detail, Hochschild explored the appeal of these services from the perspective of the people who used them, but also the potential drawbacks involved, as life becomes increasingly impersonal and commercialised. Reflecting on her study at a speaking event, Hochschild expressed her particular surprise at how many of the people she met had invested in pristine kitchen fittings or brand-new, hi-tech ovens. This seemed ironic to her, given the busyness of these people's lives, and their evident lack of time to use these facilities. Why upgrade your oven if you haven't got time to cook? Hochschild speculated that the new kitchen appliances acted like totems for the people who bought them: the brand-new oven, sparkling and unused, is a gesture towards the leisurely lifestyle people *wished* they had. We could interpret the clutter of the young professional's apartment in much the same way. The shelves full of half-read novels, the racks full of dusty CDs, and the cupboards full of mouldering camping equipment become symbols of the leisurely life that workers hoped they would have, before their jobs took over.

The topic of this chapter is leisure or, more precisely, why we seem to have so little leisure, and why the leisure time that we do have is so often suffused with a sense of responsibility and anxiety. The current popularity of self-help books coaching their readers to slow down and enjoy life (e.g., Honoré, 2004; Hodgkinson, 2004), as well as the weekly appearance of discussions on 'work–life balance' in broadsheet newspapers, are testaments to the extent to which people are feeling hurried and squeezed in their free-time. According to the International Labour Organisation, in 2013 the UK workforce (including part-time, as well as full-time workers) put in an average of 35.8 hours per week, compared with a 38.6 hour average in the USA. This is a far cry from Keynes's predictions of a radically shorter working week. Figures published by the Trade Union Congress for 2014 suggested that around 20% of the UK workforce regularly work overtime without pay. Within this 20%, the average unpaid hours per week was 7.7 (or an estimated £32bn in unpaid wages), but hundreds of thousands of workers (particularly those in education, hospitality, and mining) reported working nine to ten unpaid hours per week (Trade Union Congress, 2015). The statistics on working hours give a fair assessment of the quantitative impact of work, but in this chapter I argue that the experienced shortage of and anxiety over leisure time is a widespread cultural phenomenon with an important qualitative dimension, and not therefore the preserve of the people with the longest working hours. The degradation of leisure needs to be understood as a symptom of the broader tendency of economic demands to colonise everyday life. At a time when education risks becoming little more than a joyless pursuit of certification for work, when our interactions with others are often shaped by a need for career advancement, and when unemployment has been turned into 'jobseeking' – itself a form of work – how much of our time can we confidently call our own? When, precisely, are we genuinely released from the demand to either produce or consume economic wealth, to become truly free to experience the world and its culture?

'Free-time'

I begin with a simple-sounding question: at what point does a day's work truly end? Whilst our jobs might contractually oblige us to work a certain amount of hours per day, it is clear that we do not simply step out of our workplaces and into a world of freedom. This was brought to light by Theodor Adorno in a short but poignant essay from the 1970s called 'Free Time' (Adorno, 2001). Adorno questioned the extent to which workers are truly autonomous in their time outside work, arguing that the covert aim of non-work time is simply to prepare people for the recommencement of work: free-time is not free at all, but a mere 'continuation of the forms of profit-oriented social life' (Adorno, 2001: 189). This is because it involves activities which often have a similar quality to work (looking at screens, doing chores), but also because more alienating or exhausting forms of work produce a powerful need for recuperation. By draining people's physical and mental energies, work that is alienating ensures that much of the worker's non-work time is spent winding down, retreating to escapist forms of entertainment, or consuming treats which compensate for the day's travails.

If the recuperative or compensatory activities we undertake in our free-time are often enjoyable, Adorno would ultimately argue that they are expressions of a superficial liberty. He argues that free-time is not really free at all, so long as it remains guided by the forces that people are trying to escape. He insists on the need for a distinction between free-time and the more auspicious category of true leisure. If free-time represents a mere continuation of work, then it is true leisure which represents that sweet 'oasis of unmediated life' in which people detach from economic demands and become genuinely free for the world and its culture. Adorno argues that it is the degraded form – free-time, rather than true leisure – which prevails in affluent societies.[1] In this degraded free-time, the self-defined activities performed outside employment tend to be restricted to 'hobbies': trifling activities performed in order to pass the meagre time which is our own. Adorno passionately rejected the term *hobby*, believing that it trivialises the value of unpaid activities. In one memorable passage, he remarked proudly:

> I have no hobby. Not that I am the kind of workaholic, who is incapable of doing anything with his time but applying himself industriously to the required task. But, as far as my activities beyond the bounds of my recognised profession are concerned, I take them all, without exception, very seriously … Making music, listening to music, reading with all my attention, these activities are part and parcel of my life; to call them hobbies would make a mockery of them. (Adorno, 2001: 188–9)

Adorno has often been charged with elitism for adopting a rather militant distinction between 'high' and 'low' culture. In the above quotation, his serious interests in reading, making music and listening to music (which we can safely assume to be classical music) are being furtively contrasted with 'lower', more escapist forms of culture. I will not defend this distinction here, but I will suggest that there is a great deal of contemporary significance in Adorno's broader point about the siege on people's time. Consider the extent to which the standard eight-hour working day fractures free-time into shards. The full-time worker experiences time as a rapid series of discrete pockets: a constantly rotating cycle of work periods and free periods, in which free-time is restricted to evenings, weekends and holidays. When free-time is fragmented in this way, the cursory hobbies that Adorno denounces may be all that we have time for. Slivers of free-time offer limited scope for engagement in more substantial self-defined activities – activities which would demand steady investments of time and energy in the form of concentration, dedication, the building of communities, or the learning of new skills (Lodziak, 2002: 100). The extreme casualty of this situation is today's archetypal rushed worker, who commutes home in the dark hours with emails still to answer, feels too drained to engage emotionally with the family, and is disinclined to do very much other than drink wine and watch TV before bed. The point here is not that drinking wine or watching TV are 'low' activities, but that the worker has been deprived of the time and energy to choose otherwise.

We can find a modern representation of Adorno's point about the degradation of leisure in *The Lego Movie*, released in 2014. When he is not working, the movie's protagonist – an average joe called Emmet – spends most of his time sitting on his couch, listening to the mindless pop song 'Everything is Awesome' (a sort of Lego-world equivalent of 'Happy' by Pharrell Williams), absorbing television adverts, and religiously tuning in for a catchphrase comedy called *Where Are My Pants?* Emmet showers, brushes his teeth and exercises at the exact same time every day, before hitting the same traffic jam, having the same empty conversation with his colleagues, and returning home to his best and only friend – a potted plant. If we are willing to overlook the irony that this critique is born of capitalism's very own culture industry (and what is essentially a multi-million-dollar advert for Lego), we find in *The Lego Movie* a prescient image of the administered nature of modern life.

Adorno's broader point about free-time as a continuation of work has also taken a more literal turn in the twenty-first century, where the rise of networked technologies such as laptops and smartphones has enabled work to bleed into areas of life where it was previously absent and unwelcome. Melissa Gregg has explored how, for many of today's workers, work has broken free from its temporal and spatial confinement to the working day, and now assumes the form of a nagging and ever-present 'to do' list. Through her interviews with office workers, Gregg shows how technologies such as email or instant messaging, whose best design feature is that they allow for asynchronous communication, have ultimately had the opposite effect on today's busy employees, who feel a pressure to be always present, responsive and available, whether in or out of the office (Gregg, 2011). An article on the career tips website The Grindstone suggests that many professionals are now accustomed to the idea of being constantly on call. One reader writes in:

> Keeping up with a client in trouble or with a question via cell or Skype can turn a potential crisis into a gentle bump in the road. Clients will not tolerate an 'I was on vacation' excuse. If we do not perform, my next vacation will be in a hot bath at home with my rubber ducky. (Lepore, 2012)

Like their laptops, it seems that the plugged-in workers of today's high-commitment organisations must always remain on standby.

The pressures of employability

Adorno's broader concerns around the tendency of work to colonise our everyday lives have never been as pertinent and widely applicable as they are today. This is not only because of the fragmentation of free-time and the spillage of the workday outside its usual bounds, but also because free-time is now in jeopardy for people who are between jobs, and even for younger people who have yet to set foot into the world of paid employment. This is in large part down to the new pressures of *employability*: the responsibility of each individual to improve his or her prospects by training, acquiring educational credentials, networking, learning how to project the right kind of personality, and gaining life experiences that match up with the values sought by employers. The notion of employability has risen to remarkable prominence in the early part of the twenty-first century, where it forms the lynchpin of a neoliberal political philosophy, in which the state and employers are no longer committed to, or deemed responsible for, providing citizens with lasting and secure jobs. Those politicians who champion neoliberal policies have glorified paid employment, whilst at the same time dismantling the social protections that have traditionally insulated citizens against the uncertainties of the labour market.[2] Within this context, the capacity of individuals to work relentlessly at their employability has come to be understood as the crux of national and individual prosperity (Chertovskaya et al., 2013).

The pressure to remain employable becomes more powerful when people feel that their futures are lacking in guarantees. From the 1990s onward, influential sociologists such as Richard Sennett (1998), Ulrich Beck (2000) and Zygmunt Bauman (2000) popularised the idea that capitalist societies had entered an age of insecurity.

Among the most insecure are those people who are unprotected by unions, too poorly paid to afford necessities, caught in a debt trap, or cut off from social protections like healthcare, maternity leave and a decent unemployment benefit. This insecurity could include anybody, from the undocumented migrant worker, employed illegally and paid meagre wages, to the single parent who fears losing her benefit entitlement. It also extends to those creative or academic workers who are likely to face futures filled with short-term contracts, relocations and job hunting. We could in fact argue that precariousness is the basic condition of everybody who depends on a wage for his or her survival. Engels, in his 1840s study of the working class in Manchester, reminds us that workers have long lived in fear of becoming superfluous to the requirements of the economy: '[The English proletarian] has not the slightest guarantee that his skill will in future enable him to earn even the bare necessities of life. Every commercial crisis, every whim of his master, can throw him out of work' (Engels, 1987). In today's society, growing numbers of people live in a condition of what Gorz called 'generalised insecurity', always aware on some level that they are potentially unemployed or under-employed, potentially insecure or temporary workers (Gorz, 1999: 52).

Within this social and political climate, it increasingly falls to individuals to protect themselves from unemployment and the whirlpool of low-quality, low-paid jobs. For many people, the cultivation of employability will feel like a lifelong vocation in itself: most understand that 'the possibility of selling their labour power depends on the unpaid, voluntary, unseen work they put in continually to reproduce it anew' (Gorz, 2010: 20-1). Employability even occupies the minds of children. I recall something a twelve-year-old lad once said to me when I was assisting with research into an anti-smoking programme that had been carried out at his school. When I asked him why he had enjoyed the programme, he said 'it will look good on my CV'. This brings us back to Adorno's conviction that even areas of life traditionally thought of as 'non-work' can be seen as extensions of the demands of paid employment. The concern here is that the enjoyment of life is increasingly being subordinated to personal cultivation for the labour market. When the development of employability is a practical necessity and a main mental preoccupation, we become increasingly devoted to doing what needs to be done rather than performing activities because they are intrinsically valuable, i.e., because they develop our personal capacities, or enrich our friendships, or simply because we love to do them. There is less and less time for those autonomous activities whose aim is simply to serve the criteria of the good, the true and the beautiful, as defined by each person.

In the 1930s, Bertrand Russell wrote a series of essays in which he lamented the increasingly hurried and instrumental nature of modern life, recalling, in beautifully written passages, the inherent value of rest, play, contemplation and learning.[3] His central concern was that without a considerable amount of leisure time, humans lose their sense of reverie and become cut off from many of life's pleasures:

> There was formerly a capacity for light-heartedness and play which has been to some extent limited by the cult of efficiency. The modern man thinks everything ought to be done for the sake of something else, and never for its own sake. (Russell, 2004c: 11)

Russell's suggestion that people in modern societies always do one thing for the sake of another could almost be a reference to today's discourse of employability, which asks us to focus less on experiencing and enjoying the present, and think more about how the present can be mobilised in order to meet goals in the future. Aspirational individuals need to study the employability playbook, but be aware that everybody else has been studying it too. The most successful players are savvy in their ability to construct confident and coherent accounts about their past achievements, and about the relevance of these achievements to the world of employment (Brown and Hesketh, 2004). On the job application form, activities which were felt to be valuable in their own right are reframed in the language of employability: my charity work with the homeless must be mentioned because it has given me experience in the voluntary sector, and my hitchhike across Europe promoted because it has developed my ability to use initiative and solve problems.

Compliance in the discourse of employability is partly ensured by the imaginary figure of the future employer, who is always metaphorically looking over one's shoulder. Colin Cremin referred to this psychological apparition as 'the boss of it all': a generalised projection of future employers and their expectations, which regulates a person's actions and choices in the present (Cremin, 2011: 43). The boss of it all is a strict disciplinarian who is not easily impressed. He demands a constant labour of responsibility, rational decision-making, and self-management. If a worker does too many jobs in disparate areas, the boss of it all may see her as flaky, indecisive and unspecialised. But if the same worker languishes in the same job for too many years, the boss of it all may decide that she is complacent, unambitious or too narrow in her outlook. Any young academics reading this will have been drilled to know that in academia, the boss of it all's golden rule is that prospective employees must always remain 'research active'. 'Once you're out of the game, you're out', as an old peer of mine perversely seemed to enjoy saying. Adorno made a similar allusion to the omniscient, imaginary boss in the 1950s, when he remarked on the tense conformism of the aspiring worker:

> All these nervous people, from the unemployed to the public figure liable at any moment to incur the wrath of those whose investment he represents, believe that only by empathy, assiduity, serviceability, arts and dodges, by tradesmen's qualities, can they ingratiate themselves with the executive they imagine omnipresent, and soon there is no relationship that is not seen as a 'connection', no impulse not first censored as to whether it deviates from the acceptable. (Adorno, 2005: 23)

If economic survival means working harder, neglecting personal interests, commuting further, or working on tomorrow's meeting at bedtime, then this is what is done. Reflecting on the rhetoric of job advertisements and graduate recruitment programmes, Costea and colleagues suggest that the discourse of employability conjures in workers a restless sense of 'endless potentiality'. Each worker is taught that he or she can always be *more*, and employability becomes a tragic path whose travellers declare a constant war on themselves, questioning the suitability of their personalities and achievements, never quite satisfied that they are spending their time sensibly enough (Costea et al., 2012). Personal traits that do not fit with the image of the model employee – shyness, low moods, emotional sensitivity – must all be smoothed over in order to present a sellable self that is inoffensive, responsible, graspable and, above all, available for hire (Elraz, 2013). Employability embodies a novel power dynamic, since the personal sacrifices made in its interest are, in a certain sense, self-imposed. Unlike traditional exploitation, which is limited to clocked-in time and imposed externally, through the coercive discipline of bosses and technological control, the discipline demanded by employability is continuous and requires a constant self-policing. Employability represents a 'decentred' form of exploitation that people are forced to submit to in an almost voluntary fashion, as the spatial and temporal boundaries that previously confined exploitation to time on the work clock are dissolved (Cremin, 2011: 58).

Perhaps nowhere is the colonisation of life by work-related demands more evident and disconcerting than in the mainstream education system. Education, defined in the broadest possible sense, has the capacity to deliver a wide range of personal and public benefits: to cultivate a moral and political consciousness in the student; to foster a habit of critical thinking and contemplation; to develop in the student a taste for culture's more sublime and complex pleasures. Education might also teach the broad sets of practical skills that people require in order to become more empowered, less dependent, and able to take care of themselves, their surroundings and each other. All of these are valid and valuable goals for educators, yet the most widely accepted goal of education today is the much narrower one of stratifying the population into groups of employees, preparing and certifying young people for the assumption of a work role (Bowles and Gintis, 1976). We can once again return to Russell, who in the 1930s was already arguing that the modern emphasis on economic values had eclipsed the broader value of learning:

> Throughout the last hundred and fifty years, men have questioned more and more vigorously the value of 'useless' knowledge, and have come increasingly to believe that the only knowledge worth having is that which is applicable to some part of the economic life of the community. (Russell, 2004d: 18–19)

Even if the 'useless knowledge' Russell refers to has no direct economic or social utility, he still argues that it has a vital character, in so far as knowing things can often make life richer. Life is more rewarding when we take an interest, and what we choose to interest us scarcely matters from this point of view. Knowing something about the history of cinema may improve a person's enjoyment of films. Learning how to modify computers, make clothes, fix bikes, or cook Asian food each brings its own pleasures. Russell gives the weirder example of apricots. He says that apricots have always tasted slightly sweeter to him since he learned something about the origins and controversies of their cultivation in the Chinese Han Dynasty (Russell, 2004d: 25). As well as being economically useful, Russell believed, knowledge could be an inherent part of the *joie de vivre* and a source of mental delight in itself.

Russell is among a number of radical authors who have defended the value of a broad and general education, rather than a narrower one, geared towards the preparation and certification of students for work. Another notable supporter of this argument was Erich Fromm, who made an illuminating distinction between learning in the 'having' mode and learning in the 'being' mode (Fromm, 1979). The pressures of employability may be encouraging students to approach their learning in the first of Fromm's modes. Students who learn in the having mode will diligently memorise the key points from a lecture, but 'the content does not become part of their own individual system of thought, enriching and widening it' (Fromm, 1979: 37). Their relationship with learning is an acquisitive one: they seek to possess rather than absorb and integrate knowledge, to the ends of passing examinations and securing a qualification. Knowledge is retained, but students do not become involved in their learning or use it to address their own sets of problems. The main context of learning is anxiety. This contrasts with those students who learn in the more lively 'being' mode. Unlike the acquisitive students, these students become genuinely occupied with their learning: 'What they listen to stimulates their own thinking processes. New questions, new ideas, new perspectives arise in their minds. Their listening is an alive process' (Fromm, 1979: 38).

For both Fromm and Russell alike, it seems that the ultimate goal of education should not be to furnish students with this or that nugget of knowledge, but to foster in them a contemplative habit of mind. Education should inspire in the student a broad and humane outlook on life in general:

> What is needed is not this or that specific piece of information, but such knowledge as inspires a conception of the ends of human life as a whole: art and history, acquaintance with the lives of heroic individuals, and some understanding of the strangely accidental and ephemeral position of man in the cosmos – all this touched with an emotion of pride in what is distinctively human, the power to see and know, to feel magnanimously and to think with understanding. (Russell, 2004d: 27)

At present, the kind of broad education that Russell describes tends to be closeted in universities, or confined to the more privileged members of society – groups of people who can study freely because they are unrestricted by the urgent need to make a living. The pressures of today's labour market mean that few people who would be inclined actually manage to enjoy lives in which intellectual development and cultural activities figure as integrated, lifelong pleasures (Ryle and Soper, 2002: 183). The work ethic, along with cuts to arts budgets (and unemployment benefits, which bohemians have historically used as a sort of unofficial arts budget) have also made it less feasible for cultural creators to wing it for a few years in order to hone their craft and perhaps find a way to make a living from it.

As they leave the bosom of the university, many students are also realising that graduates are no longer free from the kinds of risks and uncertainties previously thought to be the preserve of low-paid, low-skilled workers (Brown et al., 2011). This climate of uncertainty puts a strong premium on the ability of students to take an active approach to their employability and think in practical, instrumental ways about how to secure their futures. Furthermore, the student debt caused by rising tuition fees and the abolition of student grants may be tying young people to a need to earn, long before they have had a chance to reflect on the trade-off between the benefits of a good income and the sacrifices of work. Predictions suggest that in the UK, students who started courses in 2011 will have an average debt of £23,000 by the time they graduate, with this figure rising to as much as £53,000 for 2012 entrants in England, given the latest rise in tuition fees.[4] Berardi compares the student loan to Faust's pact with the devil. In exchange for knowledge and credentials, students agree to a debt that will end up regulating their actions and shackling them to a future obligation to work (Berardi, 2009). Like the competitive graduate, the indebted graduate is more easily cajoled into doing more for less, making him ideal fodder for the thousands of unpaid internships available in today's labour market, many of which offer no guarantee of skills development or future employment (Perlin, 2012).[5]

Ultimately, the pressures of employability are bringing to fruition Max Horkheimer's lamentation on the 'loss of interiority' in advanced capitalist societies: societies in which 'the wings of the imagination have been clipped too soon', as individuals are increasingly forced to adopt a more practical and instrumental orientation to the world and others (Horkheimer, 1974: 25). A side effect of this loss of interiority is that we, as a society, may be losing our grip on the criteria that judge an activity to be worthwhile and meaningful, even if it does not contribute directly to the project of employability or the needs of the economy. Gorz poses the question: 'When am I truly myself, that is, not a tool or the product of outside powers and influences, but rather the originator of my acts, thoughts, feelings, values?' (Gorz, 1986). In a society where non-work is often merely an extension of work – time for recuperating, consuming anaesthetising products and entertainment, or sensibly cultivating one's employability – I contend that this question has become worryingly difficult to answer.

The gospel of consumption

At the beginning of this chapter, I cited Gorz's contention that economic rationality has 'no room for authentically free time which neither produces nor consumes economic wealth' (Gorz, 1989: 115). To understand fully the extent to which economic demands have taken over our time, we need to return to a basic principle of the 'end of work' argument, introduced in Chapter 1. The 'end of work' argument draws attention to the fact that advances in the knowledge and technologies of production have a natural tendency to eliminate the need for human labour. This is why Keynes and others anticipated a drastic reduction in working hours over the course of the twentieth century. Since it would take us less and less time to collectively produce the goods we needed, we would be free to enjoy a greater quantity of leisure. Less bound by necessity, man would finally have the privilege of confronting that deeper problem of 'how to use his freedom from pressing economic cares' (Keynes, 1932: 366).

In his book *Work Without End* (Hunnicutt, 1988), Benjamin Hunnicutt suggested that the shift to a more leisurely society was a realistic proposition in the 1920s, at which point the working week had already been shrinking over a series of decades, and unions had been active in the fight for shorter hours. In the USA, up until 1932 the Republican and Democratic parties had both included shorter working hours in their political agendas. The average US working week fell (depending on the sector) from around 55 to 60 hours per week in 1900, to around 40 hours in the 1950s.[6] Despite these historical precedents, however, it is clear that nothing close to the more leisurely society envisaged by work's critics has actually come to pass. From the vantage point of the twenty-first century, we would be forgiven for seeing earlier predictions for a radically reduced working week as nothing more than a historical curio – a nice but rather outlandish idea that was forgotten about decades ago. Hunnicutt explains the abandonment of the shorter hours agenda partly in terms of the fierce opposition from business leaders. In the early twentieth century, they widely recognised that the natural result of improved production techniques would be an increase in free-time, but still adamantly opposed the proposition of reduced working hours. From the perspective of business leaders, 'excessive free-time was symptomatic of economic failure, of the inability to find markets for new products and the increasing burden of surpluses' (Hunnicutt, 1988: 42). As well as the prospect of idleness being morally objectionable (an issue I take up in Chapter 4), the idea of less work and more leisure was completely counterintuitive to the dogma of economic growth.

If business leaders in the earlier part of the twentieth century were concerned about economic stagnation, these worries would be assuaged with the arrival of what Hunnicutt called the 'new economic gospel of consumption' (Hunnicutt, 1988: Chapter 2). The twentieth century was to become an age of intense consumer demand:

> If existing markets were being saturated, then the reasonable response
> would be to find new markets and increase consumption, not reduce
> working hours. Businessmen became increasingly convinced that Amer-
> icans could be persuaded to buy things produced by industry that they
> had never needed before and could consume goods and services, not in
> response to some out-of-date set of economic motives, but according to
> a standard of living that constantly improved. (Hunnicutt, 1988: 42)

It seems that predictions for a reduction of work, from Keynes and
others, had drastically overlooked the extent to which the agents of
capitalism would force us to accept the dividend of growing productivity not in the form of more leisure time, but in the form of more
consumption. Any potential gains in free-time won as a result of
growing productivity would be reabsorbed by capitalism as existing
markets expanded, new markets were created, and the commercial
sphere spread its way into hitherto uncommodified areas of life. The
story of capitalism in the twentieth century and beyond was thus not
to be a story about the liberation of humans from the need to work;
it would instead be a story about the creation of an enormous range
of dubious, previously unnecessary work tasks, based around the
manufacture, distribution and marketing of disposable consumer
goods. It would also be a story about how leisure was pressed as far
as possible into the service of consumption:

> Leisure was seen to be valuable, not because it perfected work or led
> to higher things, but because it was helpful in promoting consump-
> tion and more employment. Productivity was valued, not because it
> reduced the burden of working, but because it allowed industry to
> progress to new frontiers of goods and services. (Hunnicutt, 1988: 51)

Hunnicutt's account of the abandonment of shorter hours
in favour of the gospel of consumption allows us to clearly see

capitalism for what it really is: a system which aims to produce needs rather than satisfy them once and for all. The ongoing challenge that the market always faces is to keep consumers wanting and desiring: 'As Marx had foreseen, monopoly capitalism found itself faced with the problem of shaping subjects for the objects to be marketed; not of adjusting supply to demand, but demand to supply' (Gorz, 1967: 70). Hunnicutt quotes Charles Kettering, director of the General Motors Research Laboratory, who admitted as much when he said that the aim of businesses must be the 'organised creation of dissatisfaction' (Kettering, 1929). In Gorz's phrasing, capitalism's stakeholders would set out to promote a cultural ethos of 'the more the better', undermining people's ability to decide and stick to their own definitions of sufficiency (Gorz, 1989: Chapter 9). If a degree of consumer satisfaction was necessary for getting the wealthier members of society hooked on spending, this satisfaction should ideally have a fleeting rather than an enduring quality, so as to maintain the consumer's thirst for more. Justin Lewis has referred to modern capitalism as 'the insatiable age': an age that is 'oozing with gratification and yet underpinned by a permanent *dis*content' (Lewis, 2013: 54). We live within a system that is both economically and culturally biased towards preventing people from feeling satisfied with their material lot, to the extent that the boundless desire for consumer goods has become one of Western societies' hallmark features. The question we are left with is *how*. How has the capitalist system persuaded us to sacrifice the fight for shorter working hours and more leisure time to a desire for more stuff? What is it that motivates consumer spending today?

Perhaps the most obvious answer here is advertising. One of the most well-known texts on the power of advertising is Vance Packard's uncompromising classic *The Hidden Persuaders* (Packard,

1957). Packard was concerned with the strategies of advertisers who, in the 1950s, were beginning to refine their techniques of consumer persuasion, moving away from the traditional hard sell towards more subtle techniques of psychological manipulation and seduction. As the market for consumer goods became increasingly crowded, it was no longer enough for advertisers simply to list the positive features of the product being sold. This advertising strategy is laughable to modern viewers, who have now become accustomed to a much more diverse and sophisticated arsenal of persuasion, to the extent that it is common for modern advertisements to ignore completely the features of the product being sold. Packard was concerned about the susceptibility of audiences to the appearance of more innovative advertising techniques, and hoped to educate his readers to view advertising with a more critical eye.

Packard and other critics of advertising have often been criticised for having an exaggerated sense of the suggestibility of television viewers, with some scholars bristling at the idea that advertising wields a power to conjure false needs out of thin air. However, perhaps a more accurate way of understanding modern advertising is not as something which produces false needs, but as something that strives to promote commodified means of meeting *true* needs. Adverts often appeal to a real need for things like social acceptance, respect, self-esteem and a cultural identity, trying to persuade us that these things can be purchased.

> The craft of most contemporary advertising is to bypass informed judgements about quality and price and to juxtapose the object with an emotion or idea. The aim is to create a symbolic association between a product or a brand and something more ephemeral – images of popularity, attractiveness, family harmony, sophistication, good health or any other of the social values we hold dear. (Lewis, 2013: 82)

In the world of adverts, a certain brand of camera not only has more features, but will also identify you as a semi-pro photographer or a world traveller; a more expensive brand of dog food will not only feed your dog more nutrients, but also mark you out as a more discerning type of dog owner; a clothing range that donates a portion of its profits to charity not only will see you dressed smartly, but will also help you show the world that you are an ethically conscious consumer.

Some of today's adverts take things a step further and play on the sceptical 'knowingness' of the viewer. A long-running series of adverts for the men's deodorant Lynx, for example, comically exaggerates the old trope about scented toiletries making men more sexy. In the adverts, a spray of Lynx acts as a literal babe magnet, making the wearer instantly irresistible to all women. The media-literate viewer is made to feel smart for getting the joke, but the advert still works in favour of the brand, which comes off as a cool, humorous and sophisticated kind of brand, unafraid to mess around with the old-school conventions of advertising. A comparable strategy has long been used by Guinness, whose television adverts have often had the production values of short artistic films. The product – the pint of Guinness itself – is usually featured only minimally in the advertisement, marking out Guinness as a confident and tasteful brand that does not need to resort to the cheap tactics of persuasion (even if this is exactly what it has done). In all of these examples, the advert is less about a product than about buying into an *idea*.

We have all seen these adverts, and many of us watched them sceptically, yet this is not enough to prevent the constant exposure to the media's world of lavish and fashionable lifestyles from producing within us a powerful sense of lack: 'We watch the way television families live, we read about the lifestyles of celebrities and other public figures we admire, and we consciously and unconsciously assimilate this information' (Schor, 1998: 4). This is not to say that we mindlessly absorb media messages like a drug injection, but it is to suggest that media images of the good life are constantly working upon and exaggerating our desire for material goods. Helga Dittmar puts it well when she suggests: 'Nobody believes they will transform into a supermodel or celebrity if they can buy product X. Rather, consumer ideals have indirect but powerful effects on individuals' thoughts, feelings and behaviours, which take effect over time' (Dittmar, 2007: 25).

The aspirational imagery of advertising indeed seems almost impossible to escape in contemporary society. In the 1990s, researchers in the USA estimated that by the age of eighteen the average American will have seen around 350,000 advertisements (Law, 1994). In 2011, this level of cultural of exposure cost the advertising industry a gargantuan global total of $500 billion.[7] In addition to traditional advertising spaces such as billboards and TV commercials, there are also a range of new and more insidious formats in the form of product placement deals, commercial tie-ins, Amazon recommendations, online 'wish lists', and clickable ads tailored to the information harvested from people's Facebook profiles. If we own any kind of networked electronic device, advertising is a major part of our day-to-day experiences and extremely difficult to ignore. The message of advertising's immense landscape is ubiquitous and uniform: it tells us that no matter how much we already have, the only real way to secure happiness is to buy more.

In the more forgiving realm of cultural studies, the tendency of social critics to view the average consumer as a victim of media manipulation has produced a reactionary response. Commentaries have offered an alternative theory of consumer motivation, leaning towards the image of an active consumer who exercises choice, control and power in her consumption activities (e.g., Fiske, 1989; Willis, 1991; Featherstone, 1991). Some compare the consumer to the maker of a patchwork blanket, who stitches together the aesthetic or symbolic qualities of consumer goods in order to playfully construct a personal image. As Conrad Lodziak (a staunch critic of this approach) summarises: this new consensus 'portrays the realm of consumption as an arena of choice and individual freedom, it focuses on the meaningful nature of consumption – its symbolic rather than its material use value, and it emphasises the significance of consumption for the formation, maintenance and expression of self-identity and lifestyle' (Lodziak, 2002: 1). When trying to understand consumer motivations, we would of course be mistaken to overlook the enabling properties of many consumer goods in allowing us to enjoy some form of pleasure, accomplish a particular task, or communicate a certain sense of style. If cultural studies has done consumers a service in approaching them as agents rather than victims of manipulation, however, it has done so at the expense of drastically downplaying capitalism's systemic need for people to keep on shopping.

Reminding us of this, the philosopher Kate Soper recalls the aftermath of 9/11 and the way in which American consumers were beckoned by the government to shop 'patriotically' in order to exercise their liberty and demonstrate their allegiance to the Western way of life. Soper interpreted this desperate plea for people to stop mourning and start shopping as a remarkable reminder of the dependency of corporate power on people's loyalty to consumerism (Soper, 2008: 568). When trying to understand what motivates consumers, we need to take this on board, and we do not need to resort to an account of the consumer as a manipulated dope in order to accommodate the idea that capitalism is a system which manufactures needs. Kim Humphery proposes that we can come to an enlightened understanding of what motivates consumers by observing the various ways in which the market has come to *encircle* us, making it feel difficult or unnatural to meet many needs without recourse to spending. The concept of encirclement highlights the various ways in which the economic and temporal arrangements of capitalism have gradually reshaped our communities, dwellings and routines in ways that privilege a high level of consumption.

> Metaphorically, [the idea of] encirclement conveys the sense in which we in affluent nations live our lives through public, private, institutional and commercial space, and through a temporal arrangement of day-to-day activities, that has arisen in intimate connection with a market capitalism and that places us in a life-world utterly geared for consumption. (Humphery, 2010: 133)

With this in mind, let us pose the question again: how does capitalism produce in us a need to spend more and more, to the detriment of our freedom to work less? Humphery's idea of encirclement is faithful to Gorz's suggestion that most consumer transactions are not produced by the hidden persuasions of advertising but are actually best understood as obligatory, or made objectively necessary by capitalism. As far as the production of needs is concerned, Gorz argued that advertising and other techniques of cultural persuasion are just the icing on the cake, operating on people who are already compelled to consume due to the alienation of labour. This is to say that participating in paid employment, as well as allowing us to fund our consumption with income, also tends to *encourage* us to spend our money. The full-time working week encourages spending because it tends to devour people's time and energy, resourcing them with cash, but depriving them of the capacity for autonomy and self-production (Lodziak, 2002: 89). This explains the widespread consumption of commodities and services whose main draw is their convenience. From ready meals to dishwashers and home-cleaning services, a range of needs which people could self-furnish – had they the time and energy – are now conventionally met through commercial transactions. Gorz's suggestion that consumption is fuelled by the alienation of labour also draws attention to the fact that a certain proportion of people's spending might be explained as an effort to find solace and compensation for misery at work. It has been suggested that luxury goods provide consolation for the 'unmet needs of the spirit' (Soper, 2008: 576), or that the frivolity and impulsivity of the shopping experience are enjoyed as a contrast to the discipline of work (Bauman, 2001: 15). The home decked out with consumer goods represents a private realm over which the individual can rule, in retreat from work's relations of subordination as 'solitary sovereign' (Gorz, 1967: 68).

The explanation for consumer motivations offered here is not the consumer's materialism, simple-mindedness, or narcissistic hunger for distinction, but the gradual reshaping of society's conventions, temporal rhythms and built environments in ways which construct commodity-intensive lifestyles as the norm. Central to this process is capitalism's tendency towards commodification. Activities that were previously excluded from the economic sphere are being progressively pulled into its orbit, and the satisfaction of a growing range of needs, from social contact to knowledge, transportation, health, fun, shelter, nourishment, safety and self-distinction – needs which were previously satisfied with a lower volume or smaller range of commodities – is now increasingly reliant on financial transactions in the market. The need for exercise is increasingly satisfied through expensive gym memberships and personal trainers, and the need for hydration is met not by turning on the tap but by buying a manufactured and branded 'drink'. The withdrawal of amenities such as public libraries and subsidised leisure centres, as well as the under-maintenance of public parks, has also contributed to the process of encirclement, coinciding with the development of city centres into 'malls without walls' – places where it has become increasingly difficult to hang around without spending money (Minton, 2009: 19). This process of commodification has seen consumption slowly replace self-production as the norm, reshaping the world into which new generations are born and socialised, to the extent that it is now abnormal, impossible, and in some cases even criminal to meet many personal needs without recourse to consumption. Gorz suggests that, at their most extreme, capitalist societies are made up of 'worker-consumers', in which economic arrangements are designed so that people produce none of the things they consume, and consume none of the things they produce (Gorz, 1989: 22). In a world where children are no longer surrounded by adults who have the time, energy and know-how to do things for themselves, the persuasive power of advertisements only serves to reinforce the widely accepted idea that 'you work to earn money in order to buy the things you need and want' (Lodziak and Tatman, 1997: 72).

What all of this means is that consumers' needs are exaggerated in a variety of ways: certainly in part through the persuasive tactics of media advertising, but also through a range of other impositions to spend money, which are more accurately described as structural rather than cultural in their character. The encirclement of individuals by the market and the exaggeration of the need to consume that this entails are among the chief mechanisms through which capitalism remains mobilised against the possibility of a reduction of work. A powerful need to consume increases people's sense of reliance on the income earned through working, and also helps to vindicate the devotion of vast proportions of the economy to the production and distribution of disposable goods. In the words of J. K. Galbraith, the constant amplification of consumers' needs under capitalism represents at least one part of the 'elaborate social camouflage' that keeps societies from realising that a reduction of work is possible (Galbraith, 1958: 264). The development of productive technologies offered Western society choice: to have more leisure time, or to increase the production and consumption of consumer goods. Capitalism took us down the latter path, and the utopian dream of ease and leisure for all was buried under a mountain of commodities.

...

In the previous chapters I praised arguments for a less work-centred society for pulling apart the work dogma and addressing the fact that, for growing numbers of people, work has become an increasingly unreliable source of income, rights and security. I also framed the argument for less work and more leisure as a compelling reply to the problem of worker alienation. To these issues I would add a third reason why a concerted critique of the work dogma is relevant to us in the here and now: it is relevant as an opportunity to take stock and respond to the colonisation of our time by economic demands. When significant proportions of our time are spent working, recuperating from work, compensating for work, or doing the many things necessary in order to find, prepare for, and hold on to work, it becomes increasingly difficult to say how much of our time is truly our own. So much of our activity now seems to be geared towards securing our present and future survival, rather than engaging in activities because they are intrinsically valuable.

If the promise of less work and more time to ourselves looked possible towards the beginning of the twentieth century, those who envisioned a less work-centred future overlooked the extent to which the agents of capitalism would force us to accept the dividend of growing productivity in the form of more consumption, rather than more leisure time. If developments in productive technologies create a theoretical possibility for a reduction of working hours, the real-life possibilities for a reduction of work continue to be blocked by the principle of constant economic growth, and by capitalism's ongoing efforts to press our leisure time into the hands of consumption. The argument for a serious re-evaluation of the work dogma, and an eventual reduction of work, is an argument for a future in which a much larger proportion of our lives can be free from the pressure to produce and consume commercial wealth.

FOUR: The stronghold of work

Of course there is a humanitarian side of the shorter day and the shorter week, but dwelling on that subject is likely to get one in trouble, for then leisure may be put before work rather than after work – where it belongs.

Henry Ford (cited in Hunnicutt, 1988: 46)

In his essay 'In Praise of Idleness', Bertrand Russell wasted no time in getting to his point: 'I think that there is far too much work done in the world, that immense harm is caused by the belief that work is virtuous, and that what needs to be preached in modern industrial countries is quite different from what has always been preached' (Russell, 2004c: 1). Like the critics of work introduced in Chapter 1, Russell advocated a society-wide reduction of working hours, to be combined with a more equal distribution of the necessary labour. The joys of idleness, he argued, have been unjustly confined to an elite class of owners, whose leisurely lifestyles are built upon the exploitation of other people's labour. Against this tendency, Russell believed that leisure was a privilege that ought to be extended to everybody. In an argument now familiar to us, he argued that a radical expansion of leisure had been made possible by the time-saving capacities of modern production techniques, which had reduced the amount of human labour required to secure the necessaries of life.

The biggest obstacle to the expansion of leisure, according to Russell, was society's stubborn attachment to the belief that paid work is a noble duty. By his own admission, his call for the expansion of leisure 'shocks the well-to-do', who have historically doubted the ability of the poor to use their leisure time wisely (Russell, 2004c: 8). It was commonly thought that the poor were unworthy of leisure, and that more free-time would lead to widespread boredom and vice. (At Russell's time of writing, there was a significant moral panic around growing cinema attendance, which bourgeois society believed was corrupting the young.) Maybe more concerning, from the perspective of those in society's most powerful positions, was the prospect that increased leisure time might lubricate the political consciousness of the poor, or leave people with more time for collective action. Russell did not reflect at any length on the real-world prospects for overcoming the bourgeois work ethic in 1932, though his essay did briefly advocate the birth of a 'great public propaganda' designed to attack the sacred status of work (Russell, 2004c: 1).

The moral objections to less work were documented in more detail by Hunnicutt in *Work Without End*. Hunnicutt shows how in the 1920s, when shorter working hours seemed like an increasingly realistic possibility, business leaders reacted by developing pro-work propaganda, convincing people that paid employment was a fundamental human need:

> They spoke of work as 'a joy,' a 'critical factor of human evolution,' a 'wonder,' a 'dignity,' 'the American secret,' a cure for 'that tired feeling' and 'mental fatigue,' the 'developer of character,' an 'adventure,' a 'form of play but better,' a 'source of spiritual inspiration,' and the creator of 'saints of the workshop.' In contrast to the previous two decades, when

work as a social value was undergoing a 'crisis,' in this decade few such doubts remained, at least in business and trade publications. (Hunnicutt, 1988: 47)

Among the guardians of work was George L. Markland, chairman of the board of the Philadelphia Gear Works. Reacting to proposals to allow workers to move from a six- to a five-day week, having Saturdays to themselves, Markland declared that 'any man demanding the forty hour week should be ashamed to claim citizenship in this great country', warning Americans that 'the men of our country are becoming softies and mollycoddles' (Markland in Hunnicutt, 1988: 40). The idea that necessary labour might require a decreasing amount of human effort was terrifying to a society so ethically attached to the idea of work as a backbone of civilised human conduct.

The purpose of this chapter is to highlight the ways in which particular moral beliefs about paid employment continue to prevent a genuinely open debate on the future of the work-centred society. If the prospect of less work was morally troubling in the early twentieth century, it continues to represent a source of uneasiness now, in the context of twenty-first-century neoliberalism. In recent times, a revamped ideological focus on the sanctity of hard work has been paired with a vicious demonisation of non-workers, and others who resist the work ethic. As this chapter will suggest, the power of these ideas is the result not only of their ubiquitous presence in the media, but also of their installation in a suite of social policies which have significantly reduced the latitude for resistance to work. In the final part of this chapter, I will also think about the ways in which sociological research might be complicit in the reproduction of the work-centred society, in cases where it has reinforced the idea that paid employment represents a fundamental human need. Whilst its attempts to understand the experience of joblessness have often been valuable and empathic, the widely believed but questionable claim that employment is vital to our psychological health may be unwittingly helping to solidify the idea that there is no alternative.

Demonising the non-worker

In *The Problem With Work,* Kathi Weeks explores the legacy of the work ethic in some detail, highlighting the ethic's tremendous capacity for endurance and adaptation over the course of modern history (Weeks, 2011: Chapter 1). In the seventeenth and eighteenth centuries it was religion that demanded a life devoted to work, but the religious element had largely withered away by the nineteenth century, where it was being replaced by the promise of social mobility: the promise that through the sweat of one's brow, it might be possible to elevate the social status of oneself and one's family. By the middle of the twentieth century, a different element had been foregrounded, as work came to be idealised as a route to self-actualisation and personal development. As an ascetic ideal, the work ethic has displayed a remarkable staying presence, but no matter what its form, the behaviours which the ethic prescribes have remained consistent. In all its forms, the work ethic has promoted 'the identification with and systematic devotion to waged work, the elevation of work to the centre of life, and the affirmation of work as an end in itself' (Weeks, 2011: 46). In today's affluent societies, holding down a job is still commonly heralded as a signal of independence, maturity and good character, and hard work continues to represent a proper way of living, and proof of a commitment to the prosperity of one's nation. If there are other ways to contribute and achieve, outside the realm of paid employment, then these are not nearly as well represented or widely recognised.

For evidence of this, we need only observe the aggressive return of the work ethic in the context of neoliberalism. The British prime minister, David Cameron, came to power in 2010 relentlessly stressing the government's commitment to 'hardworking people'. In 2013 Cameron said: 'We are building a country for those who work and want to get on. And we are saying to each and every hard-working person in our country: we are on your side … This is a government for hard-working people, and that's the way it will stay' (Huffington Post, 2013). Prior to this, Cameron had routinely depicted benefit claimants as wasters, 'sitting on their sofas waiting for their benefits to arrive' (Cameron, 2010). These references to 'hardworking people' were echoed in a speech delivered by the Chancellor George Osborne at the 2012 Conservative Party conference: 'Where is the fairness, we ask, for the shift-worker, leaving home in the dark hours of the morning, who looks up at the closed blinds of their next-door neighbour sleeping off a life on benefits?' (Jowitt, 2013). These repeated references to diligent work (defined always in terms of paid employment) function to construct a rigid dichotomy in the public imagination. On one side of this dichotomy are those upstanding, hardworking citizens who help secure the country's future, whilst on the other are those morally dubious unemployed people who do nothing. Which are you? The sleeper or the employee, the shirker or the worker? Do you do something, or nothing? This technique of splitting the population into binary opposites has long been used as a method of social discipline, whether we are talking about the mad versus the sane, the normal versus the abnormal, or the dangerous versus the harmless. The New Economics Foundation has referred to this latest dichotomy as the binary of 'strivers versus skivers': a cultural myth which perpetuates the idea that those who exist outside the moral clique of 'the hardworking' are undeserving, morally suspect and likely to be criminals (Coote and Lyall, 2013).

Imogen Tyler refers to these attempts to discredit non-workers in terms of a 'culturalisation of poverty' (Tyler, 2013: 162). In spite of the structural facts of mass unemployment and deepening social inequalities, issues such as poverty and worklessness continue to be framed by governments as cultural or behavioural issues. As the discussion on social class wanes, an appreciation of the structural causes of unemployment fades away and poverty becomes regarded as a deserved result of poor self-management. Even in regions where the number of unemployed people significantly outweighs the number of available jobs, it is still maintained that were a person to present themselves a little better, put a little more effort in, or just *believe* in themselves, he or she could find work and climb out of poverty. Society's poorest are regarded as those who have failed to make the right choices in life, or who have shown an unwillingness to grasp the opportunities that society has presented to them. Financial poverty is blamed on a poverty of aspiration, and this continued foregrounding of cultural attitudes has allowed governments to ignore the structural causes of poverty and unemployment. In this new framing, society's main enemies are no longer the structural pathologies of inequality, job scarcity and the dearth of attractive jobs, but the personal pathologies inherent in a so-called culture of laziness, entitlement and dependency. Aside from the personal misery and stigmatisation they cause, perhaps the biggest crime of these cultural explanations is that they keep society's more structural or systemic issues off the table. Mass unemployment should give us occasion to question the efficacy of work as a basis for social inclusion and solidarity, but the discussion that is actually taking place is much more blinkered.

Not everybody will be convinced by the rhetoric of 'strivers versus skivers' of course, but its sheer ubiquity is cause enough for concern. The stigmatisation of unemployed people is infectious. Tabloid reports concerned with the wastage of public money seem almost uniformly obsessed with the comparatively minor cost of suspected benefit fraud. A benefits mythbuster published by Turn2Us (Turn2Us, 2012) suggested that the 'welfare burden' caused by UK unemployment has been grossly exaggerated. The report suggests that, contrary to popular opinion, public spending on welfare has stabilised since the economic crash of the year 2008/9, and was far lower in 2012 than it was in 1995, following the previous recession.[1] There is notably less anger about the public funds spent on working tax credits (which compensate for miserly employers), the high rents that force many people to depend on housing benefit, or the criminally underpublicised problem of corporate tax evasion. The media pumps out a torrent of disgust towards unemployed people, who are typically portrayed as leading empty, morally rudderless lives.

The case of Cait Reilly, unfolding in the UK over the course of 2012–13, offers a perfect example here, as a media event which brought the 'striver versus skiver' discourse to the fore. In 2012, the UK Coalition government attempted to tackle worklessness by forcing many benefit claimants to undertake periods of unpaid work. Under the rules of the new policy, Reilly, an unemployed geology graduate, was forced to leave a work experience placement in a museum, to instead work unwaged in a Poundland store. Reilly's name hit the headlines after a lawyer heard about her story and volunteered to help establish a legal case against the government. The tabloid media exploded. Responding to the suggestion that Reilly's forced labour was a violation of human rights, Jan Moir of the *Daily*

Mail wrote: 'It is hardly ten years' imprisonment without charge in Guantanamo Bay. It is hardly like being incarcerated in a Nazi prisoner of war camp for five long years, never knowing each day if you would live or die' (Moir, 2012). The Secretary of State for Work and Pensions, Iain Duncan Smith, joined the debate, labelling Reilly a 'job snob' and levelling a broader attack on those who defended her actions – a so-called 'commenting elite' who are unaware of their own intellectual conceit and sense of superiority (Holehouse, 2012). These bitter comments came just months after UK public sector workers conducted a mass strike in response to government proposals to modify pension schemes. Rather than reporting on the motivations for strike action, Tim Shipman, also reporting for the *Daily Mail,* belittled the cause by citing statistics which claimed that, on average, state workers get paid 7.5% more than private sector employees in the UK. He wrote that '[t]he findings are a blow to the credibility of union leaders who claim that public sector staff are hard done by' (Shipman, 2011).

These examples show us that the moral fence around the work ethic is not only high but also tremendously well-fortified. Any worker who steps out of line is quickly targeted as a dangerous outsider and denied a political voice. The political significance of the rebellious act is muted by portraying the rebel as pathological, diverting public attention away from the political cause and on to the supposedly deviant psychology of the rebel:

> Resistance in this context is not explained as something related to
> the inequality of the capitalist labour process, but rather a matter of
> personal problems within the worker – a negative attitude, an inability
> to be a team player or shirking one's duties. In other words, the con-
> temporary pathologies of work are pushed onto employees themselves

and are internalised as personal demeanours and characteristics that must be 'worked through' in team meetings, development assessment seminars and 'self-help' consumption in the private sphere. (Fleming and Spicer, 2003: 174)

In Cait Reilly's case, commentators variously implied that Reilly was neurotic, weird, or suffered from an unhealthy sense of entitlement. Catch-all terms such as 'job snob' work in the same vein as older terms such as 'hippy', 'wacko' or 'conspiracy theorist', being deployed in order to discredit immediately any threat to orthodox ways of thinking. Another common media response to labour disputes is the deployment of the Could Be Worse argument. If Reilly thought she was hard done by, then it was said that she should be grateful not to be a captive prisoner of war. If the UK public sector workers who went on strike in 2012 believed that they were victims of injustice, then it was said that they should have considered those who were earning less, working in poorer conditions, or struggling to find work. By providing suggestive examples of situations that are worse than the insurgent's, journalists once again peddle the message that it is individuals and their sense of entitlement that are at fault.

Whilst the moralisation of work certainly gains purchase through its ubiquity in the media, perhaps its real power derives from its installation in a suite of workfare policies designed to encourage benefit claimants out of the welfare system and into paid employment. If the moralisation of work is powerful as a cultural device, it takes on an uglier, more coercive guise when enshrined in a modern policy agenda. In the UK, the New Labour government arrived in office in 1997, resolving to 'rebuild the welfare state around work' (Department for Social Security, 1998), and previously protected welfare claimants such as lone parents and people with disabilities were increasingly expected to seek employment. The legacy of workfare continued in the UK Coalition government's 'big bold plan to Get Britain Working', which has since phased in a tightening set of conditions around who is entitled to claim benefits, along with an increasingly stringent set of audits and penalties for non-workers who fail to comply.[2]

These tightening conditions represent less a helping hand for the citizen in need than a stranglehold. In order to avoid sanctions, the claimants to Jobseeker's Allowance have been required to display a fully accountable commitment to job hunting, to accept offers of employment judged reasonable by Jobcentre Plus bureaucrats, and to attend job-seeker's training programmes deemed likely to increase the chances of finding work. The critic Ivor Southwood argues that, given the known shortage of jobs in many areas, these activities often have a performative quality, forcing claimants to project a phoney display of positivity and enthusiasm for low-status work roles: 'To refuse to go along with this performance and its mutual suspension of disbelief risks bringing the full weight of the institution down on the "customer"' (Southwood, 2011: 46).

Among the most troubling developments of the big bold plan was the controversial policy to force benefit claimants to complete compulsory periods of unpaid work. Also, the Work Capability Assessment – a test undertaken by claimants with disabilities, to verify their eligibility for benefits – was handed over to the private company ATOS in 2011. Following the handover, a controversy unfolded based on credible allegations from public investigators, whistle-blowers and failed applicants, who claimed that the flawed methodology of the Work Capability test, coupled with a punitive auditing process, was strongly biased towards a rejection of benefit applications (Franklin, 2013). It is estimated that thousands of people have been declared erroneously 'fit for work' by a system which, instead of providing support, has aimed to cap the number of welfare recipients.[3] Whilst workfare policies have undergone a complex series of changes, their underpinning morality remains consistent: paid employment is unambiguously promoted as the normal and superior state to which everybody should aspire.

What all of this ultimately means is that although we have reached a point in history where a reduction and re-evaluation of work are urgently needed, powerful moral forces remain mobilised against the development of a genuinely open discussion. A range of personal, social and environmental crises give us strong occasion to question work's function and importance in modern society, but the relentless moralisation of work is confining us to the usual circuits of thought. It is like a constant source of noise pollution – the equivalent to someone repeatedly flicking your earlobes when you are trying to think. I will show the effects of this in Chapter 7, where we will see that many of the non-workers I interviewed found it difficult to maintain conviction in their critical views inside this work-focused moral climate. Like Cait Reilly and the public sector workers mentioned here, they often found themselves stigmatised for their alternative views and actions. In a context where those who resist work are so readily disparaged, reviled and feared, it becomes increasingly difficult to foster an open-minded and intelligent debate on the future of work.

The belief that work is a medicine

When viewed in the context of society's mainstream political commitments, the critique of work clearly has a radical status. What is more surprising, however, is that the critique of work (at least as a category in itself) also remains somewhat radical in the more imaginative realm of sociology. Reflecting on the discipline, Ralph Fevre has suggested that sociology has sometimes acted more like an accomplice than a critic of work. He laments the extent to which some areas of economic sociology have grown to accept the primacy of economic rationality, neglecting classical theorists like Marx, Durkheim and Weber, whose trademark was to use 'non-economic meanings and values to critique economic behaviour' (Fevre, 2003: 3). We can make a similar observation in relation to sociological studies on the experiences of unemployment, which have also sometimes contributed to a glorification of work. Sociology has a rich and valuable history of research into people's experiences of unemployment, and has admirably documented the painful effects of the loss of income, status, identity and rights that are associated with job loss. Yet even when conducted with the best, humanistic intentions, some strands of this research may have unwittingly reinforced the work ethic, in so far as researchers have treated work unquestioningly, as a normal or natural state from which the unemployed person deviates.

I credit this insight to the sociologist Matthew Cole, who has suggested that a side effect of sociological research on unemployment has often been to reinforce the notion of employment as synonymous with a normal, healthy state of being (Cole, 2007). This assumption tends to produce a one-dimensional way of thinking by producing a fear of alternatives to the current, work-centred society. Cole focused his criticisms on the emblematic research of Marie Jahoda and colleagues, conducted in the 1930s (Jahoda et al., 1972). Jahoda and her researchers immersed themselves in the Austrian town of Marienthal, following the closure of a local textile factory. By 1932, the closure of the factory had tragically left around 77%

of the community's families without an employed member. The researchers painted a bleak picture of the town: 'from their windows at home, the workers look out on to a heap of rubble, dented boilers, old transmission wheels and crumbling walls where once had been their place of work' (Jahoda et al., 1972: 14). On the basis of extensive research, the authors concluded that Marienthal's inhabitants were on a slippery slope of despondency and resignation, displaying low expectations of the future, a dragging experience of time, and feelings of apathy. Given the fact that Marienthal's local identity was so closely tied with industry, the closure of its factory meant nothing less than the destruction of a way of life, and there is certainly no reason to doubt the credibility of these findings. Indeed, the case of Marienthal invites comparison with my home region of South Wales, which continues to suffer the miserable effects of deindustrialisation following Thatcher's closure of its coal mines in the 1980s. Such cases are proof of the power of unemployment to dismantle communities and destroy familiar ways of life.

Translated into English in the 1970s, the Marienthal study was a commendable and empathic portrayal of an unemployed community. However, at risk of using the study as something of a straw man, I agree with Cole that the research warrants our scrutiny. The study's core problem pertains to the rigid nature of its analytical framework, and the extent to which it influenced sociological understandings of employment thereafter. For the sake of ease, we can call this framework the 'deprivation model'. According to the deprivation model, paid employment fulfils a set of essential psychological needs: for shared experience and a sense of collective purpose, for a structured experience of time involving regular activity, and for a sense of status and self-identity (Jahoda, 1982). The suffering that people experience in their unemployment is explained by the model in terms of their severance from these core needs. Unemployment is thus analysed as a deficient state of being, the inverse of the normal and ideal state of employment, and a state which is fundamentally connected with misery. Whilst Jahoda and colleagues did acknowledge the relatively unique nature of Marienthal's situation (as an industrial community with an unusually sudden surge in unemployment), the deprivation model has proved widely influential, inspiring a legacy of research by a range of authors into unemployment and the deprivation of needs.[4]

The analytic simplicity of the deprivation model may have a certain appeal, but this is also the main source of its problems. One of its major failings is its ignorance of the uglier realities of paid employment. The suffering of the unemployed is taken as evidence that paid work must represent a remedy, but the benefits of employment are invoked only in the abstract, uncomplicated by any distinction between the realities of good versus bad jobs. This is a feature that the deprivation model shares with the UK government's approach to public health. Dame Carol Black's official review of public health in 2008 provides a good example of current thinking when it states, without further qualification, that 'being in work leads to better physical and mental health' (Department of Health, 2010). The government's official response to Black's report echoes the idea that work is key in 'promoting a better quality of life and allowing people to make the most of their potential' (Department for Work and Pensions, 2013). Such claims are abysmally unspecific. The health benefits of work for groups such as single mothers, for example, who have often found themselves targeted by workfare policies, are far from clear (Baker et al., 1999; Cook, 2012). These claims also ignore the entire legacy of research into the alienating, health-damaging effects of poor-quality jobs (jobs which are repetitive, prescriptive, closely supervised, and fail to provide a sense of meaning) which I explored in Chapter 2. The claim that paid employment is 'good for us' is completely without context. It is pure ideology.

A second problem with the deprivation model is that it approaches jobless people as a singular type, with predictable psychological responses. It suggests that unemployment is *inherently* miserable, and thus strongly implies that humans should work because it is normal and natural to do so. A number of studies are creditable for complicating this generalisation and shedding light on the differences in people's experiences of unemployment. A study by Fryer and McKenna, conducted in the late 1980s, provides us with an illustrative example (Fryer and McKenna, 1987). The researchers used interviews to compare experiences among a sample of unemployed men, some of whom had been made permanently redundant, and others who had been temporarily laid off for seven weeks and were expecting to return to work. The researchers found that the redundant men experienced more difficulties than the laid-off men. Many of the former reported a dragging experience of time, whereas some of the latter group developed satisfying routines, saying that they enjoyed their free-time and were racing to complete self-appointed tasks before going back to work. These findings suggest that it is not joblessness per se that causes distress, but redundancy. However, it is not valid to make this generalisation either, since the researchers also reported marked differences within the two groups of men. Variables that Fryer and McKenna considered included the personality of the jobless person, and also his or her level of anxiety about the future, with anxiety appearing to have a debilitating effect on people's ability to plan and initiate activities. Other researchers have focused on the personal consequences of a loss of income (Weller, 2012), the role of injustice in the job loss itself (Bies and

Moag, 1986), and the extent to which redundancy was a surprise (Dooley and Catalano, 1988). We can only conclude that responses to joblessness are shaped by a wide range of variables.

Like the thousands of clinical psychological studies transfixed on the isolation of particular, causal variables, there is always the risk that research into what causes unhappiness in unemployment degenerate into a tragi-comic procession of attempts to dispute or perfect an analytical model. One study might suggest that family situation is significant, whereas the next one might emphasise personality type, and the next one might factor in the individual's financial circumstances – but many will miss the truth that it is all of these, plus a much broader range of societal factors, which influence a person's experiences. When researchers study emotional trauma, it may be possible to make certain generalisations, but it is very difficult to know how people will respond to situations broadly considered to be 'traumatic' using rigid, analytical models.

> Losing a job might be a catastrophe for one person and a blessing for another, just as marriage might be a joyous occasion for one person but a tragedy for another, if, for example, it was arranged against their will … What counts as important will obviously depend on the person and their own unique history. (Leader and Corfield, 2007: 60–1)

In the case of Marienthal, perhaps it was the socialisation of the ex-workers as labourers rather than their deprivation from 'core psychological needs' that shaped their negative experiences of unemployment. Employment *itself* can be held partly responsible for the negative experiences of joblessness because, in allowing people only a limited space in which to cultivate other interests, skills and social ties, full-time jobs can often leave people with few personal and social resources to fall back on. When people profess an attachment to work, it may be that they experience their jobs as intrinsically satisfying, but it may equally be the case that they are harbouring a frustration at the lack of other opportunities for fulfilment that possess the same socially validated status as work (Gollain, 2004: 41).

I have been given occasion to reflect on this problem in my years as a university teacher. For a number of years running, I have taught annual seminars on Max Weber and his theories on the work ethic. In the seminars, I tried to get students thinking about the reasons we work today by asking them if they would still work were they to win the lottery. What is perhaps surprising is that almost all of the students usually say that they would. It is tempting to become agitated with them for this apparent lack of imagination. It was Bertrand Russell who said that, should people fear the boredom of increased leisure, we should treat this as a 'condemnation of our civilisation' (Russell, 2004c: 11). And yet in many ways the students' attachment to the idea of work is completely reasonable. In contemporary capitalism, the notion of a public life has become so synonymous with paid work that it has indeed become difficult to imagine other ways in which a person might transcend the isolation of a purely private existence. Ransome puts the problem well:

> It seems highly probable that the key reason why people continue to express such a strong willingness to participate in the labour process, stems more or less directly from the fact that there is no practical alternative available to them. (Ransome, 1995: 210)

Once again, this is not to suggest that work cannot be enjoyable. It is, however, to suggest that the felt need to work is strongly influenced by society's political, economic and moral choices (Cole, 2004: 9–10). Contrary to the convictions of the deprivation model, there is nothing in the human's innate psychological make-up that makes it necessary for him or her to be a paid employee. In today's work-centred society, unemployment is undoubtedly a terrible experience for most people, but this tells us little about how non-work would be experienced in a putative future society where work was no longer constructed as the only source of income, rights and belonging. What if income could be decoupled from work, in such a way that everyone could benefit from a greater level of financial security? What if there were a range of ways to earn respect as a citizen, other than through the performance of paid work? And what if a growing abundance of free-time gave rise to a flourishing infrastructure of informal social networks and autonomously organised production? Would my old students still feel so vitally dependent on work? I doubt that they would. The deprivation model must be treated with caution because it draws boundaries around our imaginative capacities: it fuels the mistaken conviction that employment is the only way to satisfy certain fundamental human needs, and hampers our ability to think beyond the work-centred society. When we recognise that the need to work is a product of society's political, economic and moral choices, we as a society become free to make *new* choices. We remain open to the exciting prospect maintained by the critical social theorists: that there might be other ways to meet the needs conventionally satisfied (or left unsatisfied, as the case may be) through paid employment.

Resistance to work

Concluding his extensive review of critiques of work, the sociologist Edward Granter pointed to work's 'unassailable position in politics, policy and popular discourse' (Granter, 2009: 182). Many of the topics I have discussed up to this point seem to confirm this fear. Whilst a range of critical thinkers have called for a radical re-evaluation of work and its role in society, it appears that paid employment has continued to colonise our everyday lives. The prospects for a reduction of work also seem distant in the context of a consumer economy that continues to occupy us with new reasons to work and spend, and a political ideology that continues to promote working as an irreplaceable source of good health and moral virtue. However, if the prospects for an open-minded debate on the future of work look grim, what I propose to do in the remainder of the book is to use these early chapters as a platform for a more hopeful kind of enquiry. Whilst an ever-larger proportion of our lives and minds has been colonised for the sake of capitalist production, society's grip over the individual can never be total. Everywhere one looks, there are people who feel that they differ from and exceed the roles foisted upon them by society. The problem, as Ryle and Soper have expressed it, is that the ideals promoted by society are not the same as the ideals by which it is ruled:

> It teaches altruism, but depends on egoism, approves of social responsibility, but rewards financial self-interest, advances goals of critical autonomy and all-round personal development while endorsing the system that condemns the majority to long hours of dull and undemanding labour. (Ryle and Soper, 2002: 58)

It also continues to promote an ethic of hard work, even when stable and meaningful jobs are in short supply. There is only so much of this that people will take. There is a limit to the extent to which people will tolerate the contradiction between ethical ideals and daily realities, and a critical study of work's colonising power is incomplete if it does not also recognise the opposing tradition of insurgency and rebellion, arising wherever people have refused to internalise the idea that to work is good, healthy and normal.

The rebellion against the work ethic has appeared in many forms. Going back to the 1860s, we can consider the protracted battle between workers and capitalists over the length of the working day, both in the UK and in France (a struggle that is documented by Marx in *Capital*'s chapter on 'The Working Day'). In more recent decades, we can consider the history of punks, hippies and slackers, or recall the barflies, diner bums and drifters celebrated in an artistic movement featuring the likes of Jack Kerouac, Charles Bukowski, Hunter S. Thompson, Bob Dylan, Woody Guthrie and Tom Waits. These are all figures who have in their own way stood for a rejection of the nine-to-five lifestyle. The characters that populate their books and songs bear a strong family resemblance to Generation X – a term popularised by Douglas Coupland in the 1990s, in his novel of the same name (Coupland, 1991). *Generation X* depicted a group of young adults who were grappling with their disillusionment around the trappings of the yuppie lifestyle. Coupland's novel was witty, fiercely critical, and even featured a glossary of new phrases for the Gen-Xer's arsenal: terms like *McJob* (a 'low-pay, low-prestige, low-dignity, low-benefit, no-future job in the service sector'), *Veal-Fattening Pen* ('small cramped office workstations built of fabric covered disassemblable wall partitions and inhabited by junior staff members') and *Rebellion Postponement* ('the tendency in one's youth to avoid traditionally youthful activities and artistic experiences in order to obtain serious career experience. Sometimes results in the mourning for lost youth at about age thirty, followed by silly haircuts and expensive joke-inducing wardrobes').[5]

Resistance to work has by no means been the preserve of artistic movements, however. In addition to these (notably masculine) literary refusals, we could consider a variety of alternative histories. We could consider those second-wave feminists who questioned the idea that women could be liberated simply by joining men in the sphere of work. In the 1970s, Mariarosa Dalla Costa and Selma James urged women to resist the myth of liberation through work: 'Slavery to an assembly line is not a liberation from slavery to a kitchen sink' (Dalla Costa and James, 1973: 33). We can also recall the Italian Autonomist movement, which in the 1960s and 1970s saw radical academics forming alliances with a loose coalition of workers, feminists, students and unemployed people, all in the name of a mass 'refusal of work' (Wright, 2002). Or we could consider Robin Kelley's account of segments of the black working class, whose rebellion saw them seeking meaning and pleasure outside the realm of employment (Kelley, 1994). Or perhaps think of the more radical responses to the precariousness of working life in modern-day Europe. As Kathi Weeks notes, some European activists have responded to the degradation of the work contract not by demanding a return to the world of dependable exploitation, but by calling for a completely different relation between life and work (Weeks, 2011: 80). The Euro May Day movement – a collective of flexible, temporary and migrant workers across Western Europe – is one such movement, rallying once a year to promote an alternative vision of development.[6]

A consistent theme in the works of Gorz is the idea that there exists an active, if often unexpressed, disenchantment with work in advanced industrial societies. Gorz points to the birth of the 'neo-proletariat': a demographically diverse 'non-class of non-workers' who, sensing that their time and capacities are being squandered in employment, decide to seek fulfilment in other areas of life (Gorz, 1982). Beyond the level of theory, Gorz did not expand in any great detail on who the neo-proletariat were, or where they could be found. What is important is that the neo-proletariat were understood by Gorz not as revolutionary political subjects (i.e., they were not a replacement for Marx's revolutionary proletariat), but as the embodiment of a cultural disillusionment with work that had yet to find collective expression or political purchase. The anti-work sensibilities that he believed were mounting constituted a revolution only in people's hearts and minds, but whether this supposed disaffection with work would be translated into a genuine social alternative remained to be seen.

Today, many who call for a re-evaluation of work remain confident about the existence of a cultural undercurrent in which people are actively questioning the extent to which work is worth their time. Finn Bowring argues that one of the strengths of the academic critique of work is the extent to which it harmonises with the desires of contemporary social movements. Such movements have issued a 'demand for a better quality of life … for a less aggressive and individualistic culture, for more child-friendly policies and spaces, for a recognition of the environment as a source of aesthetic and spiritual nourishment, and for more free-time and a less commodity intensive existence' (Bowring, 2011: 150). Kate Soper shares this conviction when she points towards an emerging culture of 'alternative hedonism', in which long working days and consumption-intensive lifestyles are being scrutinised as people emphasise the value of non-material goods such as free-time, well-being, conviviality, and a more relaxed pace of life (Soper, 2008). Comparably, in their manifesto for a twenty-one-hour working week the New Economics Foundation referred to 'shifting expectations or moralities regarding the use, value and distribution of work and time in society' (Coote et al., 2010: 4).

Whilst these critics are confident about the cultural resonance of their ideas, however, it is fair to say that discussions of contemporary refusal and rebellion have tended to remain on the vague side. My goal in the remainder of the book is to take a tentative step towards remedying this situation. In the next three chapters I will explore the verbal accounts of real people from the UK who have attempted to resist work, either by reducing their working hours or by trying to live without work altogether. I begin in Chapter 5 by introducing the people I met, exploring their reasons for resisting work, and outlining what they do with their time. In Chapters 6 and 7, I move on to explore some of the pleasures and difficulties they encountered trying to resist work. As we might expect within the context of a work-centred society, there are significant obstacles which block people's isolated attempts to work less. To what extent is a substantial rebellion against work achievable, given the forces that are ranged against this possibility? And might there be hidden pleasures to be found in a less work-focused, less commodity-intensive lifestyle? These are the questions that motivate the remaining chapters of this book.

FIVE: The breaking point

As an idler I pledge ... To strive not to work ridiculous hours, especially not for some corporate wankster; to not let stress intrude upon me where possible; to eat slowly; to drink real ales frequently; to sing more; to smile more; to step off the nine-to-five merry-go-round before I get queasy; to amuse myself in public as well as in private; to amuse others as well as myself; to know that work is merely for paying the bills; to always remember that friends are a source of strength; to enjoy the simple things; to spend quality time in nature; to spend less with big businesses and corporations; to make lots of nice things instead; to go against the grain; to make a difference to the world and people around you, however small ...

– selected list of pledges from the Idlers' Alliance

Between 2009 and 2013, I spent time with a range of people who were taking significant measures to prevent work from colonising their lives. Whilst some had reduced their working hours, others had given up work altogether. After locating them by various means – internet searches, local advertisements, or referrals by existing participants – I interviewed them on their views and experiences relating to work. I wanted to understand what had prompted them to resist work, to find out what they did with their time, and to gain a deeper understanding of the pleasures and difficulties that might be encountered in the process of refusal. Whilst some interviews were conducted on the phone, where possible I tried to meet people face to face in their homes. Finding that they were often generous with their time, I interviewed many for several hours (some on more than one occasion), and also accepted invitations to join them in various activities. Over the course of the research, I went for walks along the coast, gardened, helped build a barbeque, and sat behind a stall at a local music festival.

Something to bear in mind is the relatively ordinary nature of the people I met. At the more extreme end of the scale were four participants connected with an organisation called the Idlers' Alliance (Jack, Mike, Anne and Alan). This may not sound very ordinary, but perhaps 'organisation' is too strong a word here. One of the alliance's founders told me that, with one minor exception (described below), the group had never tried to 'do anything political'. The Alliance's main draw was an online message board, frequented by a loosely defined and demographically diverse group of people. Some of these people had cut their working hours a bit, some a lot, and some were trying not to work at all. Some simply seemed to be seeking an intelligent conversation. As we can see from the users' list of pledges at the start of this chapter, idling represents less a fixed set of principles than a mood or a texture, with elements ranging from the serious to the silly. A message board topic might invite people to comment on changes to welfare policy, share money-saving tips, recommend a good film, or take part in a wry conversation about the merits of different toilet seat designs. Whilst a couple of the idlers interviewed did have access to intellectual concepts and frameworks that allowed them to articulate their struggles against work in political terms, on the whole the idlers cannot be described as ideologically committed activists or members of a coherent social movement.

In addition to the four idlers, I met fifteen people each with a different background, situation and set of desires. One of these people was Eleanor, a woman in her early thirties and the only person I met whose resistance to work had seen her stepping outside of society to experiment with communal living. At this more extreme end of the spectrum I would also position Cheryl, a woman in her forties who proudly defined herself as a 'downshifter' and enthusiast of 'slow living'. I visited Cheryl at her home, where she told me that she earned part of her income by promoting her values on a local radio programme. For the most part, however, we can think of Eleanor and Cheryl as more radical exceptions to the rule. Most of the people I met had not heard of terms such as 'idler' or 'downshifter', and, when prompted, some even said that they found these terms a bit repellant. One participant, Rachel, protested that 'it all sounds a bit hippy'.

At the less conspicuously alternative end of the scale we have people such as Adam and Samantha, whose resistance to work had taken the form of a snap career change. In Adam's case, a high-commitment job as a computer programmer was ditched in favour of teaching English part-time in Japan, with a small amount of freelance programming work on the side. In Samantha's case, a well-paid job as a patent attorney was dropped (much to her mother's horror) in order to live a more leisurely lifestyle as a part-time waitress and private tutor. There were also people such as Bruce, Lucy and Emma, whose feelings of ill-health had made it difficult for them to remain in employment. For these people, resistance to work seemed to be motivated by self-preservation. Of all the people I met, perhaps Larry exhibited the most humble act of resistance. He was a social worker who had plucked up the courage to ask his managers to reduce his working week by just one hour per day – a proposition to which they had agreed. Larry's modest goal was simply to feel a bit less hurried and stressed out in his day-to-day life.

The question of whether or not these people were successful in their attempts to resist work is a complex one, which I will continue to engage with over the coming chapters. My provisional reply is that some were doing better than others. Whilst some said they were living fairly comfortably on part-time wages, previous earnings, or a partner's income, many had made significant sacrifices in order to resist work, funding their lives through some combination of dwindling savings, scraps of temporary work, mutual favours, loans and state benefits. There was also a considerable degree of variation in terms of each person's level of conviction. As we will see in Chapter 7, some were enlivened by the compassion and support of friends and family, and discussed their choices with a great deal of pride. By contrast, others were succumbing to the stigma of joblessness, and their accounts were laden with shame and self-doubt. Readers should perhaps also bear in mind the limitations of interviewing as a means of finding out how people feel about their circumstances. Like all social encounters, interviews are shaped through acts of self-presentation and selective truth-telling. This is not to say that participants are liars, but it is to recognise the fact that the interview is a social interaction like any other. I should disclose that I was left a little unconvinced by the compulsive optimism of one or two of the people I met. I wondered whether there might be less desirable aspects of their lives which they were hiding – perhaps from me, or perhaps from themselves. For the most part, however, I intuited that people were being open about the ups and downs of their lives. Many were grateful for the opportunity to participate in the research, saying that they valued it as a chance to clarify their feelings.

With these caveats in mind, this chapter, and the two that follow it, will be dedicated to exploring the accounts of the people I interviewed.[1] In Chapters 6 and 7 I will focus on the pleasures and hardships of resistance to work, but let us begin in this chapter with the more elementary question of *why*. Why did participants feel a need to resist work? Or, perhaps more accurately, why did they choose to *act* on the felt need to resist work? Feeling a need to resist is common, but far fewer people translate this feeling into a real change in their circumstances. What will become increasingly clear as we go through the accounts is that the decision to resist work was never motivated by laziness, negligence, or an aversion to productive activity. On the contrary, the decision to resist work was always motivated by a powerful set of alternative moral principles. Rather than dismissing these as eccentric or deviant, as is often the case in today's work-centred society, my goal here is to explore these moralities, taking them seriously as possible sources of inspiration in the case for a re-evaluation and reduction of work.

Farewell Santa Claus

It was one of the hottest days of summer and I had travelled to a local fair in South-East England, with hopes of meeting members of the Idlers' Alliance (hereafter *TIA*). They had plans to set up a stall at the fair and had kindly agreed to let me join them. Nobody was hollering slogans or waving banners. A couple of people were tentatively giving leaflets to members of the public who happened to drift over, but the event seemed like an excuse more to get together than to campaign. By around lunchtime most of the idlers had wandered off, and it was then that I noticed Jack lying in the sun some distance away from the stall. Jack was in his thirties, an unassuming man who initially seemed reluctant to take part in an interview. He did not seem to believe that his perspective on the world was worth my travelling halfway across the country. Shielding his eyes from the sun, Jack eventually agreed to sit down with me, beginning his interview in an apologetic tone. As we spoke, however, his mood became more philosophical. He took time to consider my questions, taking a breath, before quietly explaining his outlook on the world. In a thick regional accent, Jack explained that he had switched down to part-time hours in his job as a librarian, in an effort to gain more free-time:

> I thought 'wait a minute, life isn't just about working nine to five and commuting and things like that, there has to be more to it'. So I was quite attracted to the idea of doing less perhaps, and this model of working half a day and having the rest of the time to yourself.

Jack conveyed a strong desire to do creative work, but believed that this desire had been stifled in his previous, full-time jobs. He outlined his belief that creativity develops through a leisurely life-style, full of conversation and reading, but regretted that his previous jobs had barred him from doing these things often. The purpose of switching to a part-time role was to feel less exhausted, and hopefully rediscover a thirst for creative activities. He especially enjoyed writing, and was pleased to announce that he was finding time to do it again.

> I didn't think I'd stay with [part-time working], but it's funny that you find yourself drawn to different things at different times in your life, and at that moment I just wanted to explore this. I've stayed with it so far and I suppose, for me, it's led to greater creativity.

Jack said that his new routine of working for around four hours a day had come to feel 'perfectly natural', even if he understood that his lifestyle was unconventional. I believe he was referring to the work ethic when he described the way that the majority of people live as 'like a religion or some kind of madness'. Jack described his decision to work less using words such as 'epiphany' or 'awakening', believing he had pierced through the madness in the world around him:

> The trouble is that once it's happened you can't really see things in any other way because it's almost as if you've seen what is – it's like seeing through a *disguise* actually. It's kind of like the adult equivalent of realising that there is no Santa Claus.

Many of the people I met would describe their decision to work less in similar terms, as a result of having punctured through nurtured cultural beliefs. Sometimes this critical distance had begun developing during the person's working life, but sometimes its roots seemed to extend much further back. Another idler, Mike, talked about having reached a point in his thirties where he 'saw through' the work ethic instilled in him by his schoolteachers. The participant Eleanor started to believe that 'we are really just socially conditioned to think that we should work all the time, earn loads of money, and do all of this'. For whatever reason, the need to be employed had appeared to these people as a social construction rather than a fact of life. The question of why they worked was suddenly on the table and, as Jack said, there was no going back. It is impossible to rediscover one's belief in Santa Claus:

> … we cannot slide back and unreflectively accommodate again to routine, for by its very nature such an orientation involves the feeling that life could not be otherwise, and sadly we have already arrived at the position where our self-awareness has destroyed this fiction. There is no going back to such an unreflective condition. (Cohen and Taylor, 1992: 59)

These experiences beg comparison with Bernard Lefkowitz's research into voluntary joblessness in 1970s America, in which interviewees also regularly talked about awakenings or revelations (Lefkowitz, 1979). Lefkowitz referred to these as 'breakpoints': the point at which people decided to take a break (often a permanent one) from work, but also the point at which they 'broke' in an emotional sense. The breakpoint represents a kind of personal crisis in which a person's accustomed habits and beliefs are thrown into doubt. A biographical incident, a new moral insight, or an accumulated sense of repression leads a person to question their accustomed habits and beliefs, making their usual circumstances and routines less and less tolerable. In more heavyweight sociological terms, the breakpoint can be described as the moment at which people transcend the phenomenon known as *reification*. Originally used by Marx, the concept of reification was adapted by Peter Berger and colleagues in their analyses of human consciousness. Like Marx, Berger and colleagues began with the idea that humans are always engaged in a dialectical relationship with the world: the social and institutional order, which stands above and shapes the lives of humans, is always itself an ongoing product of human activities. In *The Social Construction of Reality,* Berger and Luckmann remind us that the social world can only ever be the result of human activity: 'It is important to keep in mind that the objectivity of the institutional world, however massive it may appear to the individual, is a humanly produced, constructed objectivity' (Berger and Luckmann, 1967: 78). Remembering that society is – and can only ever be – the product of human actions and choices is vital if humans are to experience the world as a field of open possibility, awaiting their influence. The concept of reification describes a process in which the fundamental truth that humans are the producers of the social world is forgotten.

Berger and Luckmann suggest that the development of a complex social and institutional order leads people to apprehend human phenomena 'as if they were *things,* that is, in non-human or possibly supra-human terms' (Berger and Luckmann, 1967: 106, my emphasis). This reified consciousness is an outcome of the socialisation process, which discourages disorder and promotes social cohesion by making sure that individuals take the norms, roles and structures of society to heart. It is a central principle of sociology that, through socialisation, society enters the human consciousness, moulding it into the socially desired shape and ensuring that individuals conduct themselves with a minimum of reflection. If the socialisation process is successful, society's integrated individuals accept the determinants of reality as natural and given: the world has a direct or pre-reflective presence in the mind and social roles are 'taken for granted and lived through as a necessary fate' (Berger and Pullberg, 1966: 65).

Cohen and Taylor describe this default or everyday mode of consciousness as one of 'unreflective accommodation', suggesting that it signifies a person's feeling of relaxed at-homeness in his or her role (Cohen and Taylor, 1992: 47). Yet, if reification to a certain extent represents a mental and functional necessity, Berger and Pullberg suggest that it also represents a kind of alienation. When it is represented in human consciousness as an inert or fixed entity, the social world ceases to represent an open horizon of possibility, awaiting a human imprint: 'Through reification, the world of institutions appears to merge with the world of nature. It becomes necessity and fate, and is lived through as such, happily *or* unhappily as the case may be' (Berger and Luckmann, 1967: 108). The world is encountered by man as an inert or natural 'given': 'It is *there,* impervious to his wishes, sovereignly other than himself, an alien thing opaque to his understanding' (Berger and Pullberg, 1966: 63).[2] In our everyday lives, this alienation prickles us with a sense of uneasiness. It produces a disturbing and often repressed feeling that too much of life is being conducted according to prescribed, scripted regularities. As Cohen and Taylor express it:

> Instead of being grateful that unreflective accommodation allows time to pass, helps us to get through the day, we become disturbed by the ways in which we can allow ourselves to be swept along so easily by the mundane, the trivial, the readily predictable ... This is the experience we call boredom, monotony, tedium, despair. (Cohen and Taylor, 1992: 50)

This feeling of being personally disturbed by the mundanity of conventions is a good description of the feelings of many of the people I met. Rachel, an earnest woman in her early fifties, described her decision to switch from a full-time to a part-time position (in her job as a human resources officer) as an attempt to 'take life off autopilot'. We can compare this with Anne, who had quit a high-commitment job in television to become a freelance photographer. She referred to her decision as the product of having 'woken up from a long sleep'. Several participants were disparaging towards ex-colleagues who appeared to go about their lives in a ritualistic fashion, without a clear rationale or purpose in mind. Lucy referred to people she had worked with 'who had been at work forever and just didn't have a negative thing to say about it'. Here is a quote from Adam, who had serious doubts about the modern notion of a career:

> A career is just sort of one job plugged into another job, plugged into another job, and if you don't really know why you're doing it all – not to know is to admit that you're wasting your life.

Adam said he liked to gently provoke people into clarifying their reasons for working, but identified this as an uncomfortable or taboo area of conversation:

[People] give you quite a flippant answer, which is their way of saying 'oh, don't ask me that'. They're quite happy to talk about other things and engage in small talk, but no one really wants to talk about these deep issues.

In each case, the interviewees expressed a strong desire to live with intention, often referring to some earlier period in their lives that had been conducted in a less-than-lucid state of consciousness, without them being in the driving seat. Within this context, the breakpoint represents the welcome moment at which they began to question the work role. In Berger's terminology, it represented a moment of *de-reification,* in which they became more aware of the socially constructed nature of the need to be employed. This is not to suggest, of course, that the breakpoint sees a person completely lifted from their culturally embedded position in society, or that it is tantamount to freedom from the structural and ideological impositions to work. What the breakpoint more humbly represents is the moment at which people began to reflect more clearly on the nature of cognitive power, and on their own powers of self-direction within the constraints of the society around them. The need to be employed was no longer accepted as a natural law or feature of human nature, but instead represented an object ripe for critical attention. With high spirits and a note of pride, people described a process of reflection on their stock notions and habits, a shedding of their roles, and a rediscovery of their lives as open to possibilities. They spoke out against the prescriptive world of timetables, duties, routines and rules which threatened their ability to maintain an image of themselves as unique, deliberative and responsible people. They achieved catharsis as their sense of repression culminated in a bona fide change.

What was it exactly that afforded the people I met this degree of critical distance from a previously naturalised state of affairs? The breakpoint represents the moment at which reification was punctured, with people's lives taking on a renewed feeling of malleability. But when and why do people cease to accept their social roles as natural and given? In spite of the normalising functions of socialisation, social discipline and ideology, social struggles show us that the integration of individuals into the social order is never a finished process. But if there is always an element of the self that refuses integration, then what causes this element to wake up and be heard?

The causes of a breakpoint are difficult to pin down. Critical reflection might be prompted in the most unpredictable of situations: by the vague sense of desolation that descends in a traffic jam or a crowded shopping mall; by the resentment that surfaces in a pointless team meeting; by the meditative quality of mind which can follow a trip into nature or a drive down an open road. The interviewee Eleanor talked in almost mystical terms about a kind of transcendence or flash of insight: what Cohen and Taylor, writing on the theme of escape, call a 'momentary slip through the fabric' (Cohen and Taylor, 1992). The person is briefly overwhelmed by some vague and indescribable force or spirit which leads him or her into a process of re-evaluation. Eleanor chose not to discuss her experience at length. Her inability to articulate the experience seemed to frighten, or at the very least, somewhat embarrass her:

> Maybe there was a key turning point. It's a bit difficult to go into because it's a vaguely – I haven't really spoken to anyone about this really and it was quite – I walked away from it feeling um, hmm. I should sit down some time and figure out what actually happened there.

Berger and Pullberg speculate that de-reification may occur in 'times of trouble', which rattle the world down to its foundations and allow it to be rebuilt anew (Berger and Pullberg, 1966: 69). Illustrating this idea, several of the people I met discussed the destabilising effects of having witnessed death:

> My step-dad died when I was ten and that was a kind of wake-up call. It puts a lot of things in perspective. It set me on a path of thinking, 'well, life's too short. It can be over just like that, so I'm going to do my own thing'. (Mike)
>
> I mean bereavement or redundancy – those can be good things sometimes, forcing people to make that move and realise that doing the same job for the next twenty-odd years, nine to five, is not the only option. (Rachel)

In these rare cases, interviewees isolated a key life event that had unsettled their realities, prompting a fresh perspective on the world. The sight and thought of death had acted like a jolt of electricity, prompting them to reflect on their values and priorities. This ability to isolate a key, precipitating event was a rarity among the people I met, however. More often, the breakpoint appeared to be the outcome of a more sustained, gnawing feeling of malaise or anxiety. In such cases, what we observe is not a sudden epiphany but a more gradual disillusionment with the working world, incubated in the space between desire and reality. To borrow a term from the interviewee Bruce, we witness the feeling of 'dis-ease' that breeds in the gap between personal aspirations, ethical ideals and self-perceptions, on the one hand, and the unpalatable realities of life as it is really experienced, on the other.

If we want to understand why people resist work, it seems we need to go a little deeper. This is what I will attempt to do in the

remainder of the chapter. What I present are of course simplifica-
tions of reality. Quite understandably, many participants bristled at
the suggestion that there could be one overriding cause or moment
which defined their decision to resist work. Perhaps even calling it
a 'decision' is to some extent misleading – maybe it was more like
a building feeling, or the result of a long chain of events. For those
participants who felt too unwell to work, resisting work can hardly
be described as a 'decision'. It was more like a necessity or an act
of self-preservation. I discuss the factors that led people to resist
work only in so far as any of us can really say exactly why we do the
things we do. With this in mind, I will look at three common 'routes'
into resistance to work: the rubbish job, the mini utopia and the
broken body.

The rubbish job

I encountered Larry about halfway through my investigation, having
been provided his contact details by a friend (and ex-colleague of
Larry's). Larry declined to meet me in person, so we talked about
his experiences over the phone. In his fifties, Larry was a longstand-
ing social worker who said he had been suffering from stress. He
had negotiated a reduction of his working day by one hour (bringing it down to seven, rather than the usual eight), believing that the
change would help him improve his 'chance of feeling half decent'.
The extra hour to himself meant he could dodge the rush hour during his commute, and also relax a little better: 'I'm less tired in the
evenings and I've got a bit more time to do what I want to do.' Over
the course of his interview, Larry focused on the changes he had
witnessed in his many years as a social worker. He seemed nostalgic
for an earlier time, when he had been permitted the freedom to work
on a social work case from start to finish. He valued this model of

working because he believed it had allowed him to understand his clients' needs and make a tangible contribution to their well-being. Larry contrasted this with the 'bureaucratic machine' of modern social work:

> Client contact is very small these days. We follow the set assessment and planning process, so we've got a comprehensive assessment plan. Basically, it's a whole lot of forms to do, a *lot* of paperwork, probably relating to people you've never met before. It's either very boring or quite stressful. You're trying get through all these administrative tasks, which you can never keep up with. There's so much recording and so many people you have to tell different things to: finances and forms, identifications, authorisations, contracts, and then fill in forms to say that you've *done* all these forms.

I asked Larry if he took any satisfaction from his job. He said, 'It's not satisfying at all. I used to love my job, but now I don't like it at all really.' The most troubling aspect was that the labour process had morphed over the years, so that instead of managing a relatively small number of whole cases, each social worker was assigned a narrower, more routine set of tasks across a wider range of cases. Larry believed that, as a result of these changes, he had been dispossessed of the freedom to make judgements about the best course of action for his clients. The wisdom he had gained from his years of service had become redundant: 'your experience is less valued than your typing speed'. His daily experience of work had become one of wading through administrative tasks in a state of impatience and resentment, even though he appreciated that the papers on his desk pertained to people 'with quite pressing emotional needs or crises'. As a conscientious man, he found his mounting impatience troubling. The old Larry had generous reserves of patience for his clients, but the new one was pissed off all the time. He said it was largely as a consequence of these experiences that he had come to develop a purely instrumental relationship with work, performing it without enthusiasm, only in so far as it was necessary to his survival. (Following our interview, news reached me that Larry had actually stopped working altogether.) He wondered whether he might one day be able to rediscover his attraction to social work through some other outlet, outside formal employment: 'If I needed no income I would just do voluntary work, maybe get involved with some of the voluntary bodies that do things with learning disabilities or other kinds of voluntary work, like adult literacy, or maybe even some kind of environmental group'. I wondered if Larry ever would.

Larry's account speaks to a range of broad and well-established themes from the critiques of work explored in Chapter 2. He despairs at the intensification of bureaucracy and its world of 'aims and objectives', 'outcomes' and 'mission statements', believing that standardised procedures had interfered with his ability to do the job sensitively and well. The standardisation of the labour process and a shifting division of labour had undermined Larry's identity as a social worker, destroying his ability to experience a sense of moral agency and pride in his work. He felt estranged from his younger colleagues, who were favoured for their slick efficiency, even if they were ultimately less experienced. The tragedy for Larry was being forced to observe these changes taking hold gradually, over a number of years. A job that was supposed to draw on his personal reserves of wisdom and empathy had, in Larry's view, been steadily reduced to a set of administrative procedures, in which the personal needs of the client were held at arm's length. It seems that these experiences had figured prominently in Larry's desire to push away from work.

The negative experience of work itself also figured prominently in my conversations with a participant called Matthew. Matthew was the husband of another participant, Lucy. They were a young married couple in their early twenties, and I would meet them several times over the course of the research, talking over cups of tea at their home in South Wales. Each time we met, the couple would update me on any changes in their circumstances, before going into earnest detail about their hopes and fears for the future. I always enjoyed interviewing Matthew and Lucy. Their accounts were spontaneous, surprising and often emotional. It sometimes seemed like they were explicating their views on work for the first time.

When first we met, the couple had recently moved to the area for Matthew to study philosophy at the university. Since he was studying full-time, unburdened by decisions about work, it was mainly Lucy who I had come to meet, but I will come back to Lucy a little later. At the time of our interview she did not have a job, and nor did she intend to look for one in the near future. The couple were instead financed by Matthew's student loan, plus a small amount of savings from previous employment. By the end of the research, however, the couple's circumstances had changed considerably. Matthew had finished his degree and now, like Lucy, was out of work. He claimed to have a strong sense of self-direction and said he was enjoying his jobless life: he spent quality time with Lucy, wrote articles about video games for an online magazine, attended a film club, and volunteered for the Royal Society for the Protection of Birds (RSPB), among other things, but he was also deeply worried about the couple's financial security. By the time of our last meeting, the two were claiming housing benefit, and Matthew had also begun claiming Jobseeker's Allowance.

Matthew was looking for work, but only occasionally, and largely without enthusiasm it seemed. Like all the people I met, he had a strong desire to perform work which he perceived to be meaningful. His voluntary work with the RSPB had come close to this ideal, as did a couple of one-off jobs hosting open days on behalf of his university. Matthew was happy to promote these organisations because he 'believed in them', but he generally had low hopes for finding meaningful employment. His job-seeking efforts were mostly performative. He filled out job applications – usually for high-street retailers – in order to satisfy the conditions of his benefit entitlement. He hoped that employers would not respond, especially after calculating that a minimum-wage job would leave the couple only marginally better off financially. Claiming benefits had come to represent something of a game, which Matthew was convinced they would eventually lose. The probability that he would be forced to take a menial or ethically dubious job was weighing heavily on his mind:

> Selling products that I don't care about, contributing to something that is either uninteresting or, at the very worst, contributing to something that is unethical – I don't know how I'm going to be able to do that every day without getting depressed, anxious, or a mixture of the two … I'm very worried about what the wrong job could do to me.

Perhaps he was worried about suffering the same fate as his wife, Lucy, who had previously worked in a bargain shop. Lucy said:

> I don't know if I can ever buy cushions again, because that's all my job was: *shoving* cushions into a place they didn't fit. It was like [my managers'] *lives*. They were like, 'oh the cushions have to go three that way, three that way, and three that way' … It just drove me insane.

The strength of Matthew's desire to perform work he saw as meaningful became most apparent when he admitted the full extent of the couple's financial hardships. It was very telling that, even though the couple were barely managing to pay their rent, and had often been forced to subsist on a very simple diet, buying what food they could afford day by day, Matthew had still not been driven to actively search for work.[3]

As we interrogated Matthew's attitudes in the interview, he was drawn repeatedly back to his previous experiences as an administrative assistant for a local magazine – a job he had performed without pay, over a period of several months, in order to gain work experience. He hated the role. Over the times we met, I judged Matthew to be a very congenial person. He was welcoming, enthusiastic, and seemed attentive towards Lucy, but admitted that he had struggled to exhibit similar qualities at work, especially when he felt his assignments were meaningless:

> It's like your personality's become a judgement for them, like they
> expect you to be bouncing off the walls. When I was at [the magazine],
> people on the whole were really nice, but there was a huge amount of
> pressure to be emotionally chirpy. A big part of my job was making
> phone calls, talking to people, flogging things to people, so there was
> an element of charm and charisma and stuff like that … There's quite
> a big emotional investment required to work in an office environment.

Remember that by this point, Matthew was frightened of losing his Jobseeker's Allowance. I asked him to tell me his worst-case scenario. He said it was being forced by the job centre to take a job in sales:

> The idea of working in an office and saying hello to people, being
> asked 'how are you?' when you feel terrible, having to ring people up
> – if you work in sales you have to be jumping off the walls, 'be yourself,
> be happy!' You know, there's a lot of times where I feel awful, and
> having to put on these acts really scares me.

Matthew's complaints are strongly reminiscent of Hochschild's theory of emotional labour, introduced in Chapter 2. Matthew explains his struggles to conjure up the emotional performances required by his work role. He is supposed to be 'bouncing off the walls' with optimism, but cannot summon the energy. He finds it draining to the extent that it 'scares' him, threatening his dignity and sense of authenticity. His experiences make for a very neat comparison with Larry's. If we remember, Larry's main complaint about work was that he was being forced to perform ethically sensitive tasks with the cold distance of a bureaucrat. Matthew's concerns were the inverse: he was being cajoled into performing simple bureaucratic tasks with the warm spirit of a professional.

In our interviews, I noticed that Matthew had repeatedly made a point of stressing his sociable nature. He said that one of his favourite activities was 'talking to people'. This statement reminded me of Jack, who said that one of his favourite activities was 'shooting the breeze', and it would also later be echoed in an interview with Bruce, who said that he loved 'relating to people'. Given their sociability, it may seem puzzling that these same people also said that they had felt withdrawn and inhibited in the places they had worked. Work is, after all, often valorised as an important source of sociality (recall that social contact was one of the 'key psychological functions' of work identified by Jahoda and followers in the deprivation model). Yet we can note that the people I met did not generally value work as a source of social contact. What I believe they were professing to value in their love of talking was something like a heart-to-heart or catch-up between friends, in which fully consenting people share their views, make confessions about themselves, and are richer for the experience. (Either that or something like a playful banter, or talking 'random crap', as Matthew put it.) The interactions they valued were those in which one approaches another as a common soul 'rather than as a mere useful instrument, or an obstacle to one's own plans' (Nussbaum, 2010: 6). The love of conversation is a craving for the tenderness realised when people entertain the possibility of 'relations without purpose' (Adorno, 2005: 41). Whilst some of the non-workers I met did admit to difficult feelings of social isolation, it is notable that nobody said they missed the social milieu of their previous jobs. Anne described ex-colleagues as 'back-stabbing bastards', and Rachel described a pattern of bullying at work. Lucy said she would much rather get home to her husband than drink with colleagues after five o'clock. Non-work might be isolating, but work does not necessarily represent a valued source of tender and authentic human interaction.

In the cases we have looked at (and there are many more examples I could have chosen), a purely instrumental relationship with work was forged. Following their negative experiences of work, Larry and Matthew decided that they would only tolerate paid employment in so far as it was economically necessary. This led Larry to reduce his working hours, whereas for Matthew the decision meant avoiding work as far as possible. For other people, the negative experiences of work had led to a snap career change. High-commitment careers were traded for low-commitment, part-time jobs, allowing people to pursue their thirst for productive activity in their free-time. We can consider the cases of Adam and Samantha. Adam was a lively young man in his mid twenties, who had quit a well-paid job as a computer programmer in London to work as a part-time English teacher in Tokyo, Japan. Since Adam's undergraduate degree had been in programming, a career in programming had seemed like the 'clear thing to do', but things had not turned out as expected: 'I slowly gained the feeling that, from maybe the first week, something was very *wrong*.' Adam had enjoyed computer programming a great deal at university, and had even undertaken his own, self-initiated programming projects in his free-time. This enthusiasm, however, was crushed by his job. He was dismayed when his bosses pressurised him into using a software package he did not believe was fit for purpose. He was also crushed by the length of the working day, which could be as much as sixteen hours nearing a deadline, and was outraged to discover how few holidays he was entitled to. He was only permitted twelve days of annual leave. This was not the life he had imagined for himself. He saw himself as a skilled worker and did not feel that his efforts were being recognised. His bosses saw him as a number rather than a person:

> There was no kind of 'you're a human being, thank you very much for keeping my company going', but just 'come in when you're meant to, work on this big long list, and we'll complain to you if it doesn't work'. And – oh, this is another thing! They called everyone 'resource'! I couldn't believe it! 'Yeah, we need more resource on this project', and I'm thinking, What do you mean by resource? Oh, you mean *people*!

At university, it seemed that Adam had enjoyed a sense of continuity between his work and his leisure, choosing to do programming in his spare time, but his unhappiness at work had increasingly led him to view his life in terms of compartmentalised spheres of work and relaxation: 'there was the *work* me and the *home* me'. Unsatisfied with this situation, Adam had made the drastic decision to quit the job and jet off to Japan to teach English. When we spoke, he seemed giddy:

> My job is being the face of foreign and saying 'English is very excit-ing!' People come up to me and I can *explain* things to them, and they

say 'thank you, now I understand that' ... When I started doing the English job I was like 'wow, you can enjoy yourself', so I can't go back to those earlier jobs now.

Adam's part-time hours meant that he was free to pursue his computer programming on a freelance basis. He said he was happier because he was able to take on the projects that interested him, and also have greater control over the pace and methods of his work.

We can compare Adam with Samantha, a graduate in her early thirties, whose resistance had also taken the form of a sudden shift in trajectory. Samantha had gained a PhD in genetics before working as a patent attorney in London. Like Adam, she had tried her best to find a career that would utilise the skills and interests honed in her degree. She had chosen to work in the field of biotechnology patenting, believing that this would allow her to utilise her background in genetics. She quickly became disappointed, however, finding few opportunities to draw on her specialised knowledge. Samantha was dismayed with the limited scope the job gave her to 'engage in the real world'. Compared with many of the people I met, who had performed fairly routine jobs in shops, offices and warehouses, Samantha's job was of a much higher status and skill level. Yet she seemed to have felt comparably bored. Although the job was skilled, it still felt like a 'big game': 'I felt like I was just doing hard Sudoku puzzles every day for a living ... As with a Sudoku puzzle, it just felt like a mental exercise. The only end goal was money.' Samantha's example suggests that even if a job is technically demanding and requires skill, it will not necessarily be experienced as meaningful.

Samantha described her PhD as a kind of shackle, rather than a gateway to interesting work, because it had put pressure on her to honour the qualification with a high-flying career. She recalls feeling that she had reached a 'dead end' in her life, where she should realistically anticipate no major or exciting changes. The truth, which she was gradually forced to admit, was that she was not that interested in a high-commitment job. At first she reacted in an extreme way by dropping work altogether, but this turned out to be a mistake: 'I'd always thought that what I wanted to do was nothing. I couldn't imagine anything more incredible than being completely free, but what I actually found was that it was extremely difficult.' Eventually, she took a part-time job as a waitress, working on the side as a freelance private tutor. Samantha described these jobs fondly, saying that she had 'met nice people and had nice conversations', but when we spoke she did not know what the future held. She was thinking about training to be a psychotherapist. The important thing for her was that she live with intention: 'I'm crafting my own life.'

The key point we can take from these accounts of the breakpoint is that, whether people had reduced their hours or given up work altogether, they had not done so according to some kind of crude, anti-work morality, but according to a strongly felt desire to do *more*. The stories that people told about their jobs show how the desire for resistance can be fuelled by the lack of meaning and autonomy in employment. Functional social roles such as a paid job can never be identical with the complex, fully rounded people who are forced to inhabit them. There is always an excess of self that exceeds the social role and wants to burst free. When the people I met had worked in full-time jobs, the work role had always left certain desires unsatisfied, ambitions unmet, skills dormant. Important parts of the self were denied expression and recognition. I am reminded of Matthew's statement that in his previous job roles, he had felt like 'a firework going off under a bucket'. For the most part, I doubted that there was any job that these people would be happy to perform for eight hours a day, five days a week.

The mini utopia

In order for people to reach a breakpoint and begin actively struggling against their alienation, perhaps what is first needed is a taste for autonomy. It is only through familiarity with some ideal model of engaging and meaningful activity that a person starts to really feel the pinch of their alienation, which has deprived him of this model. This describes the nature of Marx's interest in a group of skilled, multi-tasking or 'polyvalent' workers in the 1850s and 1860s. Since these workers were fortunate enough to gain a taste of what true, non-alienated work might feel like, Marx believed they would be prepared to fight for more autonomy (Gorz, 1982: 27–8). Their breakpoints would originate within the domain of work itself. What is apparent from the stories of working which I encountered, however, is that modern forms of work may provide few opportunities for workers to develop a taste for real, autonomous activity, conducted in accordance with the worker's own ideas of efficiency, beauty and usefulness. In this case, the inspiration to fight against alienation has to come from some other aspect of experience, outside the workplace. Let us once again consider the case of Matthew. In one of our later interviews, Matthew described one life event – a university trip – with particular relish:

> We went on this trip to Weynon Priory, which is this gorgeous stately home. The philosophy department went up, and the philosophy department from Newborough went up, and we all just went there. It's just this big stately home and we all stayed in rooms, and we woke up and we all had breakfast together – which is something I'd never done before. You know, there were all these interesting people like lecturers

sitting next to you, along with the students, and it was like we were all
on an equal footing. I was having a chat with this genuinely renowned
professor of philosophy, and we were talking about Pot Noodles
and instant food, and he was talking about the greatness of porridge
you can make in a cup! That sounds weird, but it was just that act of
eating together with people and talking about philosophy, or even just
random crap. Then the day was spent in lectures or just people doing
talks about things – philosophical issues, stuff about the NHS, ethics,
Nietzsche, all sorts, and then there would be tea and coffee breaks
where you could just chat. There was also a library where you could
sit and lounge. We were lucky that it was sunny when we went there,
because one of the days we went for this huge walk around the valley,
just chatting about hopes, dreams, politics, everything. And then
we got back and we would eat together – *together,* with people from
different social levels. Then we had a bit of poetry in the evening and went
to the pub, and everyone got drunk, had fun, played board games, did
quizzes. It was so amazing to be walking around, then playing football,
and then having these really deep chats. It completely changed me.
You just get a taste of what life could be like.

Matthew seemed to take a great deal of pleasure in describing his
university trip, and would later refer to it as his 'mini utopia'. He
mentions a number of desirable elements, but the most prominent
here seems to be the element of variety or multi-activity: using the
body and the mind; discussing the intellectual and the banal; being
inside and outside; routine and no routine; seriousness and silliness.
His account brings to mind one of Marx's more famous references,
to a putative future where it would be possible 'to do one thing today
and another tomorrow, to hunt in the morning, fish in the afternoon,
rear cattle in the evening, criticise after dinner', and so on (Marx,
1970: 54). Matthew lingers on the details of the trip perhaps in order

to emphasise its explanatory power, as a key life event that motivated him to resist work. The excitement and variation of the trip is favourably contrasted with his narrower experience of paid employment, which had seen him hammering away at one basic talent or capacity to the exclusion of all others. We can compare Matthew's experiences to the following story from Eleanor:

> I did a week-long environmental studies course with a charity called Operation Zissou. We went to France, and basically it's funded by the stone masons and big companies, but it's all about taking 18-to 24-year-olds away somewhere to learn about the local environment. One of the things you had to do was to prepare a ten-minute presentation at the end of the week about something you were passionate about, and again it was very much about living in a community and eating together and working together to achieve things.

As in Matthew's account of the university trip we see Eleanor tacitly contrasting certain freedoms and positive experiences with her more alienating experience of paid employment. In this case, it is the freedom to follow independent passions and the spirit of free co-operation (or 'working together to achieve things') which are emphasised. We can compare Eleanor's exotic experience with the reference of Berger and Pullberg to the de-reifying power of 'culture shock', or the 'clash of worlds', in which an encounter with foreign values and customs might lead to a disintegration of a person's taken-for-granted reality (Berger and Pullberg, 1966). In the foreign encounter, one's culture is revealed *as* one's own, relative to other possible and legitimate ways of life. So long as these encounters do not produce in the individual a xenophobic or fretful yearning for the familiar, they could represent the seeds for personal and social transformation. Not everybody, of course, has the privilege of enjoying experiences like these, but the taste for autonomy need not be developed in exotic or expensive retreats. We can consider an example from Ffion, who took inspiration from an experience much closer to home. Talking through her views on work, Ffion surprised herself with this involuntary memory about cooking a meal with the family at Christmas:

> I just remember from before – and this is just a little thing, but I remember it with a warm fuzzy feeling. Rhys's family came over here for Christmas a couple of years ago and we did the cooking, all together, and it was partly because we had time off and time to plan what we were going to do. We sort of made our own mince pies and made everything in stages you know, and had Christmas music on and a few glasses of brandy. You know, there was something really nice about being all together and it not being really frantic.

Ffion had enjoyed the leisureliness of this occasion: the joy of making things in stages, of things 'not being really frantic'. This event seemed to have stuck in her mind, where it represented the whisper of a possible alternative to her usually much busier, nine-to-five lifestyle.

In relation to these accounts, Matthew's reference to a 'mini utopia' seems entirely appropriate. Interviewees attributed a similar value to these temporary departures from the more mundane or routine aspects of daily life as academics have assigned to utopian projections of the good society. E. P. Thompson wrote that the value of utopian thinking is that it teaches us to 'desire better, to desire more, and above all to desire in a different way' (Thompson, 1976: 97). The encounter with utopian alternatives – be it the fictional utopias of literature, the theoretical utopias of academia, or those experiences of actual, fleeting escapes from the mundane – manifest themselves as unresolved desires among the habits and routines of everyday life. The utopian encounter produces in the person a sense of 'estrangement that can undercut the present social order's ascribed status as a natural artefact, necessary development, and inevitable future' (Weeks, 2011: 205). It helps people realise that the path before them is not written in indelible ink.

For graduates who today find themselves disillusioned with the world of employment, it is perhaps the experience of university that acts as the unsettling 'mini utopia'. It is perhaps for good reason that working adults often refuse to acknowledge student life as part of the 'real world'. The student's opportunities to follow her own interests, work according to her own schedule, and mix work and play are opportunities which are rarely enjoyed beyond university. Given the capitalist division of labour and the alienating qualities of many modern forms of work, those who gain a taste for creativity and variation in their education may be confronted with scant opportunities to integrate this into their later lives. As Bruce wearily told me: 'nobody is interested in talking about ideas after university'. In their university education, people like Adam, Samantha and Matthew had gained expectations and an image of themselves as autonomous workers, performing meaningful and challenging work, all the while retaining a sizeable chunk of leisure time. These expectations were to be sorely disappointed upon their graduation into the world of work. Borrowing Robert Merton's terms, we might say that higher education contributed to a disillusionment with employment by boosting each person's cultural 'frame of aspirational reference' (Merton, 1938). The breakpoint represents the moment where they registered their disappointed expectations and refocused their ambitions outside the world of careers. As Matthew said about his university trip: 'You just get a taste of what life could be like.' Matthew had enjoyed himself so much that the thought of routine work made him feel like hell.

The broken body

Up to this point, the implication has been that the people I met made a voluntary decision to resist work. It seems that for a few people, however, resistance to work was closer to a necessity, or an act of self-preservation. It was a choice made in a state of lethargy rather than energetic bravery. Several believed that to be free from the demands and routines of paid work was actually essential to their personal well-being, and we can interpret their refusals of work partly as refusals to make the bodily sacrifices often required by employment. This emotive passage from Marx is valuable as a reminder of these sacrifices:

> [In] its were-wolf hunger for surplus-labour, capital oversteps not only the moral, but even the merely physical maximum bounds of the working-day. It usurps the time for growth, development, and healthy maintenance of the body. It steals the time required for the consumption of fresh air and sunlight. It higgles over a meal-time, incorporating it where possible with the process of production itself, so that food is given to the labourer as to a mere means of production, as coal is supplied to the boiler, grease and oil to the machinery. It reduces the sound sleep needed for the restoration, reparation, refreshment of the bodily powers to just so many hours of torpor as the revival of an organism, absolutely exhausted, renders essential. It is not the normal maintenance of the labour-power which is to determine the limits of the working-day; it is the greatest possible daily expenditure of labour-power, no matter how diseased, compulsory, and painful it may be, which is to determine the limits of the labourers' period of repose.
> (Marx, 1906)

Whilst work may have generally become cleaner and physically safer since Marx's day, his concern with the disregard of capital for the limitations of the human body is no less relevant now. According to the UK Health and Safety Executive, in the financial year 2013/14, an estimated 1.2 million people began suffering from an illness they believed to be caused or made worse by their current or previous employment. Around 39% of the cases recorded were cases of stress, depression or anxiety (HSE, 2014). The social commentator Teresa Brennan argued that the productive and competitive demands of the modern world are overriding the body's capacity for self-regulation, provoking us to use our energies at a pace that exceeds their ability to regenerate: 'The deregulated body is one that goes without enough sleep, rest, proper food – taking prescribed drugs to silence its chronic illnesses and escalating allergies' (Brennan, 2003: 22). People keep on pushing when they know they should stop, overwhelmed by the myriad variables that need to be anticipated and reacted to, in the interests of productivity and survival.[4] Suffering from various symptoms – from stress, to anxiety, to fatigue – many of the people I met over the course of this research asserted a need to take back control of the deregulated body, i.e., to take their lives a little slower, to get enough sleep, to go outdoors more, to prepare a good meal, and to enjoy their leisure time free of tension.

The majority of the people I met discussed their breakpoints with at least some reference to their personal health, but it is Bruce who offers the most poignant illustration. When we met, Bruce had given up work altogether, and could not imagine himself being well enough to perform a job in the near future. Bruce had previously worked as a support worker in care homes for people with acute mental health problems, but since quitting had survived financially by claiming Employment Support Allowance – a form of disability benefit (hereafter ESA). Here, he describes a day in which his body 'broke':

> I literally just broke. That is how I think of it, a switch in me just went *psssh* and I really just broke. It was almost overnight, I started to get all of these pains and spasms and twitches. I couldn't sleep. I started to get joint pain, inflammation on my body, bowel problems, vision problems, hearing problems.

Bruce was philosophical about his symptoms, outlining his belief that sickness has a meaning which must be interpreted, rather than suppressed with stoicism, denial, or medical treatments. Bruce believed that his body was 'sending a message':

> It was just like my whole body was saying to me 'enough is enough'. My body was – in my view now, in the way I perceive mental illness – being kind to me in *shouting*. I hadn't been listening, so it shouted and said 'you really need to take some time off and kind of re-evaluate life and the way you relate to yourself'.

According to Bruce's worldview, painful symptoms can act as a valuable reminder that lifestyle changes need to be made. In a society with such a powerful moral emphasis on being a working and economically active citizen, perhaps the more conventional response to physical and psychological distress is to ignore or suppress symptoms, rather than interpret them as signals of social and environmental disharmony. However, rather than pushing on in his job, Bruce said he ended up quitting work and adopting a strategy of self-care.

As Bruce described his self-care habits, I was reminded of Gorz's definition of 'hygiene', which for Gorz means something much more than the mundane rituals of preening and cleanliness. For Gorz, hygiene consists in a more rigorous attempt on the part of individuals to understand their bodily needs and improve their well-being. Hygiene is likened to an 'art of living', and refers to the 'comprehensive set of rules that people observe *by themselves* to maintain or recover their health' (Gorz, 1980: 151, his emphasis). In Bruce's case, self-care meant a number of things, from stretching and exercising, to prioritising nutrition, and taking some time each day to rest and contemplate. To somebody else, self-care could entail a completely different set of practices. Self-care does not necessarily mean developing a strict, medically sanctioned well-being regime, but might also recognise the importance of unstructured time to relax, live in the moment, see friends, be irresponsible, and even do things commonly considered to be unhealthy. The important thing is that each person is free to decide autonomously which habits, practices, situations and environments allow him or her to flourish – a process of self-discovery which requires a degree of freedom from pressing economic demands.

Bruce recalls a previous encounter with a psychiatrist with great disdain, because the psychiatrist had suggested Bruce manage his illness with symptom-suppressing medications rather than self-care. This conflicted with Bruce's understanding of his pain as a signal of wider social and environmental disharmonies:

> I've been told by a psychiatrist before that when I was a student, I might be able to get by without medication because student life is flexible and you can get time off. But, in her words, when you are in the workforce and being employed by somebody, then you would need medication in order to keep going.

Like several of the people I met, Bruce objected to the idea that illnesses should be suppressed and ignored simply in order to keep working. Bruce and others refused to adapt themselves to an environment and a situation which they felt was maladapted to their needs, and, in their resistance to work, sought the time required to pay closer attention to their bodily needs. Anne, for example, said that her decision to become a freelancer and adopt a flexible work schedule was partly an attempt to manage her fatigue and food allergies (as well as have more free-time to care for her sick father). In Lucy's case, giving up work was explained as an attempt to live a calmer, less anxious life. In Gerald's, his early retirement was rationalised partly as an attempt to alleviate anger and tensions within his marriage.

We can note, however, that self-care means much more than securing the time necessary to cultivate healthy habits. For Bruce, especially, it also meant resisting the medicalisation of his negative experiences, such medicalisation usually being a necessary condition for exemption from the duty to work. Gorz writes:

> To be socially acceptable, [a] cry for help must take the form of an organic disorder – exogenous and independent of the patient's will. You would have no chance at all of getting your boss or supervisor to listen to you if you said 'I can't go on, I'm losing sleep, my appetite, my interest in sex; I don't have energy for anything anymore. Give me a week off.' To be acceptable, your 'I can't go on' must take the form of a somatic difficulty, of some impeachment beyond your control – in short, an illness justifying a medical exemption. (Gorz, 1980: 174)

If it is going to be seen as legitimate, a person's decision to not work generally needs to be authorised by the medical establishment, who assign the health complaint a label and prescribe a programme of recovery.[5] The pressure to adopt biomedical labels in order to secure exemption from work posed a significant dilemma for people like Bruce, Lucy and Emma – people who said they felt too ill to work, but who did not necessarily believe they were suffering from biomedical conditions. Bruce had been assigned various medical labels over the years. I asked him what these were and could tell that the interview had strayed into a sensitive area:

> I've had a long history of what they call in the profession [Bruce slowly remembers] S.E. um, what is it? S.E.M.H.P: Severe and Enduring Mental Health Problems. Bi-polar disorder, with associated major depressive disorder, with associated anxiety – so there's three labels for you there.

Bruce found these labels alienating. They conflicted with his belief that, rather than a mental disorder, he had experienced a 'crisis', precipitated by a complex cocktail of personal experiences and environmental factors. He also objected to the sense of permanence in the labels that doctors had assigned him, which conflicted with his goal to improve his health through the autonomous habits of self-care. He says the labels are 'like saying "you've got this mental illness and you will have it for life"'. We can compare Bruce's outlook with Lucy's. Lucy described a number of symptoms associated with agoraphobia (feelings of anxiety, difficulty being in busy places, and so on), but was reluctant to call herself 'disabled'.

The desire to resist medical labels posed a significant problem for these people as they began to run out of money. They were forced to file claims for disability benefit, which in the UK requires prospective claimants to undergo a Work Capability Assessment (WCA), in which a doctor conducts a series of tests in order to assess the legitimacy of the claim. Bruce's struggles had occurred around the time of the aforementioned ATOS scandal in 2012–13, when access to the sick role was controversially tightened, and the idea that claimants might be 'faking it' was prominent in the public imagination. Generally speaking, recent times have seen welfare policies expanding their definition of illnesses and impairments that are supposed to be tolerated as part of a normal, everyday working life, and shrinking the list of complaints that allow access to disability allowances. It is not entirely surprising that Bruce was rejected as a claimant after his first WCA – an experience which he said caused him to 'have a complete meltdown'. He said he felt suicidal and unable to leave his family home. Bruce contacted the Citizens Advice Bureau, which advised him (as they were advising many at the time) to treat the WCA as something of a game. Bruce arranged for a reassessment and this time 'went in wise': he made a pact with himself that he would advertise his medical labels for the sake of securing time and money for self-care, but would try his best to avoid internalising the idea that he was pathological. Bruce's second attempt at a claim was successful, and he described the Citizens Advice Bureau as 'a complete lifesaver'. Lucy had also been successful in claiming ESA, under the agreement that she was a medically recognised sufferer of 'agoraphobia'. She was more open than Bruce to the idea that medical experts might be able to help her improve her condition, but was deeply critical of the disability officer assigned to her by the job centre: 'They say "we need to help you find work," but they've never said "we need to actually help *you*"'.

We can understand self-care, resistance to work, and also the resistance to medical labels as attempts to shape lifestyles in which sufferers can feel proud and normal rather than ashamed, powerless, and medically ill. If people like Bruce are trying to actively enjoy their leisure time even though they are claiming ESA, it is because people are often willing to tolerate pain in order to do the things that they love, even if they are not prepared to tolerate it in order to work:

> There are people out there who would say – for example, I've come out here to meet you [the interviewer] today, taken the train, and there are people who would say 'Ah well, if you can do that then you can work.' But it's not that simple [sighs deeply]. There is no room for grey areas in the benefits system, yeah, there are no grey areas.

Ultimately, these examples show us that resistance to work is not always a voluntary choice, but often an act of self-preservation. Several of the people I met believed that to be free from the stresses and routines of work was essential to their well-being. Their examples perhaps sensitise us to the sacrifices that we all make when forced to keep on going, in the knowledge that we should slow down or stop.

A worthwhile ethic

My chief goal in this chapter has been to explore the experiences which can shape and precipitate the 'breakpoint': the point at which work ceases to be taken for granted as an inevitable fate and is instead opened up for critical scrutiny. We saw how sudden shock events and unhappy experiences of work prompted people to reconsider their priorities. We saw how the sense of freedom experienced in temporary breaks from the mundane routines of everyday life had made full-time working intolerable. We also saw how people began to resist work in the interests of preserving their health. What is perhaps most notable about the accounts analysed here is that they take us beyond the tired conservative stereotypes of people who resist work as shirkers and layabouts. What I discovered over the course of my research was an ethically conscientious rebellion against full-time employment, coming from a range of fairly ordinary people.

In the most general terms, it can be argued that they rejected the work ethic and replaced it with what David Cannon has called a 'worthwhile ethic' (Cannon, 1994). People were motivated by a sense of genuine utility: a desire to create, help others, and avoid ethically dubious work. They defined success not in terms of material wealth or social status but in terms of the opportunity to develop their personal capacities. They were unwilling to endure significant compromises to body and mind for the sake of earning a better wage. From their work they demanded moral autonomy and a sense of challenge and satisfaction, but they surmised that such demands were unlikely to be satisfied in the official realm of paid employment, refocusing their ambitions elsewhere. They reduced their hours, they ditched their day jobs and they freelanced, or they settled for low-commitment, part-time roles, with the instrumental aim of funding and maximising their free-time. Some used their time to take care of their elderly parents or play with their children. Those who suffered in their health used the time to take better care of themselves. Many took part in political protests and volunteered with charities. All balked at the idea that the most noble way to contribute to the wider community is to perform paid work. What I present here is a tentative first step towards challenging the idea that to live without work is necessarily to live an empty and morally rudderless existence. Rather than writing off the views of work's dissenters as eccentric or immoral, my proposal is that we study them further, taking them seriously as potential sources of nourishment for a politics against work.

Whilst the people I met over the course of my research were highly critical of work, this is not to say that they had successfully escaped its grip. The breakpoint signifies the moment at which people begin to reflect more clearly on the nature of cognitive power and their own capacities for self-direction, but it does not in itself constitute an escape to freedom. As I explored in earlier chapters, there exists a powerful set of moral and material constraints which continue to police the desire to resist work, preventing its translation into bona fide social change. Resisting work carries significant risks, from financial desolation to social castigation. In the next chapter, and the one that follows it, I will develop my investigation into the lives of people who resist work by exploring some of the difficulties and – more surprisingly – some of the pleasures that people experienced as they dealt with these constraints.

SIX: Alternative pleasures

Normal is getting dressed in clothes that you buy for work, driving
through traffic in a car that you are still paying for, in order to get to a
job that you need so you can pay for the clothes, car and house you leave
empty all day in order to afford to live in it.

Ellen Goodman[1]

Part of the way through my research, I met a man in his mid thirties called Alan. Alan's story had much in common with the stories
of others I had met. We discussed his frustration in his previous
jobs as an office administrator, as well as his powerful desire to be
identified by markers other than his occupation. He told me that
he had always found work too easy, explaining that his jobs had
represented little more to him than sources of income. At the time of
our interview, Alan was not doing paid work and he explained that
any work he had previously performed was always done in a strictly
instrumental fashion: he would work low-level office jobs until he
accumulated enough money to fund a period of leisure, at which
point he would abruptly quit the job and enjoy his free time. When
his money ran out, then it was back to work again 'in order to fund
the next adventure'.[2] This is a roundabout way of saying that the
employer was always part of Alan's plan and never the other way
around.

Alan's instrumental orientation to work was fairly commonplace in the context of my research as a whole, but what is more relevant to us here is his unique refusal to acknowledge any potential drawbacks of resisting work. Whilst most of the people I met were keen to talk about their difficulties, I occasionally felt as though Alan were delivering a sales pitch for his chosen lifestyle. My efforts to get him to reveal any less desirable aspects of his life were in vain. His unyielding optimism was wrapped up in the idea that resisting work is largely a matter of imagination and individual will: a cognitive rather than a practical challenge. Alan was particularly critical of the idea that a person's scope for rebellion might be limited by his or her class position, and talked dismissively about 'people who say that class issues still exist and blah blah blah'. My composure as an interviewer was tested when Alan insisted that 'everybody in society is kind of equal', and that people who fear unemployment are 'sad individuals' with a 'weakness of character'.

Whilst I was initially surprised by Alan's views, what later struck me was their resemblance to a lot of popular anti-capitalist polemic. In its least challenging forms, this literature has advocated happiness by calling upon individuals to change their thought patterns and adopt new forms of behaviour. It tells people (often in a rather pious fashion) that they will be happier if they choose to work less and moderate their spending. The problem here is that when the appeal for change is directed primarily towards the thoughts and habits of individuals, the broader cultural and structural restrictions on behaviour change are kept out of sight. The failure of people to resist the status quo tends to be viewed as a product of brainwashing or moral laxity, and all that is left is for the author/guru to then explain that happiness awaits those who would be brave enough to lift the veil off reality, work less, and stop shopping.[3] What is downplayed is the fact that a slower pace of life is closed off to most people because they would not be able to survive economically. When the interviewees Matthew and Lucy spoke of the very real material limits to their resistance – the constant fear of not being able to pay the rent, the dinners of plain rice, reluctantly eaten at the end of the month – I secretly wondered what they would make of Alan's idealistic view that resistance to work can be accomplished simply through imagination and individual will. If we are going to think through properly the scope for resistance to work, we clearly need to account for the material obstacles to working less.

Given that work still functions in society as a main means through which people access income, we can expect resistance to work to be accompanied by a range of material risks and losses. At the most basic level, anyone wanting to reduce their working hours will have to think about whether they can still secure such provisions as food, clothing, shelter, electricity, a telephone, an internet connection and so on. At an advanced stage of capitalism, where the goods and practices required for the satisfaction of a wider range of everyday needs have become commodified, the risks of losing income are broader. Everywhere we look, activities that were previously excluded from the economic sphere are being pulled into its orbit, with people now catering to an increasing number of their personal needs (from hydration to self-expression to leisure) by spending money. Within this context, the social theorist Zygmunt Bauman suggests that financial poverty has a cultural as well as a material dimension. He describes the 'new poor', whose suffering in the midst of affluence is twofold: the new poor are not only deprived of particular material needs but also excluded from the normal cultural life of today's consumer society. What now passes as normal life, Bauman argues, is the ability of people to 'respond promptly and efficiently to the temptations of the consumer market' (Bauman, 2005: 112). In a society where commodity relations are central, the inferior purchasing power of the poor is synonymous with a diminished ability to participate in normatively approved lifestyles. The 'new poor' suffer and become stigmatised as 'flawed consumers': people who are seen as buying the wrong things, not buying enough, or having to shamefully meet their needs by scrimping and self-producing.

The hardships of poverty, especially in the midst of consumer affluence, place very real limitations on the scope that individuals have to resist work. It is a banal kind of optimism that ignores these material realities and insists that people can resist work simply by changing their attitudes. What is also crucial to note, however, is that the encirclement of everyday life by the market is by no means a complete and inviolable process. Despite the steep financial cost of living in modern consumer societies, and the tremendous pressure this places upon people to find secure employment, it is important to remember that people also retain an agency – even if it is a compromised one – to move in and out of, and to reject and remould the conventions of the social world they inhabit (Humphery, 2010: 133). Whilst it is important to recognise the material limits to working less, we can also observe the possibility of meeting needs in less conventional ways, outside the realm of exchange relations, and the capacity of people to formulate their own ideas of pleasure, beauty, sufficiency and well-being in order to circumvent the pressure to consume (Bowring, 2000b: 315).

One of the things I was curious to find out during the course of my research was whether or not people's resistance to work had deprived them of particular pleasures. I wondered whether resistance to work was worth the hit in terms of the material deprivations and practical challenges that would have no doubt arisen as a result of losing income. The answer to this question will of course depend on how much income has been lost, and on the availability of alternative sources of income, such as a partner's earnings, savings, income from casual work, or unemployment benefits. It will also depend on things like whether or not a person has children (which introduces a huge set of financial costs) or friendships with people who lead affluent lifestyles (in which case reducing spending could mean reducing the number of one's friends). What struck me above all, however, was the extent to which even the poorest participants resisted the idea that their lives were characterised by sacrifice.

Late into our interview, Samantha (our attorney-turned-waitress) raised the issue of whether some might see her lifestyle choices as puritanical. She personally rejected this idea:

> For me it feels massively indulgent. I think I have *more*, but more of different sorts of things. Like, when I talk to my friends in London they're all knackered and working really long hours and haven't got time to have a chat on the phone and I just think god, you know, *that's* the lifestyle that feels self-hating and puritanical.

If Samantha ever felt socially excluded because of her smaller income, she also believed that there were significant penalties for *inclusion* into the work-and-spend culture of capitalist society. There were definitely one or two things she missed about her old life as a full-time working attorney, but these deprivations were less significant than the reserves of time and energy she had gained. We can compare her views with a quote from Eleanor, which also hints at the price of social inclusion. Eleanor describes the full-time working lifestyle in dismal terms, as a grinding cycle of sacrifice and compensation:

I guess it was just like, the less I worked, the more I realised I didn't have to. I guess it's just looking at friends who are still stuck in the cycle of working to pay ridiculous rent, doing Monday to Friday and then going out for the weekend and getting completely hammered, and then spending the next few days at work being really miserable and then recovering enough for the weekend to come around, and then feeling just about OK enough to do the whole thing again.

Eleanor's account recalls Adorno's insights into the way that people experience their free-time in modern societies: as a kind of vacuum between periods of work. Her views on the miseries and irrationalities of the typical affluent lifestyle are representative of a general mood among the people I interviewed. This mood, I want to argue, is consistent with what the philosopher Kate Soper has called an *alternative hedonism* (Soper, 2007; 2008; 2013).

Alternative hedonism describes a personal disposition, as well as an approach to social criticism, which focuses on reservations surrounding the subjective gratifications of affluent consumer societies. The dependency of Western consumerism on a global system of exploitation and environmental harm is increasingly acknowledged by a range of sources, but what is less often discussed and represented are the ways in which these and other problems feed into people's subjective disenchantment with affluent lifestyles. Soper argues that there are now prevalent signs that affluent lifestyles are generating new forms of unhappiness and disaffection, either because of their negative by-products or due to the fact that they often stand in the way of alternative, more robust forms of enjoyment:

It is, after all, now widely recognised that our so-called good life is a major cause of stress and ill-health. It subjects us to high levels of noise and stench, and generates vast amounts of junk. Its work routines and modes of commerce mean that many people for most of their lives begin their days in traffic jams or overcrowded trains and buses, and then spend much of the rest of them glued to the computer screen, often engaged in mind-numbing tasks. A good part of its productive activity locks time into the creation of a material culture of ever faster production turnovers and built-in obsolescence, which pre-empts more worthy, enduring or entrancing forms of human fulfilment. (Soper, 2013)

If consumer capitalism is often championed as a bastion of personal liberty – a freedom to have whatever our hearts desire (so long as we can afford it) – Soper invites us to talk about the various forms of displeasure and personal sacrifice that pervade affluent societies. Where some would emphasise the fun, the excess, the expressivity and the letting-go, Soper reminds us of the equally palpable sense of stress, pollution, routine and social isolation in modern life. In her view, consumerism corresponds with a society and a mode of living that has, in various ways, become self-denying and moribund.[4] It is to these experiences of disaffection with affluent society that Soper believes an anti-consumerist ethics and politics should appeal: for the best chances of success, countervailing voices should appeal 'not only to altruistic compassion and environmental concern but also to the more self-regarding gratifications of consuming differently' (Soper, 2008: 571). To fellow authors, her call is not for a convoluted critique of consumerism based on developing an apparently higher knowledge of what people 'really' need (something other than what they 'think' they need), but for a more grounded look at what people are themselves saying about the displeasures of modern consumerism. The hope is that such an enquiry might help to nourish the desire for social change, and it is with Soper's 'alternative hedonist' agenda in mind that I propose to explore the frustrations that might prompt people to question a commodity-intensive mode of life. I will also explore some of the new pleasures that were discovered as people began both working and consuming less.

Troubled pleasures

Elio Petri's 1971 film *La classe operaia va in paradiso (The Working Class Goes to Heaven)* contains a scene in which the character Lulù Massa, a factory worker for over fifteen years, walks around his home staring at his possessions. He sees a crystal vase, a radio, an inflatable toy, and a set of candles called Magic Moments. Like the clutter in many people's homes, these mundane objects had long faded into Lulù's peripheral vision, no longer to be consciously regarded, yet at this particular moment he gives his possessions his full attention. For the first time he sees these objects for what they truly are: trash – trash for which he has paid dearly with his labour time. As he walks around his living room, Lulù contemplates the objects one by one. An ornamental table: thirty hours of work. A painting of a clown: ten hours of work. 'Was it worth it?' Lulù seems to be asking himself. As he starts furiously kicking around the junk in his closet, we know that the answer is no.

The pleasures of wealth have become tarnished for Lulù the worker, who realises that his material luxuries have been paid for at the expense of a lifetime of exhausting and demeaning work. In this sense, Lulù's material luxuries represent an example of what Soper has called *troubled pleasures*: consumerist forms of pleasure that can only be experienced at the expense of more fundamental forms of dissatisfaction. If impulsive shopping has its own intrinsic enjoyments, these enjoyments have become troubled for many people, who are now questioning the hedonic aspects of modern consumerism on a number of different grounds – be it the anxiety and self-critical attitude brought on by consumerism's vast array of choices, awareness of the environmental costs of consumerism, or a plaguing feeling that the world has become too superficial and cluttered. In Lulù's case, the 'trouble' arose with an awareness that the pleasures of commodity consumption had become outweighed by the inertia, frustration and ill-health caused by a lifetime of devotion to alienating work.

This particular dilemma was prominent in the mindsets of the American 'downshifters' studied by Juliet Schor in the 1990s. Schor observes that 'downshifters have experienced a change in which time and the quality of life become relatively more important than money' (Schor, 1998: 138). Time and money are perceived to exist in a trade-off relationship, and whilst (like most people) downshifters would like to have more time *and* more money, their values and experiences have prompted them to make lifestyle changes that increase their free-time at the expense of income. They have decided that they are not prepared to sacrifice their time to working, simply so that they can buy more commodities.

Schor's description of the downshifter mentality is a fair approximation of the views of people I met, for whom material luxuries had also become a kind of troubled pleasure. We can see this in Mike's talk about the mental calculations involved in shopping: 'Sometimes I see things and I think "that's nice," but it's not like I can't live without it. It's not that important that I would go and get a job I detest in order to have it.' Whilst Mike did not dissociate himself from the pleasures of shopping per se, its joys had been compromised by his cognisance of the personal sacrifices involved in earning a wage. This sense of a trade-off between time and money was most clearly articulated by the participant Cheryl. She was a chirpy woman in her forties, and the only person I interviewed who self-identified with the label 'downshifter'. I invited her to take part in the study after discovering her website, which describes her as a 'committed ambassador of simple living'. When we met at her home in rural southern England, she talked at length about her belief that time is more important than money: 'There are things that you think will make your life better if you have them, but there's no point if you've got to spend all of your time out there earning money to pay for them.' Cheryl made repeated distinctions between people who have an 'outward way of being' and those who have a more 'inward focus'. The outward people are those who privilege money. They gear their lives towards material acquisition, evaluate their possessions in relation to what others have, and are engaged in a constant battle to 'keep up with the Joneses'. By contrast, the inward people (or the 'downshifters') value time. They are less competitive, value their relationships more, and spend as much time as possible with their friends and family.

Cheryl's distinction between outward and inward reminded me once again of Erich Fromm's distinction between 'having' and 'being' as two fundamental modes of engaging in the world (Fromm, 1979). The desire to *have* or acquire can be satisfied with money, whereas the desire to *be*, or experience what Cheryl referred to as the inward pleasures, can only be satisfied with significant investments of time and energy. In a real-world context these categorisations – between having/being or inward/outward – have a hollow ring to them, since it is just as difficult to imagine a person who is completely unmotivated by the pleasures of acquisition as it is to conceive of a person who recklessly values only these things. Nevertheless, these categories serve a valuable role as mental constructs that enable people, as they register the troubled pleasures of consumerism, to make sense of the choices that lie before them.

In Cheryl's case, her identification as a 'being' or 'inward' person gave her a sense of direction and moral purpose, as well as a neat way of communicating her ethics as a downshifter. Given that she valued the inward or non-material pleasures the most, she should make choices that maximised her free-time rather than her income.

If time and money often exist in a trade-off relationship, the people I interviewed were opting to privilege the former, cutting down their income in order to boost their free-time. However, a closer look at their accounts reveals that they were also questioning the *inherent* pleasures of affluent lifestyles. The pleasures of shopping had become troubled not only because of their dependency on the income earned through working, but also because they were seen as having their own internal set of drawbacks.

One of the more obvious discontents of modern affluence that comes to mind is the anxiety caused by a growing awareness of the extent to which consumerism depends on a system of human and environmental exploitation. This was particularly disturbing for Eleanor, who here talks about going to the supermarket:

> Even with just going into the supermarket you find yourself shutting down and getting really angry. You go into this massive building with so much energy being consumed – like open refrigeration – and everyone just in this miserable zoned-out world of getting overly packaged goods. It makes me feel so fucking low.

Eleanor was among several people who said that they were avoiding particular retailers because of their known reliance on sweatshop labour or environmental harm. Ffion had stopped shopping at the budget clothing store Primark, despite the appeal of their low prices. Lucy said she used to enjoy a McDonald's, but had stopped buying them after learning more about factory farming. In Eleanor's comment quoted above, supermarkets are rebuked for their high energy consumption, but what is ultimately foregrounded is Eleanor's own sense of anger and misery. Shopping in supermarkets makes her feel 'so fucking low'. She has experienced what Soper describes as that 'vague and general malaise that descends in the shopping mall or the supermarket: a sense of a world too cluttered and encumbered by material objects and sunk in waste' (Soper, 2007).

In so far as consuming less was framed as an ethical response to the dependency of consumerism on social and environmental exploitation, we get a good sense of alternative hedonism as a 'third way' of living, between the egoistic hedonism of consumer culture and the self-denying puritanism of its Green, 'simple life' alternatives (De Geus, 2009: 199). Unlike consumer hedonists, alternative hedonists derive pleasure from knowing that their enjoyments do not come at the expense of human and environmental harm. The choice to live a less commodity-intensive existence simultaneously satisfies altruistic and self-interested motives: to consume less is to try and improve one's own experience of life *and* reduce one's negative impact on the wider world, or, rather, it is to recognise that these two things – care for the self and care for others – are intertwined. Alternative hedonism suggests a vision of the good life where pleasure is partly derived from the knowledge that one's actions as a consumer have caused no unnecessary harm.

Another of the more obvious discontents of modern affluence that comes to mind is the psychic anxiety caused by the array of consumer choices on offer. Choice has become fetishised in modern consumer societies, where the majority of the things we buy must be selected from vast product ranges, and often come with their own set of customisable options. Gadgets come in a range of colours, trousers in multiple cuts, and mobile phones with hundreds of optional apps and add-ons. A survey of a branch of the supermarket Tesco in the UK found an overwhelming 188 different kinds of shampoo and conditioner on the displays, along with 161 different kinds of breakfast cereal (Lewis, 2013: 38). Marketing materials regularly promote this level of choice as a symbol of wealth and freedom, but a number of psychologists have argued that this dizzying array of choice often represents a source of anxiety rather than pleasure (Iyengar and Lepper, 2000; Schwartz, 2004). The Slovenian thinker Renata Salecl examines this idea in a story about buying cheese from a delicatessen (a slightly bourgeois example, she admits). Faced with a massive range of choices, Salecl found herself paralysed and angry. Unable to make a choice, she first chastised herself for not being a more decisive and knowledgeable consumer. She then worried about how she would be judged for her selections, questioning the suitability of her choices through the imagined eyes of others. She then also questioned the sincerity of the deli owner's advice, beginning to resent his vested interest in making the choice on her behalf (probably in the interests of profit). The simple task of buying cheese had sent Salecl down a psychological rabbit hole: 'I began to grow woozy, and not just from the smell of Camembert' (Salecl, 2011: 14). It seems that for all its superficial and apparently self-evident appeal, consumer choice may very well be one of affluent society's more troubled pleasures. Matthew's interview gives us a perfect example of the sense of anxiety, regret and self-criticism that often come bundled with the tyranny of choice. He says: 'You're in town and you've got all this stuff to buy and then you make a choice and, I don't know, sometimes I've come home and thought, Uh, did I really need that? and I've been upset.'

Other people talked about the inherent *restlessness* involved in being an affluent consumer, or what Zygmunt Bauman has referred to as the endless pursuit of insatiable desire: 'a self-begotten and self-perpetuating motive that calls for no justification or apology in terms of an objective or a cause' (Bauman, 2001). What weighed on Jack's mind was the short-lived nature of many of the pleasures accessed through shopping.

> I just see it as a route to misery. Have you ever bought a new thing? It sort of goes through a cycle, doesn't it. There's the expectation, which is the nice bit, and then there's the point where you actually get it, and then often I think there's the disappointment when it turns out to be not everything that you wanted.

Just as soon as the desire for a commodity is satisfied, it finds a new object of attention and the feeling of lack reasserts itself. Adam was similarly sceptical about the capacity of commodities to provide a lasting form of gratification. He objected to the amount of junk he seemed to have accumulated: 'The times where I have bought a treat, there's the boost afterwards of "woo yay!" but that soon disappears and then I'm thinking, Now I've just got more *stuff* in my room.'

Many said they were trying to resist this restless sense of desire associated with consumerism. Ffion said she had been developing the habit of going home and pausing for thought before buying luxury items. In the cold light of day, after the thrill of browsing had faded, she would often comfortably decide that she did not really want the desired object after all. Others said that they tried to stay away from the shops altogether. When they did buy non-essentials, they said they tried to choose items with qualities like durability and usefulness, rather than novelty. Anne had carefully chosen a mobile phone with the most useful features for her freelancing job, and she was pleased with her choice, even if it was not the flashiest model.

Rachel shunned a friend who had poked fun at the old-fashioned colour of her bathroom suite. 'What does it matter?' Rachel said. 'I've got a bathroom that works.'

These examples are interesting because they represent attempts to resist the consumerist invocation that more is always better. People appeared to take pride in their capacity to adjust to a lower level of spending – a remarkable thing given the extent to which commercial advertising tries to make us feel ashamed of who we are and what we have. Finn Bowring argues that shame is the main marketing tool of advertising, which constantly presents the public with images of lavish and fashionable lifestyles, as the norm behind which many feel ashamed to lag: 'shame is used to sell everything from cleaning products to fitness gyms, from cat food to cosmetic surgery, from mobile phones to fashion labels' (Bowring, 2000b: 315). The function of shame, Bowring suggests, is to try to get people to prioritise the opinions of anonymous others rather than develop and honour their own autonomous conceptions of usefulness, sufficiency, beauty and pleasure. With this in mind, we can see that consuming less is not necessarily about resigning to the miserable realities of a lower income, but can also be about engaging positively in a process of autonomous reflection on the nature of needs. For the people I interviewed, consuming less was about trying to live with a greater degree of intention and self-control. Self-control has a gratifying rather than a puritanical meaning here: it means feeling more discerning and empowered as a consumer, feeling less ensnared by the misery and guilt of compulsive shopping, and being less pliable in the hands of advertisers and their constant invocations to feel ashamed.

Ultimately, the examples presented here show a variety of ways in which consumerist images of the good life had become troubled – be it the reliance of consumption on the income generated in alienating work, or awareness of the tyranny of choice, or the ethical compromises involved when engaging in a system premised on exploitation, or the short-lived nature of commodified pleasures. What we are beginning to see is that consuming less did not simply represent an undesirable penalty for working less: by doing less working and less shopping, participants hoped to discover a less commodity-centred and therefore more gratifying version of the good life. In the interests of their own sense of gratification, they were questioning some of affluent society's most basic assumptions about the nature of wealth, enjoyment and sufficiency. We can get a greater sense of this if we explore some of the new pleasures that people said they discovered as they began to resist work.

Savoured pleasures

When the latest gaming console from Microsoft – the Xbox One – was unveiled, it was vigorously marketed according to the principle of speed. Gone are the days of primitive fun where a player would insert a disk, wait for it to load, and then spend a couple of hours playing. Now the games will load almost instantaneously. Bored by the game? With the touch of a button (or swish of a hand, for those splashing out on the more expensive model) you can split the display in two, allowing you to watch TV while you play. Driven a particularly fast lap? Share your achievement with your online friends by seamlessly dropping out of the game and into a social media application. Want the lowdown on your favourite TV programme? Synchronise your tablet computer with the XBox One and use it as a second screen, browsing the latest behind-the-scenes info as you watch. The Xbox One is a high-speed entertainment system for a high-speed generation. It spells the same fate for video games as the fate that has been suffered by popular music in the modern age. In his book *The Decline of Pleasure,* Walter Kerr wrote:

> We have had Music to Read By, Music to Make Love By, Music to Sleep By, and, as one humorist has had it, Music to Listen to Music By. What is interesting about these titles is that they so candidly describe the position of the popular arts in our time. They admit at the outset that no one is supposed to sit down, for heaven's sake, and attend to the music. It is understood that, whilst the music is playing, everyone in earshot is going to be doing something else. (Kerr, 1966)

The Xbox One, just like Kerr's Music to Read By or the TV dinner (Food to Watch By), is a product fit for what Staffan Linder referred to as the 'harried leisure class' (Linder, 1970). When free-time is scarce it can also become tense and fraught, and without time to spare it becomes increasingly tempting to approach leisure with the same sense of efficiency and productivity as we approach our work. The appeal of a futuristic product such as the Xbox One is that it promises to tightly schedule our fun, even allowing us to enjoy multiple activities simultaneously. It allows us to get the maximum yield out of our slivers of leisure time. The truth that the marketing spiel ignores, however, is that that no matter how much we streamline our enjoyment, this will never be enough to combat the overriding sense of tension that comes with having so little free-time in the first place (not to mention the sense of confusion brought on by trying to pay attention to two things at once). The overall point of Staffan Linder's book, written back in 1970, was that affluent societies had reached a situation in which leisure time had stopped being leisurely. The harried class are consuming at a rate that outpaces their capacity actually to savour the enjoyment of their wares. With his signature wryness, Linder writes:

> After dinner, [a person] may find himself drinking Brazilian coffee,
> smoking a Dutch cigar, sipping a French cognac, reading the *New
> York Times,* listening to a Brandenburg Concerto and entertaining his
> Swedish wife – all at the same time, with varying degrees of success.
> (Linder, 1970: 9)

When today's affluent workers come home after a hard day's
work, they find themselves in their homes, surrounded by objects
that all represent invitations for action. In my own home I find a Net-
flix account bursting with viewing choices, a set of shelves crammed
with CDs, a pile of impulse-bought books calling out to be read,
and a fridge full of ingredients that need to be cooked before they
go bad. In my less busy periods these are sources of much pleasure,
but when I am too busy to enjoy them, they are nothing but sources
of frustration. The possessions of the harried leisure class can all too
easily become anxiety-inducing reminders of how scarce free-time
can be. Crippled by choices and troubled by the scarcity of our free-
time, we often do the only thing that seems feasible – we do nothing.

This was a feeling that some of my research participants knew
well. Lucy reminds her husband, Matthew, of the anxious inertia he
experienced during his previous job with a local magazine:

> A lot of the time when you came home from there you would just
> sit there and not know what to do, but also be really annoyed with
> yourself that you were wasting time. Or you wouldn't do anything
> that wasn't *exactly* the thing that you wanted to do – like you wouldn't
> watch a film with me because it was kind of like wasting time when you
> could have been doing something better. But then you would often
> end up doing nothing anyway.

Lucy said that she had felt comparably tense in her own leisure
time, during the period she had worked at a bargain store. She said

that her free-time during that period had felt virtually worthless: 'Saturday I'd work four until eight which is horrible because it's at four o'clock and I just couldn't do *anything*, because I was depressed that I had to go to work that night.' When Lucy worked the 11 a.m. shift, 'Loads of people would say "Aren't you happy because you get a lay in?" and I'd think, Well, *no*, I don't get to do anything because I start at eleven. You can't just go out and do whatever you like.' In the context of my research as a whole, these experiences of restlessness were common. Larry (our frustrated social worker) said that he enjoyed reading novels, but had usually felt too tired to read after work: 'I've had enough of that screen.' Jack said he had reached a point in his old full-time job where he was completely 'sapped' and 'burnt-out' and 'always recovering from work'. Participants had come to the realisation that in their previous lives as full-time workers, much of their free-time had been spent in a state of preparedness or recovery, and had hence still in some senses belonged to their employers.

If a lack of quality free-time was one of the main miseries of the working lifestyle, what new pleasures were to be discovered in slowing down and working less? Cheryl believed that having more free-time had allowed her to be more spontaneous. She rediscovered the kinds of unplanned pleasures that tend to be denied in the prescriptive schedule of the working week. A discreet reference to her flourishing sex life was a great reminder that some forms of enjoyment cannot be forced to run according to a regular schedule. For all the modern sexual imagery of films, music videos and advertising, modern life seems to leave people with relatively little time to actually do the deed (Linder, 1970: 83). Arousal cannot be conjured at will in a spare half-hour before bed, any more than the urge to go outside, socialise with friends, eat good food, play games and so on can be tolerably confined to the weekend. Eros pays no heed to the time-tables of advanced industrial society.

Cheryl's sensual pleasures are also a reminder that many of life's gratifications are more sublime when they are taken slowly. In her case for alternative hedonism, Kate Soper has argued that what often gets lost as life becomes more harried are 'the aesthetic or rit-ualised aspects of consuming' (Soper, 2008: 577). We need only look to the changing practices surrounding mealtimes to get a sense of this. Soper suggests that the mealtime has a personal and cultural worth as a 'shared, convivial event having its own intrinsic value ... fostering human exchange, and providing food for thought as well as bodily renewal' (Soper, 2008: 577). The mealtime is an opportun-ity for sublime enjoyment and social intercourse, but its rituals are being whittled away by the speed of modern culture, with its ready meals and sad desk lunches.

> A primary pleasure with deep psychological dimensions is reduced to a maintenance function. The time spent in acquiring the necessary number of calories and vitamins must often be improved by reading the newspaper or looking at television. (Linder, 1970: 83)

Soper describes this as a 'de-spiritualisation of consumption', and we can note the ways in which supporters of today's 'slow food' movement have rebelled against this de-spiritualisation by celebrating the conviviality of cooking and eating.[5] The slow food movement has attempted to recapture the idea of eating as some-thing more than bodily nourishment by emphasising the more rit-ualised or sublimated pleasures of cooking, decorating and sharing meals. For some of the people I interviewed, the move to a slower pace of life seemed to embody an attempt to rescue or re-inject the spirit into certain endangered convivial pleasures. Cheryl liked to make time to cook from scratch with her children, Matthew to 'sit at the table and talk', Samantha to 'lay the table and make it a bit special', and Gerald to buy some good-quality ingredients and 'have a nice evening in'. We can also recall the warmth of Ffion's description of preparing Christmas dinner from Chapter 5.

In contrast with today's archetypal consumer, whose sated desires are always immediately replaced by new desires, what the people I met seemed to embody and celebrate was a capacity to *savour* their enjoyment. Matthew and Lucy talked at length about their love of computer gaming, explaining how even this costly hobby could be enjoyed at relatively little expense, provided you got the maximum pleasure out of each game. Lucy said that the important thing was to 'see everything in one game' before buying the next one, and we can reasonably assume that playing in this fashion did not reduce the couple's overall satisfaction. Overstuffing leisure time with toys is a fruitless way of trying to increase enjoyment, since the more luxury goods one buys, the less satisfaction one is able to derive from each object in the finite time available. As Linder puts it: 'one may possibly *buy* more of everything, but one cannot conceivably *do* more of everything' (Linder, 1970: 83). In spite of their love of video games, it is perhaps unsurprising that Matthew and Lucy said they had no interest in getting an Xbox One.

Productive pleasures

When I interviewed the participant Ffion, we were joined by her husband Rhys. Rhys said his fantasy was to work significantly less. In the fantasy, perhaps he would own a smallholding and grow his own food, but in reality he continued to work full-time as an IT technician. He was enthusiastic about computers and generally liked the job, but it troubled him to be doing it full-time. One of the things that made him want to rebel against work was the sheer expenditure involved in an average working week:

> When I think about it, I can spend less money on a week on holidays than I do on a week at work. I do it less now but certainly before: I was getting sandwiches from the café and stuff, then get a coffee in the morning with a pastry or whatever. And then after the work it was down the pub to wind down. I'd be spending the best part of a hundred quid a week.

Rhys was among a number of people who complained about the hidden expenses of the working week. Cheryl's husband Ben, for example, had changed jobs and reduced his hours after no longer being able to tolerate the irony that his commute cost a significant proportion of his wages. Gerald also complained about the transport costs he used to incur going to work, as well as the additional buying and washing of clothes he had to do because his job required him to dress formally.

Given the fact that work involves particular expenses, it appears that working less, as well as *requiring* people to lower their levels of consumption, may in some ways actually *allow* people to spend less. This principle is consistent with Gorz's theories on consumer motivation, introduced in Chapter 3. If we remember, Gorz argued that a significant proportion of everyday consumption habits can be explained as a product of the alienation of labour. This is because paid employment, by devouring time and energy and forcing people's skill sets into narrow channels, prevents people from being able to self-furnish their needs, or to meet them without recourse to expensive forms of consumption. This becomes clear when we think about the degree of modern spending that comes from a need for convenience. For people who work in stressful, time-consuming

jobs, there is a powerful temptation to 'buy' more free-time by paying for time-saving goods and services, meaning that a range of
activities from housework to gardening, to food preparation, chauf-
feuring, and even shopping itself, are now commonly executed via
commercial transactions (Schor, 1998: 162). The need to consume
is also promoted by the alienation of labour in the sense that work's
hardships often create a need for solace and compensation. The
world of consumer goods, with its escapes, luxuries and distractions, promises to fill the existential void (or at least to help us forget
about it for a while).

With Gorz's theory in mind, we can see a number of further ways
in which disconnecting from paid work actually appeared to allow
people to cut down on spending. Ben, for example, believed that
having more free-time had allowed him to disengage from the convenience industries. He gives the example of buying takeaway food:

> You come home feeling rubbish and you buy a takeaway then, don't
> you. You're too tired to cook, but that costs you fifteen quid and
> you've got to earn the money to pay for that. It's a big *cycle.*

Now that he had more free-time, he was able to shop for ingredients, learn new recipes and cook for his family. Takeaway food had lost
its luxurious status. He only bought a takeaway about once a month
now, and was usually a bit disappointed by its quality. The appeal of
takeaways was especially dubious now that Ben was more cognisant
of the 'big cycle': the fact that working produces a need to consume
convenience goods, but that the consumption of convenience goods
itself reinforces dependency on the income generated through work.
Given the extent to which many modern commodities – from pre-
prepared meals to high-caffeine drinks, car washes, repair services, care services, personal trainers, dating agencies and so on – are

capitalising on our lack of free-time, it is not surprising that many of the people I met found that working less was allowing them to save money. They were able to do more for themselves.

Interviewees also believed that they were saving money by disconnecting from what we might call therapeutic consumption – forms of consumption which capitalise on the alienated worker's need to escape from the less pleasant realities of daily life. As Gerald put it: 'When you're in a job you don't like, you need some kind of positive stroke – a frock, or buy yourself a new gadget, or you can say "come on we deserve a night out".' Whilst most people would probably feel that temporary escapes like these can never properly substitute for a more autonomous existence, these treats represent a form of compensation that is nevertheless usually accepted in the absence of genuine social alternatives (Lodziak, 2002: 158). Adam (our computer programmer turned language teacher) believed that his disconnection from the therapeutic consumption on which he had hitherto depended had allowed him to adjust to a lower income without too much trouble. In our dialogue about the practical challenges of earning less, Adam said:

> I suppose, for me, I haven't had to be tactical saving money and things like that. It's not hit me that hard because I'm happy with my life, so there's no need to spend more to sort of *boost* my happiness … The fact that I don't spend very much money probably comes from the fact that I know what I want to do, so I don't really need to spend to make my life more comfortable. I know where I'm going.

What is striking in these examples is the extent to which living with less is couched in a language of enjoyment and empowerment rather than 'coping', 'sacrifice' or 'making do'. The fact that these people had enabled themselves with the time, skills and energy to meet needs without consumption was a source of gratification. This contrasts considerably with the more conventional or consumerist imagery of the good life, in which affluence is synonymous with a high level of dependency on the market. Ffion and Rhys reflect on the ideals of affluence:

> Rhys – It's what culture tells us to do in a way. Affluence is driving places and getting lunch out. That's what the government seems to be telling us to do.
> Ffion – It's like an executive lifestyle or something.

Rhys's reference to the government brings to mind a quote commonly attributed to Margaret Thatcher who, in 1986, allegedly said that 'any man who finds himself on a bus at the age of twenty-six can consider himself a failure'. Affluence and success are associated with the ability to meet needs via private and more expensive forms of consumption. The model man drives his own car rather than getting the bus (and presumably, by extension, buys his lunch when he gets to work, rather than carrying around food, and then uses his income to get his car washed, rather than doing it himself with a sponge and bucket). What this ideal of affluence may be ignoring, however, are the alternative forms of enjoyment to be found in self-production.

These forms of enjoyment were abundant in Hannah O'Mahoney's research into a community of volunteer tourists (O'Mahoney, 2014). O'Mahoney immersed herself in the day-to-day practices of people who were temporarily living and working in Greece in aid of a sea turtle preservation project. For the duration of the project, volunteers lived in a simple, self-made, self-maintained dwelling beside the beach. O'Mahoney observed that having suddenly been confronted with a setting in which their money was worthless, it was normal for volunteers to leave the project feeling delighted by their own resourcefulness and creativity – qualities which may have otherwise remained undiscovered. Over the course of the project, initially reticent volunteers developed capacities to fix leaks, prepare food for a group, decorate their dwelling using simple tools, and make their own fun with whatever rudimentary objects they carried with them or found on the shoreline. Forced into a position where reliance on commodities was no longer an option, people began to develop and eventually celebrate their capacities for self-organisation and self-production.

Many of the people in my own study also enthused about their developing capacities for self-production. Eleanor (living on her commune) was determined to push her self-reliance as far as it would go, and she was excited to be testing the limits of her tenacity. She used words such as 'connection' and 'involvement' to talk about her relationship with the material world, and expressed a warm sense of gratitude to her granddad, who she partly credited with having given her the taste for self-reliance:

> I remember granddad would often do bits and bobs with us. He would always be working on some kind of project, and he would always make sure we had a go with the tools and learnt how to use them. I think gradually through life I've just picked up bits and bobs.

If Eleanor did ever need to call for the help of professionals (she gave the example of installing a wood-burner), she said she would always ask lots of questions and try to observe the work being done, with the hope of learning a new skill.

As the only person I met who was living 'outside' society (in a communal housing project), Eleanor represents an extreme example, no doubt. She was well aware that her lifestyle would not be to everybody's taste, yet we can note that almost all of the people

I met appeared to find some degree of joy in self-reliance. Partway through one of my interviews with Matthew and Lucy, Matthew requested a break in order to show me his bicycle maintenance tools and manuals. Similarly, the participant Rhys gave an enthusiastic account around his knowledge of computer components. He said he took pleasure in gaining the knowledge required to keep his PC up to date without having to pay a professional technician or splash out on an entirely new model. What Rhys saw when he looked inside his computer was comparable to what Matthew saw when he looked at his bike: not an alien set of components, but a set of meanings. What I believe they felt when they were fixing up their possessions was a sense of mastery – something like the 'connection' that Eleanor professed to have with material objects. What they experienced was a contrast to the frustrated impotence of the person without the time to develop a working knowledge of his or her surroundings – the person who, after whacking the problem object in irritation, calls a professional, or submits and buys a replacement.

The people I met revered their maintenance skills in a manner which reminded me of Robert M. Pirsig in his philosophical novel *Zen and the Art of Motorcycle Maintenance* (Pirsig, 1974). What Pirsig shared with many of the people I met was a sense of emotional attachment or even loyalty towards the things he owned. Pirsig talks about his motorcycle riding gloves:

> I *care* about these moldy old riding gloves. I smile at them … because they have been there for so many years and are so old and so tired and so rotten that there is something kind of humorous about them …
> They cost only three dollars and have been restitched so many times it is getting impossible to repair them, yet I take a lot of time and pains to do it anyway because I can't imagine any new pair taking their place.
> (Pirsig, 1974: 52)

When I asked people to show me around their homes or list their possessions, their inventories suggested a treasured and looked-after set of objects, treated with a sense of care and devotion. There was a comforting quality to many of the homes I visited – a quality which I have since found difficult to put into words. The home of the alternative hedonist is not decadent in any conventional sense. Its comforts have something to do with what Adorno meant when he wrote about 'the mild, soothing, un-angular quality of things that have felt the touch of hands' (Adorno, 2005: 48). I enjoyed the sensory and aesthetic pleasures of visiting homes whose inhabitants made and repaired things, conversed around tables or played games together. I enjoyed the sight of a meal being prepared and the smell of it cooking. I felt delight in witnessing people's modest displays of initiative. A makeshift system of hooks and pulleys, designed to hang wet clothes from a ceiling, replaces the need for a tumble dryer. A shelf lined with old takeaway containers serves as a cheap and neat way to separate and stow different-sized screws. A home-made cushion, stitched together from fabric scraps, speaks of the individuality of its creator in a way that a store-bought equivalent never could.

I have tried to understand the warm atmosphere of the homes I visited by thinking about the alternative – the unwelcoming, coldly clean home of the person who has no free-time, and has outsourced all of his domestic tasks to paid professionals. Gorz suggests that this kind of home is barely experienced as a home at all. Working for ourselves is what allows us to take possession of the environment; it is the mode through which 'each person comes to be rooted in the sensory materiality of the world and to share that world with others' (Gorz, 1989: 158). A person feels at home in a place only if he or she can 'participate in its development, its organisation and its maintenance in voluntary co-operation with other users' (Gorz, 1989: 158).

Hence the sense of social and environmental disconnection felt by the person who outsources all his domestic tasks to paid workers:

> The spatial organisation of the dwelling, the nature, form and arrangement of familiar objects have to be adapted to the routine attentions of service staff or robots, as they are in hotels, barracks and boarding schools. Your immediate environment ceases to belong to you in much the same way that a chauffeur-driven car comes to belong more to the chauffeur than the owner. (Gorz, 1989: 158)

Capitalism indeed now profits from the sense of environmental disconnection that Gorz describes, having established a lucrative market in the home-made aesthetics we so crave: be it global chains selling shabby chic and upcycled furniture, to the new glut of TV talent competitions about sewing and baking, or the huge range of foods and cosmetic products packaged to evoke a homey, craft-produced aesthetic. All of these are great examples of what Soper has called 'satisfactions at second remove': forms of relatively inexpensive satisfaction which the capitalist system has taken away from us, only to sell them back in a commodified form (Soper, 2008: 577). These commodified equivalents, however, can never really substitute for genuine self-production, which in Gorz's analysis represents an irreplaceable source of delight, empowerment, and rootedness in the world. Working for ourselves is what gives us a sense of connection with our environment and slots us into our communities – an affront to the idea that the decadent life is the life where a huge income means a finger is never lifted, and all needs are catered to through the market.

I am reminded of Ivan Illich, who painted the fearful image of a future in which humans have become totally dependent on commercial goods and professional services. Back in the 1970s, Illich argued that we were coming to live in an 'age of professions', lamenting the ways in which the social infrastructures in which people have historically coped, cared, played, eaten, and made friends were being eroded. Illich drives his point home by evoking the unsettling image of a baby in the womb of the market. In the extreme case: '[the] commons are extinguished and replaced by a new placenta built of funnels that deliver professional services. Life is paralysed in permanent intensive care' (Illich, 1978: 64). It is indeed curious that engagement in paid work should represent such a powerful symbol of maturity and independence, given the realities of employment as a situation of profound dependency. I speak not only of the dependency inherent in the wage relation, but also of the dependency on commercial products and services, which become the only way to meet certain needs after work has drained our time and energy. What the people I interviewed perhaps demonstrate is the extent to which many of the needs conventionally met through private and expensive forms of consumption could actually be self-furnished, perhaps even with a good degree of pride and enjoyment, were society to allow us the time.

Where things became a bit more difficult for people was in relation to society's commercialised rituals. From Christmases to birthdays, weddings and bar mitzvahs, a whole host of social rituals are now synonymous with expensive gift giving and ostentatious consumption. When we are so relentlessly encouraged to express our joy and love for others by purchasing costly commodities, it is only the grump or the skinflint who opts out in order to save money. Some of the people I met feared social occasions for this very reason, but several said they had developed solutions. On the Christmas prior to our first meeting, Matthew and Lucy had dodged the need for expensive gift buying with a bit of creativity. They had bought some plain olive oil, infused it in glass bottles with chilli, garlic and herbs, decorated the bottles, and then given the oils as gifts to friends and family. Lucy said she had enjoyed preparing the oil and that the recipients seemed to appreciate the effort taken: 'it's better than just going into Boots and buying a three-for-two present'. Similarly, Samantha told a story about her inability to afford a friend's costly birthday night out. After initially feeling bad about the situation, she opted to cook her friend a special meal at home instead. Samantha said that her friend had enjoyed and appreciated the gift. In these examples, there is a unique value attributed to the self-produced gift that contrasts with the colourless, impersonal nature of the commodity bought with money.

...

In this chapter, I have remained open to the possibility of pleasures outside the conventions of capitalism's work-and-spend culture by looking at how the people I met – people who were more or less volunteering to lose a proportion of their income – talked about and made sense of this decision. Whilst there is no syrupy suggestion here that the people I met had discovered the 'key to happiness' or an ideal model of living, their actions and choices are of interest because they contribute to a critique of the dominant mode of life in modern capitalism. What I found interesting over the course of my research was the fact that consuming less was not generally framed by people as an undesirable side effect of working less. Instead it was an expression of what Kate Soper calls an 'alternative hedonism'. Whilst we can safely assume that their lives entailed significant financial hardships (hardships that some were happy to talk about, and others reluctant), a lower level of consumption was a key component in people's attempts to discover a less materialistic version of the good life. People worked and consumed less in order to avoid the 'troubled pleasures' of affluence, hoping to discover new pleasures of the more sublime and enduring kind that can only be realised with an abundance of free-time. Resisting capitalism's constant invocations to feel ashamed and dissatisfied with their possessions, they took pride in their ability to develop their own ideas of pleasure, beauty, sufficiency and well-being. They were reflecting on the relationship between well-being and commodity consumption, and discovering a new sense of mastery and rootedness in the world, as they developed their hitherto undiscovered capacities for self-reliance. Whilst it would be absolutely blinkered to deny that the escape to a slower pace of life is a practical impossibility for many people, who would not be able to survive economically, it is equally reckless to accept the idea that high-consumption lifestyles are the fixed norm to which everybody should aspire.

SEVEN: Half a person

Idler, drone, lazybones, lie-abed, loafer, lounger, flâneur, sloucher, sluggard, slacker, skiver, clock-watcher, Weary Willie, moper, sleepyhead, dawdler, *slowcoach,* hobo, bum, tramp, *wanderer,* mendicant, *beggar,* spiv, parasite, cadger, sponger, scrounger, moocher, freeloader, layabout, good-for-nothing, ne'er do well, wastrel, slubberdegullion, floater, drifter, free-wheeler, opium-eater, waiter on Providence, *fatalist,* nonworker …

Roget's Thesaurus

As part of their art project 'Learning to Love You More' (July and Fletcher, 2007), the artists Miranda July and Harrell Fletcher asked members of the public to complete the following assignment: ask your family to describe what you do. One of the most memorable replies was from Angela Bridge from Virginia, who wrote in with responses from three different family members:

> Grandmother (91): She [Angela] spends a lot of time cooking and she brings me food and candy and Tylenol. She goes through my room cleaning a lot. She is always washing my bed.
>
> Son (7): She plays with me and goes to Hollins University and does experiments in the labs there. She plays computer games and reads books all the time. She takes me to the park and to Ian's house.
>
> Mother (65): She isn't doing much of anything right now.

Speculating with this albeit limited information about Angela's situation, we can infer that she probably does not have a paid job (somebody would surely have mentioned it). Yet she also seems like a busy person, active and generous with her time. As well as caring for her elderly grandmother and entertaining her son, she finds the time to study and play video games. Despite what the mother says, the statements from the son and grandmother confirm that Angela is not a person who 'isn't doing much of anything right now'. We can compare this assumption about Angela's lifestyle with the assumptions made by the anonymous speaker in the following exchange:

Anonymous:　You're writing a book? What is it about?

David Frayne:　It's going to be about some work I've been doing, looking at people who are trying to work less, or live a life which doesn't revolve around work. Or some of them don't work at all, and I'm looking at their values.

Anonymous:　So it's a book about tramps, about scum?

These kinds of statements, focusing on the supposed emptiness or worthlessness of the jobless life, are a feature of the work dogma and what we might call its *false dichotomy*: the prevalent idea that if a person is not engaged in paid work, then she must be doing nothing of any value. The false dichotomy essentially says that people face a choice between work and laziness. It does not register the social value of activities such as caring for children, parents, neighbours, partners and friends, and it is even more blind to the intrinsic value of non-work activities that are worthwhile ends in themselves: activities such as playing, talking, enjoying nature, or creating and appreciating cultural artefacts. If these things sit outside the serious domain of work, they also represent the more sublime possibilities of human experience. They are the things that make life more than just a slog for survival. But they are also not usually regarded as activities around which a respectable person would organise her life.

Earlier in the book, I sketched out some of the barriers that might theoretically hinder attempts to resist work. Among these barriers is the vigorous moralisation of work in contemporary society. I pointed to the stigmatisation of the non-worker in the media, which has routinely labelled those who resist the work ethic as entitled or deviant. I also argued that some sociological studies may have been complicit in work's moralisation by treating employment as a norm from which unemployed people have deviated. In both of these cases, the false dichotomy is brought into play: authorities are telling us that the choice is between employment and an empty life, between the work ethic and no ethics. This ethical objection to idleness, and to the prioritisation of activities outside the economic sphere, remains one of the major obstacles faced by those who argue for an alternative to today's work-centred society. As Kathi Weeks eloquently puts it:

> Productivist ethics assume that productivity is what defines and refines us, so that when human capacities for speech, intellect, thought and fabrication are not directed to productive ends, they are reduced to mere idle talk, idle curiosity, idle thoughts, and idle hands, their noninstrumentality a shameful corruption of these human qualities. Even pleasures are described as less worthy when they are judged to be idle. (Weeks, 2011: 170)

Taking one final excursion into the accounts of the people I met – especially those more extreme cases who were trying to live without work altogether – we can gain a sense of how the wider moralisation of work might impact upon everyday attempts to resist employment. Whilst many of the people I interviewed were comfortable with their alterity, perhaps even energised by the knowledge that their lifestyle choices were unconventional, we will see that for others, the avoidance of work represented a potential source of shame. Along with the more practical or material barriers to resisting work, this sense of shame was always lurking in the background.

Failing the moral test of work

Erving Goffman defined stigma as the situation of a person who is disqualified from full social acceptance. When a person stands before us:

> … evidence can arise of his possessing an attribute that makes him different from others in the category of persons available to him to be, and of a less desirable kind – in the extreme, a person who is quite thoroughly bad, or dangerous, or weak. He is thus reduced in our minds from a whole and usual person to a tainted, discounted one. (Goffman, 1968: 12)

In the case of the people I met over the course of my research, the stigma that threatened to present itself was joblessness. This was the discrediting fact that threatened to disrupt the person's status as a normal and acceptable member of society. Goffman refers to the account of an unemployed man taken from a study by Zawadzki and Lazarsfeld:

> How hard and humiliating it is to bear the name of an unemployed man. When I go out, I cast down my eyes because I feel myself wholly inferior. When I go along the street, it seems to me that I can't be compared with an average citizen, that everybody is pointing at me with his finger. (Zawadzki and Lazarsfeld, 1935: 239)

The unemployed man has taken his stigma to heart and become an outcast, unable to look his fellow citizens in the eye. We might say that he has experienced a crisis of social recognition. He feels that his unemployment has disqualified him as a person deserving of equal rights and esteem, and as a result he feels worthless, bewildered and isolated. Axel Honneth suggests that social recognition can be withdrawn from a person in a variety of ways. It is withdrawn when a person's body is confined or kept under control (as in the case of a prisoner or slave), and also when a person is denied particular rights which are shared by the broader population (as in cases of discrimination by race, gender, sexuality, and so on). The other kind of withdrawal – the one relevant to us here – arises in cases where society refuses to recognise particular lifestyles as culturally legitimate:

> A person's 'honour', 'dignity', or, to use the modern term, 'status' refers to the degree of social esteem accorded to his or her manner of self-realisation within society's inherited cultural horizon. If this hierarchy of values is so constituted as to downgrade individual forms of life and manners of belief as inferior or deficient, then it robs the subjects in question of every opportunity to attribute social value to their own abilities. (Honneth, 1995: 134)

In the case of the workless, the inherited cultural horizon that Honneth speaks of is one that is strongly characterised by the work ethic and its false dichotomy. In the context of a society where work is the most accepted way to gain status and a sense of identity, it is not surprising that the workless life often invites feelings of shame or inferiority, or upsurges of a desire to re-establish oneself as a 'normal' person by seeking employment.

One of the reasons work is sought after (aside from the obvious benefit of an income) is that it provides people with social recognition. We can consider the example of Gerald. Before having his fill of the harried lifestyle, Gerald had enjoyed a rewarding career as a jet-setting academic, attending conferences and receiving compliments about his publications. He said, 'you get all of these positive strokes from work', and he particularly valued the 'warm glow of appreciation' he had experienced when attending his students' graduation ceremonies. He said that students would often approach and thank him, praising him for his teaching. In today's work-centred society, it is work that is supposed to grant people a public life and a place where, like Gerald, we can have our achievements observed and rewarded. If the people in my study were going to turn away from this opportunity for recognition, they needed to make sure that they had other things lined up: new social networks, other spaces in which to achieve and interact, and alternative sources of motivation and validation to take the place of work.

One of the things that seemed to confound people's attempts to create a rewarding and respectable life outside employment was a persistent feeling that their chosen lifestyles were stigmatised. The married couple Matthew and Lucy (who had both given up work altogether) appeared to be struggling with a sense of inferiority as a result of their joblessness. Matthew believed that, in the culture of affluent societies, people usually liken being without a job to being an incomplete person:

> I think that a lot of people think that you're missing your shadow if you don't have a job. It's like being half a person, and that's quite a strong thing to say, but it's like this whole thing – like when we were introducing ourselves to people last year. They would ask 'What do you do?' and if you were unemployed it was 'brrrrrr'. People would shudder a little bit and think, Oh, so you don't do *anything* really.

One of Matthew's most valued activities at the time of our interview was writing. He enjoyed writing articles which combined his interests in philosophy and video games, and was in the process of trying to get some of his pieces published on gaming websites. Matthew spoke enthusiastically about his aesthetic sensibilities as a writer, but told me that he was often reluctant to reveal his interest in writing:

> I feel tempted more and more to just start telling people I'm a writer, even though I've not got anything published yet, because I write every day pretty much. It's all I do now. But I know what the follow-up question would be. It would be 'Who do you write for?' It's that obsession with productivity and where your writing fits in. Like, whether it has any bearing on a working, labour market type thing.

Having no obvious social utility and earning him no income, the time Matthew had spent writing represented a potential source of embarrassment. He did not think that people would accept that his identity and day-to-day routines could be constructed around a non-remunerated activity. His statements prompted reflections from Lucy, who was critical of a cultural tendency to deny recognition for activities outside the sphere of paid work:

> It's like on all these TV talent shows. The people come on stage and underneath it says their name and what they do, and in big letters it says UNEMPLOYED. It came up when Susan Boyle came on, like they don't *do* anything. They could put 'likes making cards' – I don't know, *anything*. It's in everything, even like on the news it will be 'Susan Briggs, a baker', and it's the same on game shows. I'd like to be 'Lucy, loves animals and enjoys reading'. I would love that.

Lucy had crafted a pleasant routine based around reading, spending time with Matthew, taking walks, doing crafts and looking after her pets. Whilst she said repeatedly that she was happy with her daily routine, I asked her to think about whether there were things she missed about work, and it was at this point that she raised the issue of social recognition. Lucy became visibly upset:

David: If I were to push you, out of the things you said you miss about work, which was the most important?

Lucy: Um [long pause] [sigh]. I suppose the thing I miss most is not feeling like I'm letting people down. Maybe that's because, I don't know, I just feel like I'm letting Matthew's parents down and *my* parents down. I suppose I wouldn't say – I don't know, does this make sense?

David: Yes. So do you worry about that then?

Lucy: I worry every day [long pause], all the time [sigh]. I just – I feel like I should get a job so that I don't feel like I'm letting everybody else down, but I just [sigh] – I don't know if I can *do* that.

One of Lucy's main ambitions was to have lots of children. She told a story about how her mother – a nurse – had concealed Lucy's non-work ambitions from colleagues at a Christmas party, believing that Lucy's maternal goals were too homely or old-fashioned. Lucy's lack of work-centred ambitions seemed to embarrass her mother.

Lucy was not alone. A number of participants believed that their choices were a source of shame among friends and family. We can consider the case of Emma, who had decided to stop working after being diagnosed with a severe stomach illness. Emma was convinced that people judged her negatively as a result of her joblessness:

They *definitely* do, and society does as well. And my family does. My family have been really judgemental about me not working, even when it's not my choice. They know that, but my mum completely doesn't get it. She's like: 'When are you going to get a job, when are you going to get a job, I want you to get a job.' And I've said about the sickness and she's said 'Well, you're alright now!' And I am, I am getting better since last summer, but I feel like 'Give me a break!'

In cases like Emma's, where a person feels too unwell to work, a medical diagnosis can perform a vital function in legitimating feelings of ill-health. The doctor's medical diagnosis, coming from a position of professional authority, allows the sick person to enter what Talcott Parsons called the 'sick role', in which the person in question is temporarily exempted from the responsibility to work. In Emma's case, however, not even a professional medical diagnosis was enough to validate her decision to be a non-worker. We might partially explain this as a result of the invisibility of her stomach illness. Since Emma's health problem fluctuated in terms of its severity, and had no observable surface systems, she often had a hard time communicating to others that she was sick. Without any obvious way to signal her illness, she faced an ongoing struggle to convince people of her entitlement to time off work.

We can look at one final example of the stigma surrounding joblessness by focusing on the case of Samantha (our full-time attorney in her early thirties, who ditched her career to work part-time as a waitress). Samantha's decision to quit a professional job and work part-time in a bar was taken by her parents as a sign of emotional immaturity. In their view, Samantha had left the professional world of adults and regressed back to her teenage years. Samantha's being content to work in a bar where many of the employees were teenagers was taken as an indication that she had failed to grow up. Samantha's ensuing conflict with her parents perfectly demonstrates the extent to which engagement in paid work – particularly full-time and higher-status jobs – functions as a cultural signal of maturity. One hears such sentiments expressed in the demand that young people (especially students) should 'grow up', 'knuckle down', or start living in the 'real world' – a world where people perform their adulthood by complying with the demands of work and earning a steady income.

Samantha's job as an attorney had been a tremendous source of pride for her parents, but from Samantha's perspective this pride had been nothing but a source of irritation. This is because Samantha did not really identify with her job as an attorney. Whilst she performed the practices associated with her work role, she had always resisted embodying that role, which is to say that whilst she practised as an attorney, she hated being identified as an attorney, with an attorney's outlook, an attorney's tastes and an attorney's behaviour. Samantha rebelled against her parents, refusing to accept that her decision to leave the world of professional employment was a signal of regression or immaturity. She instead forged her own conception of maturity, based on the assertion of autonomy and variety rather than the acquisition and embodiment of a work role. The biographical story that Samantha told in her interview was ultimately a coming-of-age tale, where maturity was defined in terms of a learned capacity to make deliberate choices, as opposed to being swept along by convention: 'I wanted to get in touch with what I want. I was willing to listen to myself and see my reaction to things, and to start structuring things in my way ... It felt like growing up because I was doing things I had consciously chosen to do for the first time.'

In each of the above cases, people were being negatively judged because of their resistance to the work ethic. In Lucy's case, the problem was a perceived failure to exhibit the correct kind and degree of ambition. Lucy's largely domestic goals were seen by her family as quaint and old-fashioned. In Emma's case, the issue was her perceived failure to exhibit an appropriate level of stoicism in the face of illness. Perhaps owing to the invisibility of her illness, people doubted whether Emma was really ill, and hence questioned her entitlement to be free from the demands of work. Finally, in Samantha's case, the fault was her perceived failure to grow up and accept the responsibilities of adulthood. Samantha's decision to be a part-time worker in a relatively low-status role was taken as evidence of a juvenile reluctance to enter the 'real world'. Kelvin and Jarrett describe a 'wealth ethic': a system of beliefs which stresses the responsibility of each person to make or have sufficient wealth so as not to financially depend on other people (Kelvin and Jarrett, 1985: 104). It is the wealth ethic that is evoked in accusations that jobless people are scroungers, shamelessly relying on handouts in order to live the life of Riley. What the cases explored here show us, however, is that the existence of the wealth ethic only goes part of the way towards explaining the stigmatisation of non-workers (only a few of them, after all, were actually claiming state benefits). The people I met were judged to be failing the moral test of work in a more fundamental sense. Their joblessness signified deeper weaknesses of character. In a society where work represents the chief means through which we attain a public identity, it was tough for these people to persuade others that their choices and activities were meaningful and worthwhile.

The dreaded question

What do you do? After 'What is your name?' and possibly 'Where are you from?' this is one of the first questions that strangers usually pose to one another, with convention dictating that this question is almost always an enquiry into our employment situation. 'What do you do?' means 'What job do you perform?' If we are being generous, we might say that the posing of this question is innocent enough. It represents a social custom, or an attempt to elicit information that might bring relief to the interaction by providing it with some context, pushing the conversation towards some common ground. If we are being more critical, we might view this question of 'What do you do?' as a naked attempt to measure the status of the other. 'What do you do?' means 'Summarise in a sentence what you contribute to this world, and I will judge you on the basis of your response.' Or 'Are you a person worth knowing?'

For some of the people I met, the simple question of 'What do you do?' was a considerable source of social anxiety. Bruce (who, we may recall, had quit work due to his illness) said: 'If I go to a dinner party with a friend or, say, meet somebody new, it's just that dreaded question, "What do you do?" It's horrible. I don't look forward to being asked that because I don't have an answer.' At the dinner party, Bruce assumes the position known by Goffman as the 'discreditable'. Bruce's inability to work is a piece of hidden information that might be exposed at any given moment. Goffman describes the dilemma of the discreditable as follows: 'To display or not to display; to tell or not to tell; to let on or not to let on; to lie or not to lie; and in each case, to whom, how, when, and where' (Goffman, 1968: 57). For the person with something to hide, even the most mundane social interactions can become fraught with stress:

> What are unthinking routines for normals can become management problems for the discreditable … The person with a secret failing … must be alive to the social situation as a scanner of possibilities, and is therefore likely to be alienated from the simpler world in which those around him apparently dwell. (Goffman, 1968: 110)

The discreditable person can adopt a number of strategies when under the threat of exposure, and exploring my research participants' responses to the question 'What do you do?' was almost a little study in itself. Matthew told me that he saw the question as an opportunity to assert himself. In his prouder moments, he would state without apology that he was jobless, carefully taking stock of people's responses:

> Recently I've just been telling people I'm unemployed and usually they'll get angry, but not always at me. They'll say 'oh it's terrible what you're going through', and usually I'm thinking, no actually, I'm just happy. I quite like being unemployed. Financially it's scary, but I'm doing stuff that I like *every day*. If the money wasn't a worry, and also the impending doom of getting made [by the job centre] to get a job, I would just really love it.

Matthew hoped that by taking a risk and being honest regarding his feelings about work, he might be able to change people's perceptions of joblessness in some small way. He said he had started some refreshing conversations with people using this approach, but that most people had ultimately viewed him with a sense of pity. We can compare this with Clive, who sometimes answered the question 'What do you do?' by stating: 'As little harm as possible.' Clive's intention was to use humour to denaturalise the dreaded question and raise it to a conscious level, where it could be contemplated. By breaching the normal rules of the interaction in this way, Clive hoped to sensitise people to the mundane and potentially intrusive convention of asking about work. (A friend of mine outlined a similar strategy when he proposed to walk around a wedding reception asking strangers not 'What do you do?' but 'What is your favourite Lars Von Trier film?')

We can think of these as proactive responses to the dreaded question. People assert the legitimacy of their lifestyles and use the interaction almost as an opportunity for a micro-scale political intervention. This contrasts with more defensive attempts to account for or divert attention away from the discrediting information. Matthew said that in his bitter or less confident moments, he had flippantly steered the conversation away from employment by telling outlandish lies about his occupation. When people asked him the dreaded question, he told them he was a drug dealer, a bank robber or a porn star. We can compare this with Bruce, who carried a heavy burden of shame regarding his inability to work. Bruce responded to the dreaded question by carefully managing information about himself:

> Sometimes I make stuff up, sometimes I bend the truth and say 'Oh I graduated and then I was working in mental health, but that was just a short-term contract that's come to an end so I'm sort of *in between* jobs.' Sometimes I'm honest if I think the person seems empathic, and I'll say 'Yeah, I've had some serious health issues so I'm just taking a couple of years out to focus on getting well.' But even when I answer the question in that way – and I have to be careful of this, because I don't always notice it – there's an undertone of guilt and shame in the way I answer. It's sort of defensive, you know? It's like I'm saying 'Look, I'm not a bum, I'm not a scrounger,' whereas I shouldn't have to defend myself or justify what I'm doing. I shouldn't have to justify it like that, but there is that defensiveness because the culture is so judgemental.

If Bruce thought it necessary to manage potentially discrediting information about himself when he was out there, in society, Emma saw this as necessary even in the forgiving context of the research interview. On a number of occasions, she seemed eager to convince me that she really did need the time off work, and was not just pretending to be ill.

These accounts raise an interesting question: who is really doing the judging here? I had certainly not disparaged Emma, yet she still felt a need to defend herself against an imputed judgement. Whilst Bruce was able to give a couple of specific examples of occasions where others had questioned his lifestyle, it was really his internal sense of self-doubt that represented the sternest judge. In Chapter 5, we saw Bruce talk with a great deal of conviction about his lifestyle choices, yet we can now see that his everyday experiences were still tinged with shame. He admitted that he had even experienced shame after ordering internet shopping. Whereas most people would be at their place of work during the day, Bruce would always be at home when the postman came to deliver parcels. What did the postman think? 'Does he know that I'm unemployed?' Bruce had wondered. Reflecting further on the nature and origins of his shame in a later interview, Bruce talked about his 'inner critic':

> There's this big inner critic that says you're substandard or inferior in some way, or that you don't live in the right way. Chances are, if you're having mental health difficulties your inner critic is just being ramped up to full volume, to the point where my inner critic was like 'you're such a waste of skin'.

Who is the inner critic? Drawing on the ideas of the psychologist George Herbert Mead, we might say that the people I met were experiencing shame because they were breaching the expectations of the 'generalised other' (Mead, 1962). In abstract thought or what Mead calls an 'internal conversation', the individual 'takes the attitude of the generalised other towards himself, without reference to its expression in any particular other individuals' (Mead, 1962: 155–6). Through a process of socialisation individuals come to absorb the values of the cultural climate. Cultural stigmas are internalised

and become shame – a feeling that may come to pervade all interactions, and not merely those in which there is a direct expression
of disapproval. As Bruce's postman example shows, soon every pair
of eyes becomes a potential source of judgement. We can think back
to the experience of the unemployed man quoted from Zawadzki
and Lazarsfeld's study at the beginning of this chapter. He walks
down the street with his eyes cast down because he imagines that
everybody is judging him, despite the fact that these strangers could
not possibly have any knowledge of his employment situation. His
stigma has been personally incorporated as a sense of shame, and
he believes that he really does fall short as a human being. Even in
cases where a person is essentially self-respecting, and believes that
the way he chooses to live is ethically valid, it might still be difficult
to shake off the sense of shame that society's moral authorities have
long taught us to feel about joblessness. What I observed over the
course of the research was the fragility of conviction in today's climate of stigma. Insecure about the marginal nature of their lifestyles,
people who in one breath talked confidently and coherently about
their ethics often seemed guarded and vulnerable in the next.

Insulation and support

Whilst many of the people I met were aware that their lifestyle
choices might be stigmatised, they were also engaged in an attempt
to insulate themselves from the judgements that threatened their
way of living. As Goffman observes:

> It seems possible for an individual to fail to live up to what we effec-
> tively demand of him, and yet be relatively untouched by this failure;
> insulated by his alienation, protected by identity beliefs of his own, he
> feels that he is a full-fledged normal human being, and that we are the
> ones who are not quite human. (Goffman, 1968: 17)

Reflecting on his own experiences of unemployment, Matthew Cole referred to the possibility of developing an 'outsider chic based on a celebration of the pleasures of being "unconventional" vis-à-vis the mass of workers and consumers' (Cole, 2004: 12–13). Cole specifically recalled the rebel's pleasure he had experienced when sneaking a bottle of vodka into a pub, surreptitiously topping up a single drink for the duration of the night. Just as we saw (in Chapter 6) that there are ways of managing the relative poverty of low-income lifestyles, we can note that there are also ways in which people evade stigmatising judgements about their lifestyles.

Some of the people I met were managing to do this better than others. Eleanor had eventually come to the realisation that it would be very difficult to live according to her values and remain in mainstream society: 'I feel like I'm always trying to defend how I live and I just don't want to have to do that. I hate doing that.' Her solution was to live in an autonomous rural community, where she enjoyed the company of people who shared her critical perspective on work and consumerism. She liked belonging to a social circle in which she was not forced to constantly apologise and account for her actions and choices. We can compare this with Lucy, who seemed to want to retreat from the social world altogether. Living her life mostly at home, Lucy surrounded herself with a small and tightly controlled network of people who empathised with her inability to work. Her husband Matthew appeared to be playing a particularly valuable supporting role. As a student of philosophy he was accustomed to thinking critically about accepted cultural beliefs, and encouraged Lucy to improve her self-respect by opening up the need to work as a topic of debate. When Lucy conveyed the negative judgements she had received in relation to her child-rearing ambitions, Matthew turned to her and said:

Why do the unemployed lose this respect? Obviously times have changed. Women, back in the day, would have been at home and what-not, but I hope that it hasn't completely spun where women are looked down on because they want to stay at home and look after children, because *that's* a full-time job in itself. That's something to be proud of. I'm not saying for one second that women shouldn't work, but it's a choice and neither one should be condemned.

Throughout the couple's interviews, Matthew regularly adopted the voice of what C. Wright Mills called the sociological imagination (Mills, 1959). Mills argues that one of the benefits of sociological thinking is that it allows people to conceive of their personal troubles in terms of wider cultural and structural forces. The sociological imagination promises to elevate the non-integrated person above a passively endured state of humiliation, to become a conscious critic of the norms and values that shape the cultural environment in which our lives play out. In his interventions, Matthew hoped to make Lucy feel less suspicious of herself and more suspicious of the world around her.

In the absence of physically present friends, some participants turned to their literary friends for this kind of support. Mike said: 'A few of my friends have scattered off, so I can't immediately call on them. But I've got my library books that can give me solace when need be. They're like a part of my support system.' Several people were keen to recommend books on the subject of work. The likes of Henry Thoreau, William Burroughs or Jack Kerouac – litera-ture's most celebrated free agents and non-workers – as well as a number of popular critical texts – Tom Hodgkinson's *How To Be Idle* (Hodgkinson, 2004) or Bob Black's *The Abolition of Work* (Black, 1986) – were repeatedly recommended to me by members of the Idlers' Alliance. These texts offered people opportunities to feel recognised and validated as non-workers, as well as a chance to develop a more coherent and articulate sense of their ethics. These texts helped people, in their abandonment of the work ethic, to find their bearings as non-workers and hammer out a new moral code. The benefits of reading perhaps explain Eleanor's sense of regret that she had not taken more time to read and write things in connection with her values. She expressed a strong desire to clarify and formalise her ethics as a non-worker, which is perhaps one of the reasons why she relished taking part in the research process.

Beyond personal or literary friends, those people I met who were affiliated with the Idlers' Alliance benefited from a wider circle of recognition. What quickly became apparent as I spent time with TIA was that the group was less a social movement with political objectives than a social network, valued by its members as a source of camaraderie and validation. One of the Idlers' Alliance co-founders, Anne, talks about the appeal of TIA from the perspective of its members:

> I think that for a lot of people – they don't have anyone in their day-to-day life who understands what their philosophy is, or the way they look at the world, and they become quite introverted because they don't have anyone they can talk to. I feel very sorry for them because then they might become quite isolated. They might stop giving people a chance because 'they're not going to be on the same wavelength' or, you know, 'no one's ever going to understand me'. That's why, for a lot of people, TIA is like a refuge, it's where they are understood.

Illustrating Anne's point, a couple of the idlers I met said that whenever they were at home they usually left TIA's online message board running in the background. The message board was very active, with 2,037 members at my time of writing, as well as hundreds of unregistered users. As well as providing a forum for people to share practical tips on money-saving, self-sufficiency and so on, the message board represented a valued opportunity to experience the sense of belonging and comfort that comes when mingling with like-minded others. Aware of the emotional benefits of community, the founders of TIA were hoping to organise a more regular programme of physical meet-ups at various locations across the UK. On those occasions where I was able to attend personally and observe these meet-ups, it was quickly evident that the events were not geared towards political mobilisation and stern ethical debate, but towards having a good time. The atmosphere reflected the description by Haiven and Khasnabish of social movements as 'islands of refuge in a tempestuous world': spaces that provide a sense of friendship, community, romance and empowerment (Haiven and Khasnabish, 2014: 10–11). Whilst the idlers did not actively campaign for social change, they did work at prefiguring the world they wanted to see on a small-scale level – a world that valued both individuality and commonality, both passion and reason, and a world that made people feel accepted. People munched food, got drunk, listened to live music, and enjoyed the feeling of belonging to a community of like-minded people. TIA's emphasis on making people feel included, above all else, is perhaps reflected in the name of the organisation. As a banner under which people are invited to unite, 'idling' is suggestive of a light-hearted and humorous kind of resistance. It defiantly reappropriates a derogative term and uses it for radical purposes. My impression was that, divorced from ideas of class, political causes, or notions of Right and Left, the catchword 'idling' had been successful in uniting a broad spectrum of people, with a variety of backgrounds and sensibilities.

Without the warm light of recognition provided by a community such as TIA, it is all too easy for the will to resist to wither away. We can note the case of Rhys, who believed that his decreasing contact with people who shared his values had dampened his determination to live differently: 'Out of my close friends and family, [alternative ways of living] are not on their radar, and I suppose that's why it's gone on the back burner really, and I've gone off and got a job at the university.' Jack summarises the predicament of the isolated idler:

> For me, community is completely key to everything and if you don't have it, then everything that happens to you happens in isolation. Any group of people need to define themselves, and they need reinforcement from each other. Without it, you just lose a sense of where you're going and then you just revert to guess what: working nine to five and all the kind of negative things in our society.

The benefit of a culture of resistance is that it offers people an opportunity to move out of a state of passively endured humiliation, towards an active defence of their ethics and practices. Ultimately, however, it appears that there exists no social movement with the capacity to knock work from its pedestal at the centre of society. For the immediate future at least, work will continue to creakily function as people's main source of income, rights and belonging, and there appears to be no community with the necessary following, resources, and level of organisation required to challenge this significantly. The problem I am left with at the end of my investigation is whether and how the individual cases of resistance to work, observed growing in the interstices of society, can be translated into a meaningful and desirable social change for all.

EIGHT: From escapism to autonomy

The life plan maps our existence. Ahead of us run the career lines of our jobs, our marriage, our leisure interests, our children and our economic fortunes. But sometimes when we scan these maps, traverse these routes, follow the signs, we become strangely disturbed by the predictability of the journey, the accuracy of the map, the knowledge that today's route will be much like yesterday's. Is that what our life is really about? Why is each day's journey marked by feelings of boredom, habit, routine?

Cohen and Taylor – Escape Attempts (1992: 46)

In the above quotation, Cohen and Taylor reflect on the sense of dread that sets in when we realise that our lives are governed by pre-scribed regularities. 'The route we take to work, the clothes we wear, the food we eat, are visible reminders of an awful sense of monotony' (Cohen and Taylor, 1992: 46). Without warning, we are filled by the horrible feeling that our lives are predetermined, first by the managers, targets and procedures that shape our working lives, and then by the restrictions of our depleted time and energy when we arrive home. For the people whose lives I have explored in this book, this sense of monotony was palpable enough to provoke a search for alternatives. As much as their practical circumstances would allow, they fought to push work out of their lives and behave in ways which were more consistent with their values and priorities. They rekindled neglected interests and developed new ones. They spent more time relaxing and breathing fresh air. They became more active members of their communities, and they spent more time caring for their elderly parents, their children and themselves. Some of these people had even given up work altogether.

For most of us, and for good reason, giving up work seems like an extreme solution, and working less is not always a practical option. When the periodic sense of dissatisfaction swells within, most of us resort to a more familiar set of escape strategies. We fight the demon of routine in our minds. Some common strategies are those we might place in the category of 'refrains': mental tics and transitory fantasies that remove us momentarily from the mundane reality in front of us. A refrain could be playing a song over and over in one's head, or it could be having daydreams. Cohen and Taylor write that, at any moment, we can 'throw a switch inside our heads and effect some bizarre adjustment to the concrete world that faces us' (Cohen and Taylor, 1992: 90). We can strip people naked, assassinate bosses, or conjure in the mind an altogether different and more pleasant scene than the one set before us. Drink and drugs provide a comparable break from reality, whereas some people rely on an annual holiday overseas. So unhappy are many of us with our daily routines, that even illnesses are sometimes greeted as a welcome refrain. A friend of mine recently sent me a text message in which he celebrated the fact that he had come down with a nerve infection: 'Been trying to enjoy my time today, reading *Jest* [a novel], cycling, making a Spanish crepe, perusing the bookshelves. The free time is reminding me of the creativity in my head I long to set loose. So many ideas and thoughts now.' One of our guiltiest collective secrets in the working world is that we often crave incapacity as a welcome break from responsibility. The problem with refrains, however, is that their buzz never lasts long. A holiday overseas might provide us with a

refreshing sense of distance from our usual circuits of possibility –
we might arrive home pledging to relax more, eat more interesting
food, and reconnect with old friends – but it is never long before life
takes over and we are once again overwhelmed by the ordinary business of living. Try to make the temporary escape more permanent
and one runs into trouble.

What other escape routes are available to us? Perhaps one of
the more common modes of escape is the one that Goffman called
the practice of 'role-distancing' (Goffman, 1972). Role-distancing
involves an attempt to demonstrate to others that we are dissatisfied
and uncomfortable in our role. Goffman gives the example of an older
child who clowns around on a merry-go-round, openly flouting the
ride's safety rules in order to show others that, whilst he might be
riding the merry-go-round, he is doing so flippantly, having outgrown
the childish role of 'merry-go-round rider'. In the working world,
role-distancing might take the form of similarly petty acts of non-
compliance: slouching in a team meeting, doing paperwork sloppily
or wearing a measured expression of incredulity (as perfected by
Martin Freeman's character Tim in the British version of *The Office*).

Drawing on their research into modern organisational cultures,
Fleming and Spicer discuss the related strategy of cynicism (Fleming and Spicer, 2003). Cynicism is perhaps one of the more common
escape strategies in the context of today's emotionally demanding
workplaces. When opportunities to genuinely change the system
seem to be beyond us, cynicism represents a last-ditch attempt
to create a free space in which we can feel less confined by work
demands. As we saw back in Chapter 2, in relation to Catherine
Casey's study of Hephaestus, managerial attempts to engineer identification with work sometimes produce the opposite feeling in the
worker (Casey, 1995). Workers try to preserve their individuality

with a sense of disbelief, cynically dis-identifying with the work culture. A study by David Collinson records manual workers referring to the push to build a culture of excellence as 'Yankee propaganda'. The company newsletter became known as the 'Goebells Gazette' (Collinson, 1992). These cultures of cynicism can undoubtedly act as important weapons in labour struggles, though they will only be effective if workers are also committed to the idea that an alternative is really possible. Fleming and Spicer argue that, by itself, cynicism can actually represent a very conservative force:

> ... cynical employees are given (and give themselves) the impression that they are autonomous agents, but they still practice the corporate rituals nevertheless. When we dis-identify with our prescribed social roles we often *still perform them* – sometimes better, ironically, than if we did identify with them. (Fleming and Spicer, 2003: 160, emphasis in original)

Cynicism is a form of rebellion that often leaves the foundations of power intact. Much like the 'culture of fun' management styles mentioned earlier in this book, cynicism can accommodate workers to their subordinate position by allowing them to enjoy a modicum of superficial freedom. Fleming and Spicer give the memorable example of a McDonald's worker who dis-identifies with the company values (of teamwork, cleanliness, customer service and so on) by secretly wearing a 'McShit' T-shirt underneath her uniform. The authors argue that whilst her transgressive taste in fashion may allow her to preserve a sense of individuality, her dis-identification is ultimately superficial, so long as she continues to act *as if* she believes in the company values (Fleming and Spicer, 2003: 166).

Escape attempts in the form of role-distancing, cynicism and dis-identification provide a valuable breathing space in which we can feel less trammelled by work demands and more like ourselves, yet they also allow us to go on tolerating the confines of our roles: 'The fact that we can regard with amusement the conventions of university or office life and our roles as teachers or managers, actually ensures that we remain within those conventions and these roles' (Cohen and Taylor, 1992: 56). Like watching a profitable anti-capitalist film at the weekend, wearing a Che Guevara T-shirt, or 'liking' a political page on Facebook, cynicism often represents what Mark Fisher calls a 'gestural' type of rebellion – an act of resistance that provides an illusion of empowerment, whilst ultimately leaving the world unchanged (Fisher, 2009).

As a method of getting away from the more troubling aspects of work, consumer escapes embody many of the same weaknesses as refrains or cynicism. Whilst buying consumer goods is often very pleasurable, providing wonderful opportunities for relief, expression and enjoyment, Chapter 6 stressed that consumerist forms of pleasure also have a more troubling side. Like refrains, commodified pleasures tend to be fleeting and temporary, not to mention the fact that their enjoyment depends on a steady source of income. Whilst I do not want to submit to a kind of 'no way out' pessimism, I think it is important that we continue to ask ourselves whether the escape routes conventionally offered and sanctioned by capitalism represent an authentic form of liberation, or whether they only serve to reinforce our tolerance of the toxic situations from which we seek escape. If the desire for social alternatives is a fire that burns within us, I posit that the relatively harmless escape routes described above are like a fine mist of water over the flames – a mist that suppresses them, if never fully putting them out. While we are busy cynically mocking our bosses in our minds, convincing others that we are more than the job we do, or shelling out hard-earned money on distractions from our alienation, time is passing us by and our bodies are getting older. The sanctioned escape routes from reality may often be enjoyable and therapeutic, but they are also self-negating and temporary, cultivating our tolerance and engraining us more deeply into the very situations from which we are seeking reprieve. Today's most readily adopted escape routes may allow for short periods of respite or a momentary glimpse of freedom, but they generally embody a superficial kind of liberty. It is a liberty to criticise work privately, to escape its demands temporarily, and to choose between consumer goods, but not a liberty to choose a different way of life, to participate democratically in the creation of genuine social alternatives, or to protest against the fact that we are being forced to sell our lives simply in order to live.

It is against the follies and contradictions of society's most conventional escape routes that I want to position the anti-workers I met over the course of my research as representatives of a more redemptive alternative. These were people who believed that, through their own actions, it might be possible to change their lives for the better. I believe that what they were pushing for in their resistance to work – successfully or unsuccessfully – was a more permanent kind of escape than those described above. Perhaps 'escape' is not the right word at all: what they strove for was a more authentic sense of *autonomy*. For all the propaganda we hear about work as a source of good health and a way to 'meet potential', work so often seems to stand in the way of people realising what they are capable of in terms of their capacities for creation and co-operation. The people I met all felt themselves limited by their work roles, and were trying to carve out a space in which they were free to develop a range of interests and capabilities.

Whilst there are several conclusions to be drawn from the case studies presented here, one of the main things they have helped me to reflect upon is the extent to which human felicity depends upon developing a sense of continuity between values and actions. It was, after all, in the painful gap between these two things – between ideals and reality – that unhappiness had bred and the breaking point had sprung. In the simplest possible terms, we can note that people are happier when they have more time to do the things they want to do. Depending on how seriously we are willing to take it, this realisation has the capacity to be incredibly banal or incredibly profound:

> It may seem somewhat obvious to suggest that people are happier when they are doing things that satisfy them physically and mentally, but despite the ostensible banality of this statement, it is amazing how few people seem to achieve this in their daily lives, how little time people manage to have for themselves, how few sunrises we see, how minimal the proportion of time we spend with our loved ones is. (O'Mahoney, 2014: 242)

Over the previous few chapters of this book, I have tried to show the good moral sense in people's reasons for resisting work. By paying attention to the self-understandings of anti-workers, I have tried to provide a revitalising break from prevailing social stereotypes of the non-worker as a social deviant, lacking a moral compass and leading an empty life. My hope is that the insights contained in these chapters contribute to a denaturalisation of work and its centrality in modern society. Over the course of the analysis, we have seen some of the ways in which resistance to work can be made tenable. We have seen the ways in which dependency on income can be happily reduced, and we have seen some of the strategies that people use to insulate themselves against the stigma and sense of isolation that come with resisting work in a work-centred society. Overall, it appeared that some of the people I met had been successful in pushing work out of their lives, and would continue to enjoy this success for at least the immediate future. Their stories are a testament to the power of individual agency. Whilst I recognise this, however, I ultimately maintain that attempts to resist work on an individual basis are very limited.

No matter how critical we become of today's work-centred society and its hold on the imagination, this does not in itself alter the fact that work is still socially constructed as a chief source of income, rights and belonging. In the context of today's work-centred society, it is fair to say that any substantial resistance to work will likely remain the preserve of the brave, the determined, people with a contingent source of income, or people whose health and personal circumstances leave them unable to work and without much choice. In view of the social constraints on working less, the question we must ask is whether and how society can be organised so that *everybody* can benefit from the time saved by capitalism's productive development. For thinkers such as André Gorz, introduced towards the beginning of this book, resistance to work was always conceived as a collective rather than an individual project. It follows that any serious attempt to engage in a critique of work must always go beyond questions of individual ethics and enjoyment to consider the prospects for a more widespread revaluation of work, as well as the establishment of structural changes that might provide the basis for everybody to enjoy a greater degree of freedom. Ethical reflection and self-critique are an important part of any confrontation with the work dogma. But challenging this dogma must also be about social critique and collective political action. Where to go next is not an individual but a social choice.

Towards a politics of time

Perhaps the closest thing we have seen to an organised movement for less work in recent years is the campaign for better 'work–life balance'. In the UK, the discussion around work–life balance peaked in the early 2000s with the launch of the Department of Trade and Industry's official work–life balance campaign. The stated aims of the campaign were 'to convince employers of the economic benefits of work–life balance by presenting real-life case studies, and to convince employers of the need for change'. With particular focus on those sectors with the longest working hours, the campaign pledged to strive for five years to 'help employers provide people with more choice and control over their working time' (DTI, quoted in Shorthose, 2004). Around the time of the campaign, a range of voices (from journalists to sociologists and HR gurus) were taking part in a broader discussion about the importance of dividing time equitably between work and non-work activities. The discussion focused mostly on the priority of family time, with the phrase 'work–life balance' passing rather unremarkably into everyday usage.

The research inspired by the official campaign provided a wealth of evidence to demonstrate the negative effects of long working hours on health and family life, and the campaign can be praised for making some of the issues around work time more intelligible. Ultimately, however, it is hard to see the rhetoric of work–life balance as a vehicle for promoting a genuine alternative to today's work-centred society. Melissa Gregg describes work–life balance as an 'ideological ruse', whose overall effect has been to place the responsibility for managing work demands at the feet of the individual. The raft of training initiatives it has inspired – workshops on 'coping with stress', 'dealing with change' and 'time management' – have all ultimately pushed the same message: that it is you alone who is responsible for your commitments, and you personally who is at fault if you are struggling to cope (Gregg, 2011: 4–5). Fashionable ideas such as 'work–life balance' or 'life simplification' are in most cases consistent with neoliberal ideology: an ideology that teaches us that everything is in our hands and that we are free to make what we want out of our lives. If you are struggling, this ideology insists that you have simply made bad choices, and must therefore begin the work of personal rehabilitation that will allow you to make the correct choices (Salecl, 2011). It is this ideology that has seen Western populations turning away from politics and collective action, to instead become obsessed with ideas of self-improvement, personal happiness, and peak health (Cederström and Spicer, 2015).

Perhaps the lasting effect of the work–life balance campaign has been to depoliticise workers rather than encourage them to demand substantial changes. In its most anodyne form, the campaign has framed balance as a 'win–win' situation for workers and employers: the worker wins because she gets to feel less stressed, and the employer wins because the enterprise then benefits from her increased focus and productivity. What is disguised in this framing is any potential conflict of interests between workers and their employers (Shorthose, 2004). Co-opted by management, work–life balance represents yet another example of capitalism's remarkable ability to take a potentially radical idea, soften it up, and serve it back to us in the interests of commercial gain. The failing of the work–life balance rhetoric is that it does not ask fundamental questions about the purpose of work, nor does it question work's ability to fulfil its societal functions; it only gives us permission to ask quietly that we be allowed to work a bit less (usually to pursue other responsibilities such as taking care of our families). It tries to accommodate our disaffection with the current system *within* that system, hindering our ability to really compare alternatives in an open way. It also has little to offer those people who are forced to work long hours because their economic circumstances compel them to do so.

If we are to offer up a genuine challenge to the work-centred society, I believe we need to get beyond telling people about the benefits of 'balance'. We need to be much bolder and start discussing different ways of organising and distributing work, so as to give everybody more free-time. Rather than a campaign for work–life balance, what I am arguing for here is an uptake of what André Gorz called a *politics of time*: a concerted, open-minded discussion about the quantity and distribution of working time in society, with a view to allowing everybody more freedom for their own autonomous self-development. What must be stressed is that problems with work are political by nature, and therefore also require politically engaged solutions:

> [The solution lies] in the definition of new rights, new freedoms, new collective guarantees, new public facilities and new social norms, in terms of which chosen working time and chosen activities will no longer be marginal to society, but part of a new blueprint for society. (Gorz, 1999: 65).

Gorz often chose to call his new society a 'society of chosen time' or of 'multi-activity', but we can choose whatever name we like. One of the single most important features of this society would be a society-wide policy of shorter working hours. This policy would reduce the rate of unemployment by improving the social distribution of necessary work. By spreading the available working hours more evenly across the population, the goal is to reverse the escalating division of society into occupational elites on the one hand, and a mass of unemployed, underemployed or casually employed people on the other (Gorz, 1989: 92). Each of us would work less, so that more of us could work:

> Rather than furiously scrambling to make new work that is often meaningless and of low or no social utility, we should seek to share more

equitably the work that needs to be done, the leisure dividend from the work we choose to no longer do, and the wealth generated. (Hayden, 1999: 34)

The longer-term goal would be to re-create society so that work was no longer an inviolable source of income, rights and belonging. As periods of free-time became longer, people would use it to perform a wide variety of productive and non-productive activities, each according to their own autonomous standards of beauty and utility. Non-working time would be transformed into something much more than the mirror image of our working time: it would be 'something other than time for rest, relaxation and recuperation; or for activities secondary and complementary to working life; or idleness – which is but the obverse of compulsory hetero-determined wage slavery; or entertainment – the counterpart of work which, by its monotony, is anaesthetising and exhausting' (Gorz, 1989: 92). The guiding ideal of social development would be the extent to which people were free to pursue and develop a range of interests and capacities. With more time to ourselves, we would have more time to work for ourselves, and hence would no longer depend on the economic sphere to cater to our every need. The number of everyday activities that would need to be formalised into paid jobs in the economic sphere would drastically contract. New cultural values would be reflected in new approaches to architecture and urban design, which would encourage and assist with the autonomous co-operation of individuals. Cities, towns and apartment blocks would become open spaces for communication, collaboration and exchange, with shared workshops and communal areas fostering the development of voluntary networks and informally organised production (Gorz, 1999: 100–2). This would constitute a reversal of the current trend in North America and the UK, which sees an escalating shift towards the commercialisation and privatisation of city spaces, designed primarily for isolated and dependent consumers (see Zukin, 1995; Minton, 2009).

These ideas of a multi-active or culture-based society may seem lofty and remote from the perspective of the here and now, but their primary function in the present is to stimulate the imagination. What is demanded is not an instant, top-down change in policy, but a more gradual process of collective exploration and open debate. Indeed, perhaps one of the reasons why democratic debate is currently in such a moribund state is that our busy lives leave us with so little time to study policies, collectively organise, or find out what is going on in our communities. The strength of democracy depends on people having the time to engage and participate in this process. The difference between the politics of time and the prescriptive utopias of the past is that the former does not seek to enrol people in some pre-planned utopian scheme, but to gradually free them from prescribed roles, furnishing them with the time to become politically active citizens. The demand for shorter hours 'prescribe[s]' neither a vision of a revolutionary alternative nor a call for revolution, serving rather to enlist participants in the practice of inventing broader methods and visions of change' (Weeks, 2011: 222). The hope is that an increasing amount of free-time will allow people to forge new relations of co-operation, communication and exchange, and thereby become participants in the construction of their own futures.

The call for a politics of time represents an invitation to begin dismantling the work dogma according to a humane set of ideals, and a range of academics and activists are already leading the charge. We can consider the growing group of economists who are now

questioning the validity of GDP growth as a measure of social prosperity (Jackson, 2009; Lane, 2000; Sen, 1999; Stiglitz et al., 2010), or
those social researchers and philosophers who are questioning the
relationship between human flourishing and capitalism's fixation on
material gain (Schor, 1998; Soper, 2008). On the specific issue of
working hours, we can point to a range of agencies who are pulling
apart the five-day, nine-to-five norm. In the UK, the New Economics Foundation argues that a shorter working week proffers a range
of potential social and environmental benefits (Coote et al., 2010;
Coote and Franklin, 2013). Its publications contribute to an effort
to denaturalise our attachment to the forty-hour norm, by pointing
both to our sixty-hour past and towards a suggested twenty-one-
hour future. The real strength of contributions like those from the
New Economics Foundation, however, is that they are helping to
move the debate beyond the terrain of critique and speculation.
Their publications capture something of Erik Olin Wright's suggestion that social and political justice should be pursued by envisioning 'real utopias'. This involves moving beyond critical diagnosis
and futuristic fantasies to incorporate systematic analyses of which
alternatives would be the most feasible and desirable. It also involves
studying the present in order to discern the most effective vectors
for resistance and social transformation (Wright, 2010). One hopes
that arguments for a less work-centred society will continue to move
in this more grounded direction, and also to become more public
and spirited in the process.

The discussion will be more persuasive if it can incorporate les-
sons from existing experiments with alternatives. Some European
countries are already gaining a reputation as innovators in the area
of work time. In France, two laws (one in 1998 and one in 2000)
established a thirty-five-hour week as the new norm, as opposed

to the typical forty. By 2004 in Germany, labour unions had also achieved a thirty-five-hour week for an estimated one fifth of the workforce. Germany's shorter working week was resisted by many employers in the mid 2000s, though shorter working hours are now once again on the country's agenda as a method of combating unemployment (and there are also many examples of smaller victories in countries including the Netherlands, Denmark, Norway and Belgium (Hayden, 2013)). For a more recent example we can turn to Sweden, and the city of Gothenburg's proposal in 2014 to trial a six-hour workday for public sector workers, without a reduction in pay. Gothenburg's deputy mayor Mats Pilhem was confident that the proposal would not have a negative impact on productivity, owing to the undeniable fact that most workers struggle to maintain focus over a typical eight-hour day (Withnall, 2014).

For a final example we can look to the UK's Green Party, for whom a shorter working week already exists as an official, costed social policy. Aiming to share out the available work more equitably and allow people to enjoy more free-time, the party has pledged to work towards establishing a thirty-five-hour week in the UK, as well as oppose any weakening of government regulations on maximum working time. The policy is a key element of the Green Party's broader commitment to recognising the value of activities and forms of self-organisation outside the formal economy, with their official policy outline defining work as 'all the activities that people undertake to support themselves, their families and communities' (Green Party, 2014b). A statement from the Wales Green Party adds that 'our capacity for knowledge, invention, interaction and improvisation is almost limitless' (Green Party, 2014a), and the party's policy of shorter working hours has been designed to create a larger space for these activities and capacities to flourish.

One of the bigger dilemmas faced by innovators in work time is of course the puzzle of how to reduce working hours without low-paid workers experiencing a loss of income. For most who support the shift to a less work-centred society, an integral element of any policy of shorter hours is the dethronement of work as society's main method of income distribution. Recognising that the scarcity and insecurity of work have rendered it unfit as a means of distributing income, many argue that work and income should now be decoupled, and alternative systems of wealth distribution explored. The most popular alternative among academics and activists in Europe and North America is the Basic Income.[1] The principle is simple enough to understand. As Bertrand Russell explained it back in 1918: 'A certain small income, sufficient for necessities, should be secured for all, whether they work or not' (Russell, 1918). The Basic Income is based on a belief that everyone deserves access to the resources required to meet basic needs, and is designed to establish a baseline below which income would not be allowed to fall. Citizens wanting to increase their earnings or pursue a professional career would still be able to do so through the conventional channels of paid employment, but the Basic Income would protect everybody in society from the threat of destitution. The hope is that, freed from the threat of hunger, people would be able to develop a range of interests and capacities, to campaign for better working conditions without fear, and to lead richer and more varied lives outside work.

The policy has two novel and integral elements that distinguish it from today's welfare policies. The first is that the Basic Income is *universal,* received by everybody as a right of national citizenship, and the second is that it is *unconditional,* received regardless of whether a person performs work or any other form of social contribution. It is also usually argued that the Basic Income should be an individual entitlement and paid to each person, according to his or her personal right, rather than to the designated head of a family unit. Further details of the policy remain open to debate, including questions such as what constitutes a reasonable amount to meet basic needs, whether this amount would need to change over the life course, and how children would fit into the scheme. If Basic Income seems wildly unconventional, it is worth noting that for a number of political parties across Europe (among them, the UK's own Green Party), it already exists as an official, costed social policy.[2] Now that it is no longer an academic curio, interest in Basic Income seems to be growing. Academics and activists alike are studying proposals for Basic Income from a range of angles, discussing its moral and philosophical justifications, its economic and political feasibility, and also its potential benefits for freedom and social justice. (A wide range of contributions to the debate can be found in the anthology put together by Widerquist et al. (2013).)

It is beyond the scope of this book to undertake a detailed analysis of policies for shorter hours or alternative methods of income distribution, but it is fair to say that such policies cannot be treated as magical cures for all society's ills. The potential benefits of less work would not be won automatically, and the feasibility and official purpose of any policy changes would need to be carefully debated. In so far as it is difficult to imagine a radical reduction in working hours for the time being, it is also important that activists continue to campaign for better working conditions and the living wage. There is clearly still some thinking to be done on the matter of whether and how demands for a less work-centred future can be fruitfully combined with immediate demands for better working conditions and for a wage that can keep up with living costs. That said, I believe that the above alternatives represent a refreshing glimmer of hope in an otherwise murky puddle of business-as-usual. They are reminders that 'normal' is a flexible category that is always ripe for reinvention, and act as a promising sign that many are now considering alternatives to the work-centred society. Taking inspiration from a range of dissenting voices (be it activists, philosophers, researchers, or the anti-workers featured in this book), let us together begin to dismantle the work dogma, scrutinising the societal attachment to work as an irreplaceable source of income, rights and belonging. Let us point out the pathological features of today's work-centred society and insist that the future could be different.

The road ahead

If the prospect of a less work-centred society sounds appealing, the negative side is that there appears to exist no cultural movement that currently has the potential to develop a politics of time. The resistance to work that I have been exploring in this book is more accurately described as a mentality or potentiality than a formed and coherent political project. Those who resist work, however we might choose to define them, have no overall mission, no public voice, and no real unity beyond their common set of experiences. They embody a cultural disillusionment with work that has yet to find collective expression or political purchase, and whether the mounting disaffection with work-and-spend lifestyles can be translated into a genuine social alternative remains to be seen. A change in mentality has already taken place, but what is 'cruelly lacking is a public translation of its meaning and its latent radicalism' (Gorz, 1999: 60). With this in mind, what can we do to help build a resistance to the work dogma?

1. Open the doors of the discussion

My first proposal is that we open the doors of the discussion. First and foremost, opening the doors would entail critics of work making a more concerted attempt to appeal to the public rather than a minority group of academics. What we might hope to see is a more public enquiry into the lived realities of work and worklessness, helping to show the dissonance between the mythical sanctity of work on the one hand, and the troubling realities of people's actual experiences on the other. Such a project might involve an explicit commitment to demonstrating to a wide range of people that the problems with work have a common structural basis, and are not specific to particular employers or workplace antagonists.

Opening the doors of the discussion also entails showing just how many doorways there are through which to enter into a critical conversation. Many of the most recent contributions have foregrounded the ecological case for a less work-centred society, recognising the potential environmental benefits should growth in productivity be channelled towards time affluence instead of the production of more consumer goods. It has also been speculated that people with more free-time might be more able and inclined to participate in environmentally sound but time-intensive practices, whether cycling instead of driving, repairing instead of binning, or self-producing instead of purchasing packaged goods (Hayden, 1999; 2013). As we saw in Chapter 6, some initial evidence of the benefits of time for the leading of more environmentally friendly lifestyles was found in my own case studies, which showed people happily cutting down on convenience or compensatory forms of consumption as they gained more free-time.

If ecology represents one potential doorway into the discussion, others might enter the conversation in the interests of public health.

In 2014 John Ashton, a leading figure in public health, recommended a four-day working week as a solution to a range of health problems, from high blood pressure, to stress and depression. He suggested that the troubling rates of these illnesses could be partly explained in terms of a maldistribution of work, which is causing some people to suffer the health impacts of long hours, while others suffer the anxiety of worklessness and destitution (Campbell, 2014). What one might hope to see developing in the near future is a discussion on public health that more insistently confronts the societal causes of illness. The critic Mark Fisher refers to this as a drive to 're-politicise' illness, arguing that stress and other modern affective disorders are forms of 'captured discontent': localised signs of wider systemic disharmonies, which it is the job of the social analyst to unpack and develop into a broader critique of the political status quo (Fisher, 2009: 80). From this perspective, problems such as stress, anxiety and depression are less personal issues than profound indictments of today's work-centred society and its incumbent problems of insecurity, alienation, and the enforcement of a tempo of living that often outpaces the body's capacity to thrive and regenerate. Instead of approaching modern illnesses as personal pathologies that must be professionally evaluated and medically cured, we should recognise that the strains of the work-centred society have created a situation in which it may actually be mad to be sane. In other words, we should recognise that the limits of our bodies, as well as the limits of our planet, are now alerting us to the need for social change.

There are also a number of other possible routes into the discussion. Some feminists have become interested in shorter working hours, believing that such a policy could allow for a more equal distribution of paid and unpaid labour between women and men. The idea is that shorter hours, combined with a more equitable distribution of work, could increase the rate of women's participation in the labour market, as well as leave men with more time to participate in family life. Shorter hours therefore represents a possible solution to the notorious 'double shift' worked by many women, whose right to perform paid work has still yet to be matched by a complementary right to be free from domestic duties (see Hochschild, 1990). As rhetorically tempting as it might be to emphasise the importance of family life, however, we should be wary of building the case for less work on 'family values' alone. One weakness of emphasising family time is that it keeps the case for less work imprisoned in a vocabulary of responsibility and duty: 'The problem, it seems to me, is that using the moralisation of nonwaged work to argue for a reduction of waged work precludes a broader or more insistent interrogation of dominant work values' (Weeks, 2011: 159).

The vocabulary of my own book has not been a vocabulary of responsibility and duty, but a vocabulary of freedom. My main focus has been on our troubled desire to escape the realities of working life, and my belief is that the most crucial advantage of less work is its promise to allow us to live more varied and convivial lives. For my part, the call for less work is at its most compelling as a celebration of the human capacity for autonomy: 'the capacity to represent and recreate oneself and one's relationships, the freedom to design, within obvious bounds, our own lives' (Weeks, 2011: 168) – a capacity that the work-centred society has blocked through processes of alienation and colonisation. Ultimately, however, if we want to build a strong case against work, we should take a moment to recognise the breadth of today's critical contributions. Activists would do well to stress that a resistance to the work dogma can simultaneously be a resistance for the environment, for health, for gender equality, for the family, for personal autonomy, and, let us also not forget, for fun.

2. TAKE AN ACTIVE INTEREST IN SOCIETY'S OUTSIDERS

A research intervention into the work dogma would require researchers to take an active interest in the values and practices of people on the margins of society. The role I imagine for the researcher here is a person who uses her skills and insight to work in solidarity with movements for the refusal of work. Max Haiven and Alex Khasnabish have argued that today's monopolisation of social research by academic institutions has too often seen researchers working *on* rather than *with* social movements. Too often the role of the researcher is to 'swoop in' from above, applying a disciplinary perspective and generating grist for the academic mill (Haiven and Khasnabish, 2014: 13). As Michael Billig argues, the publications tied to these research endeavours are often unintelligible and highly self-referential (and, in any case, often fail to see the light of day outside the academy) (Billig, 2013). Like Haiven and Khasnabish, I would like to see a confident defence of the researcher who works in solidarity with social movements for the purposes of transformative social change, as opposed to working *on* social movements for the purposes of generating academic capital.

In order to foster a longer-term research project on the refusal of work, researchers would need the good mind to approach people on the margins of society not merely as excluded individuals, in need of reintegration, but as potential sources of inspiration for a case against work. An emancipatory social science would resist normalising lifestyles based on work and consumerism, and avoid the suggestion that deviation from this norm always necessarily entails an experience of deprivation and shame. What we might hope to see are more research projects that think through those exemplary experiences and practices that explore ways of living, co-operating, expressing and creating, outside the de-skilled and micro-managed sphere of employment. What we might hope to see are more research projects that remain open to the possibility of meeting needs in less conventional ways, outside the ambit of economic exchange relations. Through their investigations, perhaps researchers will be able to shed more light on the unsung inventiveness of people who are already developing their own conceptions of pleasure, sufficiency, wealth and well-being, fit for a less work-centred society. And if researchers are willing to communicate their findings in clear style, perhaps readers will draw inspiration from these examples, with once disparate or fragmented groups of refusers and outsiders achieving a greater sense of unity and collective purpose.

3. JOIN THE BATTLE OF WORDS. AND TURN UP ARMED

The battle against the work dogma is to some extent a battle over language. Throughout this book, we have seen several examples of society's ability to chew up and swallow resistance, either by taking possession of radical language, or by closing off critical communications prematurely. If it was once thought that capitalist ideologies could be challenged by asserting a right to 'be ourselves', Chapter 2 showed how this idea has been co-opted by today's managerial cultures of fun. If many have spoken out against work, Chapter 4 showed how dissenting voices have been suppressed and humiliated by the media's tendency to discuss acts of resistance in a language of deviance and individual pathology. If critics of the work dogma want to join this linguistic battle, they had better turn up armed. For example, how about responding to the moral panic around today's so-called 'culture of entitlement' by developing a critique of today's more prevalent 'culture of gratitude'? It is the culture of gratitude that thrives when, buckling under the pressure to survive, people begin to hurl themselves into any form of work that promises to boost their career profile, whether the work in question is paid or unpaid, suitable or unsuitable. The culture of gratitude flourishes in my own field of academia, where fierce job competition leaves junior academics with little choice but to dive headfirst into any possible work openings. In this hyper-competitive context, it has almost become a matter of bad taste to fuss about issues like contracts, payment, and working conditions. You should just be grateful to have an opportunity in the first place (see Brunning, 2014). Instead of frowning upon people who resist work for their supposed sense of entitlement, how about we *all* get a little more entitled, and build a bold new critique of today's culture of gratitude?

Overall, it seems we need to become more creative with our language and steer the discussion in ways which expose the outdated nature of the work ethic. We need to challenge economic rationality by finding ways of talking about the intrinsic, cultural and societal value of non-work activities. We need to reinvent the term *work* to describe a far wider range of activities than paid employment, and we need to dispel the false dichotomy which says that a person is either working or doing nothing of any value. The question of what we might choose to call a movement against work seems quite important, too. At several points in this book, I have referred to my interviewees' motivations using David Cannon's notion of a 'worthwhile ethic'. Adopting a 'worthwhile ethic' means questioning the sanctity of paid work and insisting that there are other, potentially more worthwhile, activities around which life might be organised. I borrowed this term because it seemed to have certain benefits as a way of describing resistance to work. The most obvious is its deliberate mirroring of the concept it hopes to replace – the work ethic – but it also has several other strengths. First of all, the notion of a movement based on the 'worthwhile ethic' avoids the pitfall of trying to unite people on the basis of existing social categories such as class or gender. A range of people stand to benefit from the shift to a less work-centred society, and the desire for a more self-determined life does not belong to any single demographic. The desire to transcend a work-centred existence germinates wherever people experience a gap between their ideals and realities, and wherever people sense a rift between their socially prescribed roles and their sense of self. This is true whether these people are old or young, male or female, with or without families, working or not working, rich or poor. As a banner under which people could potentially unite, an advantage of the 'worthwhile ethic' is that it is broad, and does not confine the struggle to any particular cultural group. What counts as 'worthwhile' is up to each person to decide.

Another conceptual advantage of the 'worthwhile ethic' is that it stresses a point I have been making throughout this book: that those who resist the work ethic are not necessarily without morals, as the stereotypes often suggest. The reference to an *ethic* insists that there are principles other than dedication to work that might allow people to give their lives meaning and a sense of direction. In this sense, the notion of a worthwhile ethic could be considered an improvement over the concept of 'idling', as a rallying cry against the work dogma. Even though the latter is intended to be humorous (and, in the case of the Idler's Alliance, had succeeded in capturing the imaginations of a diverse range of people), it is counterintuitive if it ends up reinforcing the belief that resisting work is always about leading a lazy life. Several interviewees in my study who were not affiliated with the Idler's Alliance were actually somewhat dismayed to be participating in the same study as people calling themselves 'idlers', because they felt this to be a misrepresentation of their active lifestyles. Where possible, we should try to show that a life without work is not necessarily empty and morally rudderless.

4. DEFEND THE IMPORTANCE OF IMAGINATION

To finish, I would also like to stress the importance of an ongoing commitment to a utopian style of thinking and analysis. Ruth Levitas defines utopia as 'the expression of the desire for a better way of living' (Levitas, 1990: 9). Instead of extrapolating from the present, utopian thinking prompts us to think first about where we might *want* to be, and then about how we might get there. Imagining an alternative and more desirable future helps us to reflect upon the desires which our present social conditions have generated but left unfulfilled. If this sounds like a worthwhile project, however, the adjective 'utopian' is just as commonly used in a pejorative sense, to refer to a person who advocates unrealistic reforms, or nurses an absurd desire for societal perfection. As Levitas points out, this dismissal ranges from the good-humoured to the deadly serious. At one end of the scale, the utopian is labelled a dreamer, whereas at the other end, the utopian is seen as a tyrant, having forgotten the historical links between utopianism and totalitarianism (Levitas, 1990: 3). In my own experience, it is in the derogative sense that the word *utopian* is usually heard.

Against this trend, I would like us to defend the value of a more utopian mode of thinking and talking. If the recent economic crises have shown us anything, it is that crisis alone is not enough to bring about genuine social change. No matter how much crises escalate, positive changes cannot occur unless we as a society remain open to the idea that an alternative might actually be possible. The point of utopian thinking is to remind us that there are always ways of doing things differently; it prompts us to assemble something new out of a crisis instead of seeking ever more absurd ways of accommodating social problems within the present system. It seems to me that no matter how broken the work-centred society becomes – no matter how bad the rates of unemployment and underemployment get, no matter how stressed and downtrodden today's workers feel, no matter how much this stress bleeds out in the form of racism, violence and addiction, and no matter how much strain economic growth places on the environment – a positive social change cannot occur unless we begin actively to entertain and explore the possibility of alternatives. To once again borrow a phrase from Kathi Weeks, the importance of utopian thinking is in 'neutralising the hold of the present' (Weeks, 2011: 205). It is designed to help us think beyond our all-too-familiar horizons of possibility.

This does not mean providing and enforcing a prescriptive blue-print for social change, and nor is there any suggestion here that less work could be a cure for all societal ills. What I have wanted to do in this book is simply present an opportunity to raise questions about aspects of the social world that might otherwise be taken for granted or seem unalterable. Developing a new imaginative attitude does not entail denying the present necessities and gratifications of work, but it does mean creating some healthy critical distance between our-selves and the work-centred society. Utopian commentary should attempt to provoke, incite and inspire, to educate the reader's sense of desire and, without succumbing to bland optimism, appeal to a feeling of hope. If others would point out the unrealistic nature of utopian thinking, the critic should retort by pointing out that our notions of what is realistic are socially structured, as well as the deluded nature of believing that things could comfortably go on as they are.

Ultimately, it is undeniable that working grants access to a range of vital pleasures – if not always in the production process itself, then in the form of social interaction, monetary rewards, a sense of status, or the opportunity to have a public existence. The question I pose, however, is why must our entitlement to these things depend on our submission to work – an activity that is often exploitative and environmentally harmful, not to mention scarce? Why can't we begin a political discussion by thinking about other ways in which the need for income, rights, and a sense of belonging could be satisfied? To any who would suggest that there is no alternative to the work-centred society, I submit that it is a profoundly sad society that cannot envisage a future where a sense of social solidarity and purpose are achieved through anything other than commodity relations.

Notes

INTRODUCTION

1. The arguments of thinkers under the banner of critical social theory represent a significant source of inspiration for this book. Where a choice has been necessary, however, I have generally opted to avoid exhaustive summaries of the academic literature in favour of maintaining narrative focus. Whilst this book is not the place to deliver a detailed account of critical social theory, interested readers may benefit from two excellent academic commentaries: Edward Granter's *Critical Social Theory and the End of Work* (Granter, 2009), and Kathi Weeks' *The Problem With Work* (Weeks, 2011). Other key sources of inspiration include the works of André Gorz – especially *Critique of Economic Reason* (Gorz, 1989) and *Reclaiming Work* (Gorz, 1999) – as well as Franco Berardi's Autonomist piece *The Soul at Work* (Berardi, 2009). I have also written a brief overview of critiques of work in *The SAGE Handbook of the Sociology of Work and Employment* (Frayne, forthcoming).

CHAPTER 1

1. Whilst autonomous activities are performed as ends in themselves, this does not necessarily mean that the products of autonomous activities never benefit anybody else, or have no exchange value. A musician, for example, might bring pleasure to others and also make a living by selling recordings of her music. So long as the musician remains internally motivated by her own conception of the Good, her activity remains autonomous. For Gorz, it appears to be the main intention of the activity that is decisive in whether or not it can be classified as autonomous. Should the musician be tempted, perhaps by the promise of fame or fortune, to tailor her music to the aesthetic styles that she believes the market wants, then she risks transforming her autonomous activity into an economic one.

2. The political project usually attributed to Marx is what we might call socialist modernisation. According to this well-rehearsed theory, the impoverishment of workers is approached mainly as a problem of ownership: labourers (or the proletariat) are alienated as a result of their inferior position in the relations of production. Owning no capital, they are forced to work for wages, with little or no control over the goals and conditions of their work. They are exploited: paid less than the true value of their labour, so that an elite class of owners (the bourgeoisie) may profit from the fruits of their work. The Marx who students usually first encounter is the one who calls for 'collective appropriation': abolition of the class system and an end to exploitation, via a workers' struggle to take collective ownership of the means of production. Alienated work can then become non-alienated work – a true expression of the workers' productive capacities. However, Marx's call for collective appropriation – or the 'Plain Marxist Argument' (Booth, 1989: 207) – can be contrasted with ideas in his later writing, where some believed he tempered his earlier enthusiasm for work. It has been suggested that Marx himself 'could not clearly decide if communism meant liberation from labour or the liberation of labour' (Berki, 1979: 5). For a more detailed discussion of the distinction between the 'plain' and the 'post-work' Marx, see Granter (2009: Chapter 4).

3. Curious readers can find more detailed summaries of Marcuse's connection with the argument for shorter working hours elsewhere (for example, Granter, 2009: Chapter 5; Bowring, 2012; Frayne, forthcoming).

4. For a more detailed overview of the ideas of André Gorz, see the accessible introduction by Lodziak and Tatman (1997) or the more in-depth treatise by Bowring (2000a). The latter deals in a detailed fashion with Gorz's connections to social theory, as well as his early work in existential philosophy.

5. Bertrand Russell made a similar argument in relation to the work of teachers. Russell suggested that teachers should work far less than they do at present, enjoying activities and making social contacts outside the world of education. He argued that the 'spontaneous pleasure in the presence of children' vital for a healthy pedagogical relationship is difficult to sustain over long periods: 'it is utterly impossible for overworked teachers to preserve an instinctive liking for children; they are bound to come to feel towards them as the proverbial confectioner's apprentice does towards macaroons … Fatigue, in the end, produces irritation, which is likely to express itself somehow, whatever theories the harassed teacher may have taught himself or herself to believe' (Russell, 2004b: 146). Gorz suggests that the purpose of a professional sabbatical is to avoid this kind of slump:

to get workers (teachers included) 'to take on fresh ideas, to get a fresh perspective on their own situations, broaden their horizons, liven up their imaginations' (Gorz, 1989: 194).

6. The International Labour Organisation is responsible for communicating the official rate of unemployment and uses the Labour Force Survey as its data source. For an explanation of the differences between official measures of unemployment and the more comprehensive measures used by the Trade Union Congress, see Trade Union Congress (2013).

7. A recent report by the Joseph Rowntree Foundation found that in the UK in 2013 around 13 million people were living in poverty. (The report classifies a household as 'low income' or 'in poverty' if its income after tax is less than 60% of the national median household income over a particular year.) What is surprising is that around 6.7 million of these people were actually living in households with at least one working member. The same report found that in 2012 around 27% of female employees and around 15% of male employees were paid less than the UK living wage of £7.45 an hour. Significant numbers of people are also facing poverty because they are *under*employed, seeking full-time work but only able to find part-time jobs. The 2013 JRF report estimated that, shortly before its publication, 1.4 million UK citizens were in this category (MacInnes et al, 2013). The working poor form a significant but largely overlooked proportion of the population in supposedly affluent societies, their experiences proving that work is not always a ticket out of poverty. Many of the working poor are employed through agencies or on a temporary basis, and may be insufficiently protected by employment legislation or trade unions. These workers are therefore likely to be excluded from the benefits of permanent employment contracts, such as paid holidays or sick leave. Such exclusions are a particular concern in the USA, where it is employers rather than the state who grant access to social insurances such as healthcare (Markova and McKay, 2008).

8. Many low-wage workers, particularly in the retail and fast-food industries, are on controversial zero-hours contracts, kept on call but given no guaranteed hours, and paid only for the hours that they work. According to the Office for National Statistics, 116,000 people were on zero-hours contracts in the UK in 2008, with this figure rising to 200,000 in 2012. Figures produced by the Chartered Institute of Personnel and Development, on the other hand, advise that this is a conservative estimate. Their own survey suggested that by August 2013, over 1 million people in the UK were on zero-hours contracts.

9. In the UK, a number of attention-grabbing headlines have illustrated the fallout caused by the shortage of skilled jobs. The *Telegraph* reported that

one branch of the coffee franchise Costa received a desperate 1,701 applications for only eight jobs. According to the report, many of these applicants were 'vastly overqualified' (Silverman, 2013). Another story suggested that unemployed graduates in Scotland are routinely being told to 'dumb down' their résumés in order to find work (BBC News, 2012).

CHAPTER 2

1. In one memorable example from my own employment history, a training session required trainee checkout workers to role-play a range of customer service scenarios. Fake customers were brought in and instructed to behave belligerently towards the trainees. Under the watchful eye of the managers, who were scoring the performance on clipboards, the trainee staff were expected to confront the customer-actors whilst remaining composed and continuing to smile. After the exercise, the trainees were notified of their mistakes via a training video, which dispensed the company's customer service policies over the soundtrack of Natalie Imbruglia's top-ten pop hit 'Wrong Impression'.

CHAPTER 3

1. Marcuse made the same argument about the compromised nature of time outside work in *One-Dimensional Man,* though what is interesting is that Marcuse inverted Adorno's terminology. For Marcuse, 'free-time' is the rarity and it is 'leisure' that 'thrives in industrial society, but ... is unfree to the extent to which it is administered by business and politics' (Marcuse, 2002: 52).
2. For an informed introduction to neoliberalism I recommend David Harvey's excellent book *A Brief History of Neoliberalism* (Harvey, 2005).
3. I am not referring to Russell's more heavyweight works as a philosopher here, but to his more accessible contemplative essays – primarily those collected in the volumes *In Praise of Idleness* (Russell, 2004a) and *The Conquest of Happiness* (Russell, 2006). My reference to the aesthetic appeal of Russell's prose in these works is not incidental: Russell argued that one of the costs of a society increasingly enthralled by efficiency is that the 'conception of speech as something that is capable of aesthetic value is dying out, and it is coming to be thought that the sole purpose of words is to convey practical information' (Russell, 2004d: 19). Russell's own words resist this trend and are a joy to read in their own right.
4. These figures are based on projections from the student debt survey by Push. The survey was conducted with 2,808 students at 115 UK universities,

and accounts for the money owed to parents, banks, and student loan providers. See www.push.co.uk

5. A 2014 survey by savoo.co.uk asked 1,505 graduates whether they would be willing to work in an unpaid internship to gain experience. Some 85% said they would, with 65% saying that they would do so even if there was no job guarantee at the end (HR Review, 2014).

6. Figures from the Economic History Association, 'Hours of work in US history' (available at http://eh.net/encyclopedia/hours-of-work-in-u-s-history/).

7. Figures from eMarketer Digital Intelligence, 'Mobile Shines Amid Rising Digital Ad Spending', 13 October 2011 (available at www.emarketer.com/Article.aspx?R=1008639).

CHAPTER 4

1. Among other myths, the Turn2Us report also busts the idea that the welfare state is clogged by 'problem households', characterised by high numbers of children and multiple generations of welfare dependants. It also offers evidence to challenge the pernicious belief that people regularly *choose* a life on benefits because it is financially cushy.

2. A report by the Citizens Advice Bureau provides a more detailed summary of the relevant policy changes in the UK (Citizens Advice Bureau, 2013).

3. Even the most cursory internet search turns up an abundance of upsetting stories about the consequences of failed applications, from people with disabilities having their benefits cut off because they were doing occasional volunteer work, to people with degenerative and chronic illnesses being told by ATOS that they would 'get better', to stories of extreme poverty and, ultimately, suicide. The Citizens Advice Bureau collected some of these stories in their 2013 *Punishing Poverty* report, cited above.

4. For a sense of this legacy, see the article by Waters and Moore (2002), which provides a range of references to studies which directly investigate one of the psychological needs identified by Jahoda and colleagues.

5. Some more examples are worth noting. *Consensus Terrorism:* 'The process that decides in-office attitudes and behaviour'. *Emotional Ketchup Burst:* 'The bottling up of opinions and emotions inside oneself so that they explosively burst forth all at once, shocking and confusing employers and friends – most of whom thought things were fine'. *Overboarding:* 'Overcompensating for fears about the future by plunging headlong into a job or lifestyle seemingly unrelated to one's previous life interests' (Coupland, 1991).

6. See http://www.euromayday.org/

CHAPTER 5

1. In accordance with common ethical practice, participants were reassured that they would be kept anonymous, although interestingly several of the people I met protested this decision. These people were a lot like the non-workers interviewed by the journalist Bernard Lefkowitz back in the 1970s. Lefkowitz wrote: 'Most of the people I interviewed did not ask anonymity in return for their candor. They believed that the transition from work to not working had taken courage. They felt that if I disguised them it would imply some guilt or shame on their part' (Lefkowitz, 1979: foreword). People were proud of their lifestyle choices and they wanted to be identified in the book. Whilst I understand their reasoning, I have ultimately gone against their wishes and do not believe that they should be held accountable for the stories they have shared. All the names here are pseudonyms, and many identifying details have been altered. Aside from these minor alterations, all extracts from the interviews are quoted verbatim.

2. Berger and Pullberg argue that sociology itself contributes to reification, in so far as it often treats social roles and social laws, rather than intentional human beings, as its prime reality. A reifying sociology depicts a world in which '[no] one exists any longer'. Social intercourse is envisaged in almost mechanical terms as a world of roles, spontaneously colliding in a sort of 'ectoplasmic exchange' (Berger and Pullberg, 1966: 66).

3. This had changed by my time of writing, with both Matthew and Lucy having taken jobs as customer assistants for a well-known chain of opticians.

4. The health risks of a work-centred society are particularly concerning in a climate of job insecurity. See Nolan et al. (2000) and Benach and Muntaner (2007) who cite a range of studies which, among other things, have connected job insecurity with feelings of helplessness, sleep disturbance, marital breakdown and a diminished ability to form and execute plans.

5. Students of sociology may note the link between Gorz's observation and Talcott Parsons' classic theory of the sick role. According to Parsons' theory, the medical establishment acts as a social authority which assigns labels to health conditions and essentially decides who is sick and who is not. A medical diagnosis from a doctor is generally needed if a person is to enter what Parsons called the 'sick role' and gain exemption from his or her usual responsibility to work. This right to not work will usually depend on the patient's agreement to commit to a new set of responsibilities, which include exhibiting a tangible effort to get better. The patient must follow the advice of the doctor, take his medicines, and devote all of his time to rest and recuperation, in order that he can quickly reassume his work role.

CHAPTER 6

1. Although the original source of this quotation is unclear, multiple websites attribute it to the American journalist Ellen Goodman.

2. To borrow a droll turn of phrase from a good friend of mine, we might say that Alan was a representative of *Bullshit Incorporated*. Representatives of Bullshit Inc. do not care a great deal about the social utility of their work roles. They take on jobs that are low-commitment and offer little opportunity for identification and moral agency, performing these jobs congenially and proficiently, but ultimately without passion. Since the ultimate goal is always to fund leisure time, the most important thing is the pay: the ultimate Bullshit Inc. scheme is mentally undemanding but high in remuneration.

3. Kim Humphery offers an excellent critique of this style of anti-capitalism in his book *Excess* (Humphery, 2010).

4. Soper is clearly inspired by the critiques of the Frankfurt School (see Soper, 1999). She seems deliberately to echo Marcuse's concept of 'repressive tolerance' when she speaks of a certain 'anti-hedonist tolerance' in modern society: 'our almost unconscious capacity to adjust to the impact of technological change and to the ways in which it often detracts from sensual enjoyment whilst simultaneously deadening us to the sense of what it is we may have lost, or be in the process of losing' (Soper, 2008: 579).

5. See http://www.slowfood.com/

CHAPTER 7

1. Basic Income is also sometimes known as a Citizen's Wage, Guaranteed Income, Social Dividend, Universal Grant, Demogrant, or a number of other names. A good place to start for readers who want to learn more would be the Basic Income Earth Network – an international coalition committed to the promotion of Basic Income. Its website is at: www.basicincome.org

2. The following proposal is taken straight from the UK Green Party's official policy statement: 'A Citizen's Income sufficient to cover an individual's basic needs will be introduced, which will replace tax-free allowances and most social security benefits. A Citizen's Income is an unconditional, non-withdrawable income payable to each individual as a right of citizenship. It will not be subject to means testing and there will be no requirement to be either working or actively seeking work ... The Citizens' Income will eliminate the unemployment and poverty traps, as well as acting as a safety net to enable people to choose their own types and patterns of work. The Citizens' Income scheme will thus enable the welfare state to develop towards a welfare community, engaging people in personally satisfying and socially useful work' (Green Party, 2014b).

Bibliography

Adorno, T. (2001) 'Free Time', in T. Adorno, *The Culture Industry*, London: Routledge. (Original work published 1977.)

Adorno, T. (2005) *Minima Moralia: Reflections from a Damaged Life*, London, Brooklyn: Verso. (Original work published 1951.)

Anthony, P. D. (1977) *The Ideology of Work*, London, New York: Tavistock Publications.

Arendt, H. (1998) *The Human Condition*, Chicago: University of Chicago Press. (Original work published 1958.) http://dx.doi.org/10.7208/chicago/9780226924571.001.0001.

Bains, G. (2007) *Meaning Inc. The Blueprint for Business Success in the 21st Century*, London: Profile Books.

Baker, D., K. North and The ALSPAC Study Team (1999) 'Does Employment Improve the Health of Lone Mothers?', *Social Science & Medicine*, 49, 1, pp 121–131. http://dx.doi.org/10.1016/S0277-9536(99)00104-5

Bauman, Z. (2000) *Liquid Modernity*, Cambridge: Polity.

Bauman, Z. (2001) 'Consuming Life', *Journal of Consumer Culture*, 1, 1, pp 9–29. http://dx.doi.org/10.1177/146954050100100102

Bauman, Z. (2005) *Work, Consumerism and the New Poor*, Maidenhead: Open University Press.

Baumberg, B., K. Bell and D. Gaffney (2012) *Benefits Stigma in Britain*, London: Elizabeth Finn Care / Turn2Us.

BBC News (2012) 'Scottish Graduates Told to Dumb Down CVs', 27 July (available at: www.bbc.co.uk/news/uk-scotland-19006651).

BBC News (2013) 'Amazon Workers Face Increased Risk of Mental Illness', 25 November (available at: www.bbc.co.uk/news/business-25034598).

Beck, U. (2000) *The Brave New World of Work*, Malden: Polity Press.

Beder, S. (2000) *Selling the Work Ethic*, London: Zed Books.

Beecher, J. (1986) *Charles Fourier: The Visionary and His World*, Berkeley, London: University of California Press.

Bell, D. (1973) *The Coming Post-Industrial Age: A Venture in Social Forecasting*, London: Heinemann.

Bell, D. (1976) *The Cultural Contradictions of Capitalism*, New York: Basic Books.

Benach, J. and C. Muntaner (2007) 'Precarious Employment and Health: Developing a Research Agenda', *Journal of Epidemiology and Community Health*, 61, 4, pp 276–277. http://dx.doi.org/10.1136/jech.2005.045237

Berardi, F. (2009) *The Soul at Work: From Alienation to Autonomy*, Los Angeles: Semiotext(e).

Berger, P. and T. Luckmann (1967) *The Social Construction of Reality*, Harmondsworth: Penguin.

Berger, P. and S. Pullberg (1966) 'Reification and the Sociological Critique of Consciousness', *New Left Review*, 35, pp 56–71.

Berki, R. N. (1979) 'On the Nature and Origins of Marx's Concept of Labour', *Political Theory*, 7, 1, pp 35–56.

Bies, R. J. and J. Moag (1986) 'Interactional Justice: Communication Criteria of Fairness', in R. J. Lewicki, B. H. Sheppard and M. H. Bazerman (eds) *Research on Negotiation in Organizations*, vol 1, pp 43–55. Greenwich, CT: JAI Press.

Billig, M. (2013) *Learn to Write Badly: How to Succeed in the Social Sciences*, Cambridge: Cambridge University Press.

Black, B. (1986) *The Abolition of Work and Other Essays*, Port Townsend: Loompanics Unlimited.

Blauner, R. (1964) *Alienation and Freedom: The Factory Worker and His Industry*, London: Pluto Press.

Booth, W. (1989) 'Gone Fishing: Making Sense of Marx's Concept of Communism', *Political Theory*, 17, 2, pp 205–222. http://dx.doi.org/10.1177/0090591789017002003

Bowles, S. and H. Gintis (1976) *Schooling in Capitalist America*, London: Routledge.

Bowring, F. (1999) 'Job Scarcity: The Perverted Form of a Potential Blessing', *Sociology*, 33, 1, pp 69–84. http://dx.doi.org/10.1177/S0038038599000048

Bowring, F. (2000a) *André Gorz and the Sartrean Legacy: Arguments for a Person-Centred Social Theory*, London: Macmillan. http://dx.doi.org/10.1057/9780230288744.

Bowring, F. (2000b) 'Social Exclusion: Limitations of the Debate', *Critical Social Policy*, 20, 3, pp 307–330. http://dx.doi.org/10.1177/02610183000 2000303

Bowring, F. (2011) 'Marx's Concept of Fettering: A Critical Review', *Critique: Journal of Socialist Theory*, 39, 1, pp 137–153. http://dx.doi.org/10.1080/03017605.2011.537457

Bowring, F. (2012) 'Repressive Desublimation and Consumer Culture: Re-Evaluating Herbert Marcuse', *New Formations*, 75, 1, pp 8–24. http://dx.doi.org/10.3898/NewF.75.01.2012

Braverman, H. (1974) *Labor and Monopoly Capital: The Degradation of Work in the Twentieth Century*, New York, London: Monthly Review Press.

Brennan, T. (2003) *Globalisation and Its Terrors: Daily Life in the West*, London, New York: Routledge.

Brown, P. and A. Hesketh (2004) *The Mismanagement of Talent*, Oxford, New York: Oxford University Press. http://dx.doi.org/10.1093/acprof:oso/9780199269532.001.0001

Brown, P., H. Lauder and D. Ashton (2011) *The Global Auction: The Broken Promises of Education, Jobs and Incomes*, Oxford, New York: Oxford University Press.

Brunning, L. (2014) 'Higher Education and the Culture of Gratitude', *Times Higher Education* website, 7 August (available at: www.timeshigher education.co.uk/comment/opinion/higher-education-and-the-culture-of-gratitude/2014988.article).

Cameron, D. (2010) 'Leader's Speech', Conservative Party Conference, Birmingham (available at: www.britishpoliticalspeech.org/speech-archive.htm?speech=214).

Campbell, D. (2014) 'UK Needs Four-Day Week to Combat Stress, Says Top Doctor', *Guardian Online*, 1 July (available at: www.theguardian.com/society/2014/jul/01/uk-four-day-week-combat-stress-top-doctor).

Cannon, D. (1994) *Generation X and the New Work Ethic*, London: Demos.

Casey, C. (1995) *Work, Self and Society: After Industrialism*, London, New York: Routledge.

Cederström, C. and Fleming P. (2012) *Dead Man Working*, Alresford: Zero Books.

Cederström, C. and A. Spicer (2015) *The Wellness Syndrome*, Cambridge: Polity.

Chertovskaya, E., P. Watt, S. Tramer and S. Spoelstra (2013) 'Giving Notice to Employability', *Ephemera*, 13, 4, pp 701–716.

Citizens Advice Bureau (2013) *Punishing Poverty: A Review of Benefits Sanctions and Their Impact on Clients and Claimants*, Manchester: Manchester CAB Service.

Cohen, S. and L. Taylor (1992) *Escape Attempts: The Theory and Practice of Resistance to Everyday Life*, London: Routledge.

Cole, M. (2004) 'Unemployment and the Moral Regulation of Freedom'. PhD thesis, University of Bristol.

Cole, M. (2007) 'Re-Thinking Unemployment: A Challenge to the Legacy of Jahoda et al', *Sociology*, 41, 6, pp 1,133–1,149. http://dx.doi.org/10.1177/0038038507082319

Collinson, D. (1992) *Managing the Shop Floor: Subjectivity, Masculinity and Workplace Culture*. Berlin: de Gruyter. http://dx.doi.org/10.1515/9783110879162

Cook, K. E. (2012) 'Single Parents' Subjective Wellbeing Over the Welfare to Work Transition', *Social Policy and Society*, 11, 2, pp 143–155. http://dx.doi.org/10.1017/S1474746411000546

Coote, A. and J. Franklin, eds (2013) *Time on Our Side: Why We All Need a Shorter Working Week*, London: New Economics Foundation.

Coote, A., J. Franklin and A. Simms (2010) *21 Hours*, London: New Economics Foundation.

Coote, A. and S. Lyall (2013) *Strivers v. Skivers: The Workless Are Worthless*, London: New Economics Foundation.

Costea, B., K. Amiridis and N. Crump (2012) 'Graduate Employability and the Principle of Potentiality: An Aspect of the Ethics of HRM', *Journal of Business Ethics*, 111, 1, pp 25–36. http://dx.doi.org/10.1007/s10551-012-1436-x

Coupland, D. (1991) *Generation X*, London: Abacus.

Cremin, C. (2003) 'Self-Starters, Can-Doers and Mobile Phoneys: Situations Vacant Columns and the Personality Culture in Employment', *Sociological Review*, 51, 1, pp 109–128. http://dx.doi.org/10.1111/1467-954X.00410

Cremin, C. (2011) *Capitalism's New Clothes: Enterprise, Ethics and Enjoyment in Times of Crisis*, London: Pluto.

Csikszentmihalyi, M. (1990) *Flow: The Psychology of Optimal Experience*, New York: Harper and Row.

Dalla Costa, M. and S. James (1973) *The Power of Women and the Subversion of the Community*, Bristol: Falling Wall.

De Geus, M. (2009) 'Sustainable Hedonism: The Pleasures of Living Within Environmental Limits', in K. Soper, M. Ryle and L. Thomas (eds) *The Politics and Pleasures of Consuming Differently*, pp 113–129. Basingstoke, New York: Palgrave Macmillan.

Department for Social Security (1998) *New Ambitions for Our Country: A New Contract for Welfare*, London: Department for Social Security.

Department for Work and Pensions (2013) *Improving Health and Work: Changing Lives*, London: Department for Work and Pensions.

Department of Health (2010) *Healthy Lives, Healthy People: Our Strategy for Public Health in England*, London: Department of Health.

Dittmar, H. (2007) 'The Costs of Consumer Culture and the "Cage Within": The Impact of the Material "Good Life" and "Body Perfect" Ideals on Individuals' Identity and Well Being', *Psychological Inquiry*, 18, 1, pp 23–31. http://dx.doi.org/10.1080/10478400701389045

Dooley, D. and R. Catalano (1988) 'Recent Research on the Psychological Effects of Unemployment', *Journal of Social Issues*, 44, 4, pp 1–12. http://dx.doi.org/10.1111/j.1540-4560.1988.tb02088.x

Ehrenreich, B. (2002) *Nickel and Dimed: Undercover in Low-Wage USA*, London: Granta Books.

Elraz, H. (2013) 'The Sellable Semblance: Employability in the Context of Mental Illness', *Ephemera*, 13, 4, pp 809–824.

Engels, F. (1987) *The Condition of the Working Class in England*, Stanford: Stanford University Press. (Original work published 1845.)

Featherstone, M. (1991) *Consumer Culture and Postmodernism*, London: SAGE.

Fernie, S. and D. Metcalf (2000) '(Not) Hanging on the Telephone: Payment Systems in the New Sweatshops', in D. Lewin and B. Kaufman (eds) *Advances in Industrial and Labour Relations*, Greenwich, CT: JAI Press.

Fevre, R. (2003) *The New Sociology of Economic Behaviour*, London: SAGE.

Fisher, M. (2009) *Capitalist Realism: Is There No Alternative?* Alresford: Zero Books.

Fiske, J. (1989) *Reading the Popular*, London: Routledge.

Fleming, P., B. Harley and G. Sewell (2004) 'A Little Knowledge Is a Dangerous Thing: Getting Below the Surface of the Growth of "Knowledge Work" in Australia', *Work, Employment and Society*, 18, 4, pp 725–747. http://dx.doi.org/10.1177/0950017004047951

Fleming, P. and A. Spicer (2003) 'Working at a Cynical Distance: Implications for Power, Subjectivity and Resistance', *Organization*, 10, 1, pp 157–179. http://dx.doi.org/10.1177/1350508403010001376

Fleming, P. and A. Spicer (2004) '"You Can Checkout Anytime, but You Can Never Leave": Spatial Boundaries in a High Commitment Organisation', *Human Relations*, 57, 1, pp 75–94. http://dx.doi.org/10.1177/0018726704042715

Fleming, P. and A. Sturdy (2011) '"Being Yourself" in the Electronic Sweatshop: New Forms of Normative Control', *Human Relations*, 64, 2, pp 177–200. http://dx.doi.org/10.1177/0018726710375481

Franklin, K. (2013) *How Norms Become Targets: Investigating the Real Misery of 'Fit for Work' Assessments*, Centre for Welfare Reform (available at: www.centreforwelfarereform.org/library/type/pdfs/how-norms-become-targets.html).

Frayne, D. (forthcoming) 'Critiques of Work', in S. Edgell, H. Gottfried and E. Granter (eds) *The SAGE Handbook of the Sociology of Work and Employment*, London: SAGE.

Fromm, E. (1979) *To Have or To Be?* London: Abacus.

Fryer, D. and S. McKenna (1987) 'The Laying Off of Hands: Unemployment and the Experience of Time', in S. Fineman (ed) *Unemployment: Personal and Social Consequences*, London: Tavistock.

Galbraith, J. K. (1958) *The Affluent Society*, London: Hamish Hamilton.

Goffman, E. (1968) *Stigma: Notes on the Management of Spoiled Identity*, Harmondsworth: Penguin.

Goffman, E. (1972) *Encounters: Two Studies in the Sociology of Interaction*, London: Allen Lane.

Gollain, F. (2004) *A Critique of Work: Between Ecology and Socialism*, London: International Institute for Environment and Development.

Gorz, A. (1967) *Strategy for Labor*, Boston: Beacon Press.

Gorz, A. (1980) *Ecology as Politics*, London: Pluto Press.

Gorz, A. (1982) *Farewell to the Working Class*, London: Pluto Press.

Gorz, A. (1985) *Paths to Paradise: On the Liberation from Work*, London: Pluto Press.

Gorz, A., with R. Maischien and M. Jander (1986) 'Alienation, Freedom and Utopia: Interview with André Gorz', *Telos*, 70, pp 199–206. http://dx.doi.org/10.3817/0386067199

Gorz, A. (1989) *Critique of Economic Reason*, London, New York: Verso.

Gorz, A. (1999) *Reclaiming Work*, Cambridge: Polity Press.

Gorz, A. (2010) *The Immaterial*, Calcutta: Seagull Books.

Graeber, D. (2013) 'On the Phenomenon of Bullshit Jobs', *Strike! Magazine Online*, 17 August (available at: http://.strikemag.org/bullshit-jobs/).

Granter, E. (2009) *Critical Social Theory and the End of Work: Rethinking Classical Sociology*, Farnham: Ashgate.

Green Party (2014a) 'How many of us would like to work shorter hours, spend more time with the family, more time in self advancement? The answer is most of us', Wales Green Party website. (Available at: wales.greenparty.org.uk/news.html/2014/09/22/luddite-at-the-end-of-the-tunnel/.)

Green Party (2014b) 'Workers' rights and employment', Green Party website. (Available at: http://policy.greenparty.org.uk/wr.html.)

Gregg, M. (2011) *Work's Intimacy*, Cambridge: Polity.

Haiven, M. and A. Khasnabish (2014) *The Radical Imagination*, London: Zed Books.

Harvey, D. (2005) *A Brief History of Neoliberalism*, Oxford: Oxford University Press.

Hayden, A. (1999) *Sharing the Work, Sparing the Planet*, London: Zed Books.

Hayden, A. (2013) 'Patterns and Purpose of Work-Time Reduction: A Cross-National Comparison', in A. Coote and J. Franklin (eds) *Time On Our Side: Why We All Need a Shorter Working Week*, pp 125–142. London: New Economics Foundation.

Hochschild, A. (1983) *The Managed Heart: Commercialisation of Human Feeling*, Berkeley, Los Angeles: University of California Press.

Hochschild, A. (1990) *The Second Shift: Working Parents and the Revolution at Home*, London: Piatkus.

Hochschild, A. (2012) *The Outsourced Self*, New York: Picador.

Hodgkinson, T. (2004) *How To Be Idle*, London: Hamish Hamilton.

Holehouse, M. (2012) 'Iain Duncan Smith: It's Better to Be a Shelf Stacker Than a Job Snob', *Telegraph Online*, 21 February (available at: www.telegraph.co.uk/news/politics/9095050/Iain-Duncan-Smith-its-better-to-be-a-shelf-stacker-than-a-job-snob.html).

Honneth, A. (1995) *The Struggle for Recognition*, Oxford, Cambridge: Blackwell.

Honoré, C. (2004) *In Praise of Slowness*, New York: Harper Collins.

Horkheimer, M. (1974) *Critique of Instrumental Reason*, New York: Continuum.

HR Review (2014) 'Most Graduates Happy to Take on Unpaid Internships, Even With No Job Guarantee', *HR Review* website, 30 July (available at: www.hrreview.co.uk/hr-news/l-d-news/graduates-happy-to-take-on-unpaid-internships/52291).

HSE (2014) 'Health and Safety Statistics: Annual Report for Great Britain' (available at: www.hse.gov.uk/statistics/overall/hssh1314.pdf).

Huffington Post (2013) 'Benefit Reforms Are Putting Fairness Back at the Heart of Britain', 6 April (available at: www.huffingtonpost.co.uk/2013/04/06/benefit-reforms-cameron-welfare-_n_3029737.html).

Humphery, K. (2010) *Excess: Anti-Consumerism in the West*, Cambridge: Polity.

Hunnicutt, B. (1988) *Work Without End*, Philadelphia: Temple University Press.

Illich, I. (1978) *The Right to Useful Unemployment*, London, Boston: Marion Boyars.

Iyengar, S. and M. Lepper (2000) 'When Choice Is Demotivating: Can One Desire Too Much of a Good Thing?', *Journal of Personality and Social Psychology*, 79, 6, pp 995–1,006. http://dx.doi.org/10.1037/0022-3514.79.6.995

Jackson, T. (2009) *Prosperity Without Growth: Economics for a Finite Planet*, London, New York: Earthscan.

Jahoda, M. (1982) *Employment and Unemployment: A Social-Psychological Analysis*, Cambridge: Cambridge University Press.

Jahoda, M., P. F. Lazarsfeld and H. Ziesel (1972) *Marienthal: The Sociography of an Unemployed Community*, London: Tavistock. (Original work published 1933.)

Jowitt, J. (2013) 'Strivers v. Shirkers: The Language of the Welfare Debate', *Guardian Online*, 8 January (available at: www.theguardian.com/politics/2013/jan/08/strivers-shirkers-language-welfare).

July, M. and H. Fletcher (2007) *Learning to Love You More*, London, New York: Prestel.

Kelley, R. (1994) *Race Rebels: Culture, Politics and the Black Working Class*, New York: Free Press.

Kelvin, P. and J. Jarrett (1985) *Unemployment: Its Social Psychological Effects*, Cambridge: Cambridge University Press.

Kerr, W. (1966) *The Decline of Pleasure*, New York: Simon and Schuster.

Kettering, C. (1929) 'Keep the Consumer Dissatisfied', *Nation's Business*, 16, p 31.

Keynes, J. M. (1932) *Essays in Persuasion*, New York: Harcourt Brace.

Lafargue, P. (1975) *The Right To Be Lazy*, Chicago: Charles H. Kerr. (Original work published 1883.)

Lane, R. (2000) *The Loss of Happiness in Market Democracies*, London, New Haven: Yale University Press.

Law, A. (1994) 'How to Ride the Wave of Change', *Admap*, January

Leader, D. and D. Corfield (2007) *Why Do People Get Ill?* London: Penguin.

Lefkowitz, B. (1979) *Breaktime: Living Without Work in a Nine to Five World*, New York: Hawthorn.

Lepore, M. (2012) 'I Have Never Taken a Vacation Because of My Job', *The Grindstone* (available at: www.thegrindstone.com/2012/03/29/work-life-balance/people-who-have-never-taken-a-vacation-579/2/).

Levitas, R. (1990) *The Concept of Utopia*, Oxford: Peter Lang.

Lewis, J. (2013) *Beyond Consumer Capitalism*, Cambridge: Polity.

Linder, S. (1970) *The Harried Leisure Class*, New York, London: Columbia University Press.

Lodziak, C. (2002) *The Myth of Consumerism*, London: Pluto.

Lodziak, C. and J. Tatman (1997) *André Gorz: A Critical Introduction*, London, Chicago: Pluto.

MacInnes, T., H. Aldridge, S. Busche, et al. (2013) *Monitoring Poverty and Social Exclusion 2013*, York: Joseph Rowntree Foundation.

Marcuse, H. (1998) *Eros and Civilisation*, London: Routledge. (Original work published 1956.)

Marcuse, H. (2002) *One-Dimensional Man*, New York: Routledge. (Original work published 1964.)

Markova, E. and S. McKay (2008) *Agency and Migrant Workers: Literature Review*, London: TUC Commission on Vulnerable Employment.

Marx, K. (1906) *Capital*, Chicago: Charles H. Kerr and Co. (Original work published 1867.)

Marx, K. (1959) *Economic and Philosophical Manuscripts of 1844*, Moscow: Foreign Language Publishing House. (Original work published 1844.)

Marx, K. (1970) *The German Ideology*, London: Lawrence and Wishart. (Original work published 1845.)

Marx, K. (1972) *Grundrisse*, London: Macmillan. (Original work published 1939.)

Marx, K. (1981) *Capital*, vol 3, Harmondsworth: Penguin. (Original work published 1894.)

Mead, G. H. (1962) *Mind, Self and Society*, London: University of Chicago Press. (Original work published 1934.)

Merton, R. (1938) 'Social Structure and Anomie', *American Sociological Review*, 3, 5, pp 672–682. http://dx.doi.org/10.2307/2084686

Mills, C. W. (1956) *White Collar*, Oxford, New York: Oxford University Press.

Mills, C. W. (1959) *The Sociological Imagination*, New York: Oxford University Press.

Minton, A. (2009) *Ground Control: Fear and Happiness in the Twenty-First Century City*, London: Penguin.

Moir, J. (2012) 'A Human Right Not to Stack Shelves? She's Off Her Trolley', *Daily Mail Online,* 13 January (available at: www.dailymail.co.uk/debate/article-2086000/Cait-Reilly-Human-right-stack-shelves-Poundland-Shes-trolley.html).

More, T. (1962) *Utopia*, London: Dent. (Original work published 1516.)

Morris, W. (1983) 'Useful Work Versus Useless Toil', in V. Richards (ed) *Why Work? Arguments for the Leisure Society*, pp 35–52. London: Freedom Press.

Nolan, J., I. Wichert and B. Burchell (2000) 'Job Insecurity, Psychological Well-Being and Family Life', in E. Heery and J. Salmon (eds) *The Insecure Workforce*, pp 181–209. London: Routledge.

Nussbaum, M. (2010) *Not for Profit: Why Democracy Needs the Humanities*, Princeton: Princeton University Press.

O'Mahoney, H. (2014) 'Volunteer Sea Turtle Preservation as a Hybridisation of Work and Leisure: Recombining Sense-Making and Re-Visioning the Good Life in Volunteer Tourism', PhD thesis, Cardiff University.

Offe, C. (1985) *Disorganised Capitalism*, Cambridge: Polity.

Ollman, B. (1971) *Alienation: Marx's Conception of Man in Capitalist Society*, London, New York: Cambridge University Press.

Packard, V. (1957) *The Hidden Persuaders*, Harmondsworth: Penguin.

Perlin, R. (2012) *Intern Nation: How to Earn Nothing and Learn Little in the Brave New Economy*, London: Verso.

Pirsig, R. M. (1974) *Zen and the Art of Motorcycle Maintenance*, London: Vintage.

Ransome, P. (1995) *Job Security and Social Stability: The Impact of Mass Unemployment on Expectations of Work*, Aldershot: Avebury.

Rifkin, J. (2000) *The End of Work: The Decline of the Global Work-Force and the Dawn of a Post-Market Era*, London: Penguin.

Russell, B. (1918) *Proposed Roads to Freedom*, New York: Blue Ribbon Books.

Russell, B. (2004a) *In Praise of Idleness*, Abingdon, New York: Routledge. (Original work published 1935.)

Russell, B. (2004b) 'Education and Discipline', in B. Russell (ed) *In Praise of Idleness*, pp 141–147. Abingdon, New York: Routledge. (Original work published 1935.)

Russell, B. (2004c) 'In Praise of Idleness' in B. Russell (ed) *In Praise of Idleness*, pp 1–15. Abingdon, New York: Routledge.

Russell, B. (2004d) '"Useless" Knowledge', in B. Russell (ed) *In Praise of Idleness*, pp 16–27. Abingdon, New York: Routledge. (Original work published 1935.)

Russell, B. (2006) *The Conquest of Happiness*, Abingdon: Routledge. (Original work published 1930.)

Ryle, M. and K. Soper (2002) *To Relish the Sublime? Culture and Self-Realisation in Postmodern Times*, London, New York: Verso.

Salecl, R. (2011) *The Tyranny of Choice*, London: Profile Books.

Schor, J. (1998) *The Overspent American*, New York: Harper Perennial.

Schwartz, B. (2004) *The Paradox of Choice: Why More Is Less*, New York: Harper Collins.

Sen, A. (1999) *Development as Freedom*, Oxford, New York: Oxford University Press.

Sennett, R. (1998) *The Corrosion of Character: The Consequences of Work in the New Capitalism*, New York: Norton.

Shipman, T. (2011) 'State Workers Get Paid 7.5% More Than Private Sector Staff', *Daily Mail Online,* 1 December (available at: www.dailymail.co.uk/news/article-2068378/State-workers-paid-7-5-private-sector-staff.html).

Shorthose, J. (2004) 'Like Summer and Good Sex? The Limitations of the Work Life Balance Campaign', *Capital and Class*, 82, pp 1–8.

Silverman, R. (2013) 'Desperate 1,701 Fight for Eight Costa Jobs', *Telegraph Online*, 19 February 2013 (available at: www.telegraph.co.uk/finance/newsbysector/retailandconsumer/9881606/Desperate-1701-fight-for-eight-Costa-jobs.html).

Soper, K. (1999) 'Despairing of Happiness: The Redeeming Dialectic of Critical Theory', *New Formations*, 38, pp 141–153.

Soper, K. (2007) 'The Other Pleasures of Post-Consumerism', *Soundings*, 35, pp 31–40.

Soper, K. (2008) 'Alternative Hedonism, Cultural Theory and the Role of Aesthetic Revisionsing', *Cultural Studies*, 22, 5, pp 567–587. http://dx.doi.org/10.1080/09502380802245829

Soper, K. (2013) 'The Dialectics of Progress: Irish "Belatedness" and the Politics of Prosperity', *Ephemera*, 13, pp 249–267.

Southwood, I. (2011) *Non-Stop Inertia*, Alresford: Zero Books.

Stiglitz, J., A. Sen and J. P. Fitoussi (2010) *Mis-Measuring Our Lives: Why GDP Doesn't Add Up*, New York: The New Press.

Taylor, P. and P. Bain (1999) '"An Assembly-Line in the Head": Work and Employee Relations in the Call Centre', *Industrial Relations Journal*, 30, 2, pp 101–117. http://dx.doi.org/10.1111/1468-2338.00113

Terkel, S. (2004) *Working*, New York, London: The New Press. (Original work published 1972.)

Thompson, E. P. (1967) 'Time, Work-Discipline and Industrial Capitalism', *Past & Present*, 38, 1, pp 56–97. http://dx.doi.org/10.1093/past/38.1.56

Thompson, E. P. (1976) 'Romanticism, Moralism and Utopianism: The Case of William Morris', *New Left Review*, 99, pp 83–111.

Thompson, P., C. Warhurst and G. Callaghan (2001) 'Ignorant Theory and Knowledgeable Workers: Interrogating the Connections Between Knowledge, Skills and Services', *Journal of Management Studies*, 38, 7, pp 923–942. http://dx.doi.org/10.1111/1467-6486.00266

Thoreau, H. (1962) 'Life Without Principle', in H. Thoreau, *Walden and Other Writings*, edited by J. Krutch, New York: Bantam Books.

Toynbee, P. (2003) *Hard Work: Life in Low-Pay Britain*, London: Bloomsbury.

Trade Union Congress (2013) '"Total" Unemployment in the UK is Nearly Five Million – Almost Double the Official Figures', 5 September (available at: www.tuc.org.uk/economic-issues/economic-analysis/labour-market/%E2%80%98total-unemployment-uk-nearly-five-million-%E2%80%93-almost).

Trade Union Congress (2015) 'Workers Contribute £32bn to UK Economy from Unpaid Overtime', 27 February (available at: www.tuc.org.uk/economic-issues/labour-market/fair-pay-fortnight-2015/workplace-issues/workers-contribute-%C2%A332bn-uk).

Turn2Us (2012) *Read Between the Line: Confronting the Myths About the Benefits System*. London: Elizabeth Finn Care / Turn2Us.

Tyler, I. (2013) *Revolting Subjects: Social Abjection and Resistance in Neoliberal Britain*, London, New York: Zed Books.

Waters, L. E. and K. A. Moore (2002) 'Reducing Latent Deprivation during Unemployment: The Role of Meaningful Leisure Activity', *Journal of Occupational and Organizational Psychology*, 75, 1, pp 15–32. http://dx.doi.org/10.1348/096317902167621

Weber, M. (2002) *The Protestant Ethic and the Spirit of Capitalism*, New York: Charles Scribner's Sons. (Originally published in 1904; first published in English in 1930.)

Weeks, K. (2011) *The Problem with Work*, Durham, NC, London: Duke University Press. http://dx.doi.org/10.1215/9780822394723.

Weller, S. (2012) 'Financial Stress and the Long-Term Outcomes of Job Loss', *Work, Employment and Society*, 26, 1, pp 10–25. http://dx.doi.org/10.1177/0950017011426307

Whiteside, N. (1991) *Bad Times: Unemployment in British Social and Political History*, London: Faber and Faber.

Widerquist, K., J. A. Noguera, Y. Vanderborght and J. De Wispelaere, eds (2013) *Basic Income: An Anthology of Contemporary Research*, Chichester: Wiley-Blackwell.

Willis, P. (1991) *The Common Culture: Symbolic Work at Play in the Everyday Cultures of the Young*, Milton Keynes: Open University Press.

Withnall, A. (2014) 'Sweden to trial six hour public sector workday', *Independent Online*, 9 April (available at: www.independent.co.uk/news/world/europe/sweden-to-trial-sixhour-public-sector-workday-9248009.html).

Wright, E. O. (2010) *Envisioning Real Utopias*, London, New York: Verso.

Wright, S. (2002) *Storming Heaven: Class Composition and Struggle in Italian Autonomist Marxism*, London: Pluto Press.

Zawadzki, S. and P. Lazarsfeld (1935) 'The Psychological Consequences of Unemployment', *Journal of Social Psychology*, 6, 2, pp 224–251. http://dx.doi.org/10.1080/00224545.1935.9921639

Zukin, S. (1995) *The Cultures of Cities*, Cambridge: Blackwell.

Index